COMBATING CORPORATE CRIME

Northeastern University ■ *1898–1998*

THE NORTHEASTERN SERIES

ON WHITE-COLLAR AND

ORGANIZATIONAL CRIME

EDITED BY KIP SCHLEGEL

AND DAVID WEISBURD

COMBATING CORPORATE CRIME

Local Prosecutors at Work

MICHAEL L. BENSON

FRANCIS T. CULLEN

Northeastern University Press

BOSTON

NORTHEASTERN UNIVERSITY PRESS

Library of Congress Cataloging-in-Publication Data
Benson, Michael L.
    Combating corporate crime : local prosecutors at work / Michael L. Benson, Francis T. Cullen.
        p.   cm. — (The Northeastern series on white collar and organizational crime)
    Includes bibliographical references and index.
    ISBN 1-55553-353-1 (cl. : alk. paper). — ISBN 1-55553-352-3 (pa. : alk. paper)
    1. Corporation law—United States—Criminal provisions.   2. Corporations—Corrupt practices—United States.   3. Prosecution—United States.   4. White collar crime—United States.   I. Cullen, Francis T.   II. Title.   III. Series.
    KF9351.B46   1998
    345.73'0268—dc21   97-45999

Composed in Berkeley Old Style by Graphic Composition, Inc., in Athens, Georgia. Printed and bound by The Maple Press Company in York, Pennsylvania. The paper is Sebago Antique Cream, an acid-free stock.

Manufactured in the United States of America

02   01   00   99   98   5   4   3   2   1

Contents

TABLES

ACKNOWLEDGMENTS

This book took a long time in the making, and, as is often the case in long-term projects, many people helped along the way. Neal Shover provided invaluable substantive and editorial criticism during the preparation of our proposal to the National Institute of Justice for a study of local prosecutors and corporate crime. We are indebted to the Institute for its willingness to fund our research and especially to our project manager, Lois Mock. She was consistently helpful, supportive, and most of all patient, as we slowly completed our work and filed our reports. Of course, neither she nor the Institute is responsible for any of the interpretations, positions, or conclusions found herein. Special thanks also must go to Kip Schlegel and David Weisburd, who invited us to present the initial results of our research at a conference on white-collar crime held in honor of Edwin Sutherland and who then encouraged us to expand them into this book.

The project could never have been completed without the help and cooperation of local prosecutors around the country. Literally hundreds of them took the time to fill out our questionnaire. Many others sat through interviews with us and helped us gain access to other local officials who deal with corporate crime. Field research is always an imposition on the people whose field is being invaded. Yet, throughout our field work, these very busy people were for the most part graciously willing to talk to us. We came away impressed by the dedication and enthusiasm of local prosecutors. They work under exceedingly difficult conditions, and they care about what they are doing against corporate crime.

The original research team for the project included Professor William J. Maakestad of Western Illinois University. Professor Maakestad, a lawyer, was primarily responsible for the interviews with local prosecutors and representatives of the state attorney general's office in each of the field sites we visited. His expertise in the area of corporate criminal liability was instrumental in helping us to establish credibility and rapport with our research subjects.

Finally, it is traditional for authors to acknowledge their families, and this is a tradition well worth perpetuating. For their love, humor, and understanding, we dedicate this book to Shelley L. Paden and Christopher Michael Benson and to Paula J. Dubeck and Jordan Cullen.

COMBATING CORPORATE CRIME

1

INTRODUCTION

■ *On November 10, 1988, in Milwaukee, Wisconsin, a machine boring a tunnel for a new sewer system automatically shut down as an alarm sounded. The alarm signaled the presence of methane gas in the tunnel. Workers quickly evacuated, but the project manager, frustrated with construction delays, ordered employees Tony Bell, Ron Kohne, and Rick Sochacki back into the tunnel to check for the gas. The men reluctantly entered the shaft, hoping that the methane had been ventilated. Suddenly, flames exploded through the tunnel, and all three men were incinerated. The Milwaukee County district attorney, outraged at this senseless loss of life, filed criminal charges against the project manager and other company executives for criminal homicide (Kinney et al. 1990).*

■ *In Los Angeles a woman reads an advertisement in the* Los Angeles Times *promoting an apartment-finding service. She goes to a small storefront office, pays a fifty-dollar fee, and receives three addresses, which, she is told by the saleswoman, identify locations where apartments are available for rent. At the first two sites, the apartment complex managers tell the woman that there are no vacancies and that they have never heard of the apartment-finding ser-*

vice. At the third site, she finds an empty lot, overgrown with weeds. A few days later, she goes back to the service and is given another list of three addresses. These turn out to be no more fruitful than the first three. When she returns to the office a week later to demand a refund, she finds its door padlocked and the windows boarded up. The woman files a complaint with the Consumer Affairs Division of the Los Angeles County District Attorney's Office.

■ In Chicago, two men operate a metal-plating business out of a small, filthy garage. Barrels containing residues of the toxic chemicals used in the plating process stand rusting and leaking in the backyard of the shop. A sanitary district inspector warns the men that they are in violation of the law and that the barrels of toxic chemicals must be properly disposed of or a citation will be issued. Shortly thereafter, the metal-platers load the barrels in a pickup truck, drive to a deserted lot in South Chicago late at night, and pitch them over the side. Neighborhood children use the barrels the next day to play hide and seek. A mother, worried when her daughter comes home with oily and smelly stains on her clothes, calls the Illinois Environmental Protection Agency (EPA) to ask for advice.

■ The owners of a chain of stores specializing in electronic appliances advertise in the Sunday paper that they have obtained a limited quantity of a soon-to-be discontinued model of television. The televisions are being offered, for one day only, at less than half price. The advertisement does not mention that only one of the discontinued televisions will be available at each of the chain's outlets. When customers ask about the specially priced televisions, a salesperson says that they are sold out already. The salesperson then strongly encourages the customers to buy a much more expensive model that is in stock. Although many customers are upset at having missed out on the half-price televisions, no one complains, and the company makes a nice profit selling the new model.

These four examples represent different varieties of what criminologists call corporate crime—that is, illegal acts committed for the benefit of business corporations or other types of business entities. Some of the examples may seem outrageous, but they are not unique. Similar incidents, some worse and others more trivial, occur every day throughout the United States. In some cases, a large, complex, and highly structured corporation is involved, and the effects of the offense spread from one coast to the other, harming thousands of victims. In other cases, the offender is a small business enterprise—say a small retail outlet or manufacturing operation—and the crime is a relatively minor affair. Regardless of the size or complexity of the corporations involved, these offenses make up part of our crime problem and part of the workload of the criminal justice system.

Just as the crimes, themselves, vary a great deal, what happens after corporate crimes are committed also varies enormously. In some cases, such as the half-price television rip-off, no one other than the perpetrators may be aware that a crime (consumer fraud, in this particular instance) has occurred. At other times, a victim (e.g., the worried mother) may be aware that something is wrong and decide to seek help from a regulatory agency (the Illinois EPA). In other cases, the victim (e.g., the apartment-hunting woman) files a complaint with a criminal justice agency (the district attorney's office), and an investigation starts, much as would happen with an ordinary street crime. Finally, in some notable cases, government officials (e.g., the Milwaukee County district attorney) proactively initiate proceedings against the offenders. Official responses to corporate crimes range from none at all to the most serious criminal charges possible.

The examples given above portray a diverse range of crimes and reactions, but they have one element in common. In the three cases where the crime was uncovered, the initial response came from a local or state agency, not from the federal government. It may strike some readers as atypical or unusual for local and state agencies to be involved with corporate crime, because this type of crime is widely thought to be the domain of federal law enforcement and regulatory officials. However, as this book illustrates, local prosecutors are playing an increasingly important part in efforts to control corporate crime. This book is about how they and other local agencies respond to the problem of corporate crime.

Theoretical Themes and Objectives

Of the variety of concerns that motivated us to undertake this project, one of the most important was our desire simply to describe what local prosecutors are thinking and doing about corporate crime. When we began this study, most research on official responses to corporate crime focused on the federal system. What little research existed on local handling of corporate crimes was limited to case studies of particularly notable or egregious cases, often reported in strongly polemical tones (e.g., Cullen et al. 1987; Schudson et al. 1984; Vandivier 1992). Although valuable for drawing attention to the problem of corporate crime in local communities, these case studies tell us little about the extent of the problem nationwide or about how local prosecutors handle more routine cases (assuming, of course, that there are routine cases). Another shortcoming of the case study approach is that cases often are selected because they represent failures of control rather than successes. Hence, little was known about what, if anything, works in the control of corporate crime. Our first objective, therefore, was to provide a more systematic and comprehensive empirical view of the attitudes and activities of local prosecutors regarding corporate crime. Another objective was to address issues of general and longstanding interest among those who study the criminal justice system. Particularly important among these general issues are discretion, interagency interactions, and the influence of community context on decision making.

Discretionary decision making by legal actors is a central and unavoidable component of the law in action. It is central because legal and administrative officials are expressly granted authority to attain broad legislative goals. It is unavoidable because the process of translating rule into action cannot be accomplished unless legal actors interpret and make choices (Hawkins 1992, 11). In contemporary legal systems, discretionary behavior is compelled by "the vagaries of language, the diversity of circumstances, and the indeterminacy of official purposes" (Galligan 1986, 1).

The exercise of discretion by criminal justice officials is a vexing practical and theoretical problem (Hawkins 1992). For some, discretion is an evil to be rooted out of the legal system. It leads to bias and discrimination, and it prevents fairness and equality of treatment (Davis 1969). Yet, for others, discretion is what permits bureaucracies to be flexible, enabling the unique features of each case and each person to be recognized by the system (Handler 1986). Discretion also raises difficult theoretical questions. What are the factors that influence its exercise? Is there an underlying pattern or rationale to the exercise of discretion, or is discretion synonymous with anarchy? How do discretionary decisions made at one stage of the justice process link to and influence other stages?

It would be difficult to find a position in the justice system which has more discretion than that of local prosecutor. The prosecutor has virtually unreviewable discretion (Jacoby 1980). As the chief law enforcement officer of the jurisdiction, the prosecutor alone decides which cases will or will not go to court. By making the decision to prosecute or to ignore potentially sanctionable behavior, the prosecutor defines the moral boundaries of the community. The problem of defining boundaries is especially difficult and ambiguous in cases involving harmful behavior by business corporations. How do prosecutors decide whether to pursue civil, criminal, or other forms of remedy in a corporate case? How do they decide whether to prosecute individual corporate executives, the corporation itself, or both?

Since the control of corporate crime often involves multiple agencies, another theme of our investigation was the creation, maintenance, and operation of local control networks—formal and informal working relationships among criminal justice and regulatory agencies. Although the use of control networks has been promoted as a strategy for corporate crime control for several decades, little is known about how widespread this strategy is or how control networks actually operate. How many prosecutors' offices routinely work with other agencies on corporate crime cases? How are relations with other agencies established? Whom do prosecutors work with most often, and why? How are cases transferred from one agency to another?

Since James Q. Wilson's (1968) pioneering work on the police, the influence of community context on the operation of criminal justice agencies has been increasingly recognized. Context appears to influence all stages of the justice process, from arrest to sentencing and beyond. Who is arrested and for what? Who goes to prison and for how long? The answers vary over time and place. Like other criminal justice officials, prosecutors do not make decisions in a vacuum. They operate within a context of other officials, other governmental agencies, and, most importantly, the community at large. The community elects the prosecutor, and it is the community's values and norms that the local prosecutor must reflect to attain and retain office. Indeed, the nature of the population represented by the prosecutor, its resources, and its social and cultural patterns may be the single most important influence on the local prosecutor (Jacoby 1980, 47). Thus, the influence of community context on prosecutors' reactions to corporate crime is a third theme in our investigation.

Policy Issues

Since the beginning of the nineteenth century, the rise of the corporation as a form of business association has provoked great controversy. Americans typically fear unbridled power, and as business corporations have grown in number and size their potential to concentrate economic power has been distrusted by substantial segments of the general public and lawmakers alike (Evans et. al 1993; Lipset and Schneider 1987; Friedman 1985a, 188–201). Not surprisingly, as business corporations have proliferated so have efforts to develop reliable and effective means of controlling them.

Controversy surrounds the use of the criminal law to regulate corporate conduct. Some argue that criminal penalties are entirely appropriate for corporate criminals (Geis 1972), and they suggest that prosecutors should treat corporate offenders just as they do other types of offenders and try to get as many off the streets as they can through prosecution, conviction, and sentencing. An opposing view claims that in the case of corporate crime it makes more sense to focus on prevention and remediation rather than on punishment. Corporate offenders often make important contributions to local communities by providing employment and paying taxes. The process of prosecution carries the potential to disrupt business operations, and criminal prosecution may force some businesses to close or move to another location, costing people jobs and reducing the local tax base (Moore 1987; Wheeler 1981). Thus, the potential spillover effects from corporate criminal prosecutions may complicate prosecutorial decision making.

Another important policy issue concerns the role of the federal government in helping local governments respond to corporate crime. In the United States, criminal justice has always been primarily a local responsibility. Yet, because of their complex nature, corporate crimes often can severely tax the abilities of local authorities to respond effectively. For example, some environmental crimes, such as illegal disposal of toxic substances, require sophisticated and expensive laboratory tests to identify the substances. Many local governments cannot afford such laboratories and, hence, may have a difficult time prosecuting such violations when they occur. The potential ineffectiveness of local law enforcers makes it tempting to suggest that the federal government ought to take over the job of controlling corporate crime. After all, the federal government has vastly greater technical, financial, and personnel resources than do isolated local governments. Despite its appeal, however, such a shift in responsibility for law enforcement has its drawbacks.

One problem with simply ceding complete responsibility for corporate crime control to the federal government is that the federal government, itself, has inadequate and shrinking resources. In this era of smaller government, federal regulatory and law enforcement agencies have not been exempt from budget cuts. They have taken their hits in reduced operating budgets and diminished staffs. It is also important to remember that the sheer geographic and population size of the United States works against centralized control. Even if federal regulatory and law enforcement agencies were doubled or tripled in size, it is difficult to imagine that they could ever be made large enough to police every city and county in the nation. Vast though they may be, federal resources are dwarfed by the combined resources that state, county, and local governments devote to law enforcement.[1] Discussing the potential for greater local involvement in corporate crime control, a local prosecutor interviewed for this study observed that "there's only fifty attorney generals in the country, but there's thousands and thousands of DAs, with even more thousands of local police departments that could be the eyes and ears on these things." In recent years, many of the landmark prosecutions have been initiated by local prosecutors, whose intolerance of corporate misconduct has moved them to the forefront in trying to use the criminal law to punish corporations and business executives (e.g., Farber and Green 1988; Cullen et al. 1987, 312–19; Frank 1985; Wright et al. 1995).

But what about the supposed size and complexity of corporate crimes? Is it realistic to expect local officials to handle complex, multijurisdictional offenses committed by powerful corporate behemoths? Probably not. Although local prosecutors occasionally do take on national and multinational corporations, the odds of winning clearly are not in their favor (Cullen et al. 1987). Winning in court against the likes of the Ford Motor Company, IBM, or U.S. Steel is very difficult and very expensive. Except in the really large jurisdictions, such as Los Angeles County, most local prosecutors would not be evenly matched against the big Fortune 500 companies. In cases involving such companies, only larger governmental entities—such as states, consortiums of states, or the federal government—have the financial, legal, and personnel resources to contest effectively in court. However, as we hope to show in this study, in a majority of corporate crime cases, the offender is not a large, multinational corporation. More likely, the offender is a much smaller business entity, such as a sole proprietorship, a business partnership, or a small, locally based corporation. The offenses committed by such business entities tend not to be overly complex. They typically are not widespread geographically, nor do they usually involve large numbers of victims. Although the offenses may be quite serious and harmful, their effects often are concentrated in a single community or geographic area. Federal law enforcement and regulatory agencies have neither the resources nor, in many instances, the jurisdiction to go after these all-too-numerous, smaller corporate crimes. Understandably, federal agencies have to concentrate on the larger cases. Consequently, it is up to local prosecutors to take charge of the smaller ones.

Not surprisingly, local prosecutors have reasons for wanting to take these cases. Local prosecutors often are physically and psychologically closer to the victims of corporate crime than are federal authorities. When a worker dies or a consumer is swindled, these victims or their families and friends may be known to the local prosecutor. Victims are also voters. They constitute a very motivated part of the local prosecutor's political constituency, giving the prosecutor a personal stake in their cases. This investment in the welfare of the community's citizens may strengthen beliefs that punitive action should be taken against corporations, especially when prosecutors believe that federal or state regulatory agencies have been lax in their supervision and have permitted the victimization to occur (Cullen et al. 1987).

There are, then, a number of reasons why the federal government's role in local corporate crime control is limited. Inadequate resources, a historical tradition of local criminal justice, a large and spread-out population, and too many small offenses—all of these factors combine to limit what federal agencies can do directly against corporate crime. Rather than calling for greater federal involvement in investigating and prosecuting corporate crime, we think it makes more sense to explore ways in which the federal government can help local prosecutors be more effective. Thus, an important policy-related goal of this project is to develop suggestions for increasing and improving federal assistance to local prosecutors in their fight against corporate crime.

Finally, although local prosecutors are becoming more active against corporate crime, it is still a relatively new and unexplored area. Prosecutors in many of the country's larger jurisdictions have had considerable experience in preparing such cases, but the same cannot be said for their counterparts located in smaller jurisdictions. Prosecutors in large jurisdictions have learned what works and what does not. They have had experience in working with other agencies, and experience often is crucial for successful corporate crime prosecutions. They know what it takes to be, for example, a good environmental law prosecutor. In short, local prosecutors in large jurisdictions have a wealth of personal experience and knowledge regarding corporate crime control, and this knowledge and experience need to be disseminated. Thus, a final policy-related goal of this project is to learn from local prosecutors, themselves, about how to improve local responses to corporate crime.

Concluding Note

For the most part, this book focuses on what *is* rather than on what ought to be. We are interested in providing valid information and analysis of what prosecutors actually do regarding corporate crime rather than castigating them for not doing more. The prosecutors, investigators, and regulators who were kind enough to participate in our interviews came across to us as dedicated public servants, as people who understand and take seriously the harm caused by corporate criminals and who really want to do something about it. Yet, they work under difficult circumstances, often with grossly inadequate resources. Perhaps because their situations have forced them to innovate in order to accomplish anything at all, they were able to give us a number of suggestions on improving local corporate crime control. In the final chapter, we bring these suggestions together and provide a few of our own.

Notes

1. See chapter 2 for documentation of this point.

PART I

Local Prosecutors
and Corporate
Crime

2

LOCAL CRIMINAL JUSTICE
AND CORPORATE CRIME

The criminal justice process in America has been variously described as a system, a loosely coupled system (Hagan et al. 1979), a nonsystem (Skoler 1977), and, perhaps most accurately, as simply a mess. In the words of Patrick V. Murphy of the Police Foundation, "What is supposed to be a system of criminal justice is really a poorly coordinated collection of independent fiefdoms, some ridiculously small, which are labeled police, courts, corrections, and the like" (Skoler 1977, xvii). This "poorly coordinated collection of fiefdoms" is made up of distinct agencies having "no chain of command, no single line of authority, no central policy-making source, to run the criminal process" (Newman 1986, 71). Criminal justice in America is pursued by a patchwork of decentralized, fragmented agencies of overlapping authority, often working at cross-purposes with one another. The most significant characteristic of the criminal justice process in America, and certainly the feature most responsible for its apparent lack of organization, is that it is primarily a local responsibility. The bulk of the money spent on the justice system is spent by local governments. In fiscal year 1988, the reference year for this study, local government expenditures for the justice system amounted to more than $33.5 billion. At the federal level, justice-related expenditures that same year amounted to not quite $7.8 billion (U.S. Department of Justice 1990a). Local criminal justice is also a major employer. The Bureau of Justice Statistics estimates that, in 1987, 11,989 local police agencies provided employment for nearly a half-million people (U.S. Department of Justice 1989).

Approximately 2,300 of the people working in local criminal justice systems hold the position that, for simplicity's sake, we will call "the local prosecutor" (Dawson 1992). The occupants of this position go by a variety of titles—district attorney, county attorney, commonwealth attorney, prosecuting attorney, and state attorney. In all but a few states, the local prosecutor is an elected public official, a uniquely American mixture of politics and law (Jacoby 1980, 5–7; Kress 1976).[1] Generally, local prosecutors are county officials, though about one in five serves judicial districts that encompass multiple counties (Dawson 1992). In this study, we use the terms *local prosecutor* and *district attorney* interchangeably.

Local prosecutors administer offices that vary dramatically in size, resources, and the types of jurisdictions served. Most local prosecutors serve rural counties (Jacoby 1980). In many such jurisdictions, the local prosecutor's office is, literally, a one-person show and part time at that. A prosecutor in this type of office may not see more than a dozen or so felony cases per year. On the other end of the scale, the District Attorney of Los Angeles County supervises a staff of over six hundred attorneys and administers a multimillion-dollar budget. Felony prosecutions in Los Angeles annually number in the thousands.

Not surprisingly, an important factor determining the size of the local prosecutor's office is the size of the population served. Population correlates directly with crime, and as crime increases, the number of felonies the local prosecutor must handle increases, in a predictable manner. The volume of the felony caseload, in turn, correlates strongly with the number of assistants a local prosecutor is likely to have. According to one observer, the size of an office's annual felony caseload can be closely approximated by multiplying the number of assistant prosecutors by 100 (Jacoby 1980, 63). On average, local prosecutors have about eight full-time assistant prosecutors (Dawson 1992).

The Position of Local Prosecutor

Americans are so familiar with the idea of a locally elected prosecutor that they may not realize that such an individual can be found in no other justice system in the world (Jacoby 1980). The historical origins of the position are murky (Jacoby 1980; Kress 1976). Some scholars think that one source for the public prosecutor was an official known as the *schout*, who acted as both a kind of sheriff and public prosecutor in colonial Dutch settlements (Van Alstyne 1952). Another theory traces the origin of the position to the French *procureur du roi* (National Commission on Law Observance and Enforcement 1931, 7). But both of these theories seem inadequate. Dutch settlements were neither numerous nor long lived, and it is not clear how the institution of the *schout* was picked up by other colonies (Friedman 1993, 30). Unlike the American prosecutor, the French *procureur* works for a centralized government and is not locally elected. Neither the *schout* nor the *procureur* appears to have the historical pedigree to claim title as the forebear of the American prosecutor. Hence, scholars now believe that the prosecutor we know today evolved from a combination of historical events and circumstances unique to America and is not the historical descendant of any other legal official (Kress 1976; Jacoby 1980; Friedman 1993).

Regardless of origin, American prosecutors differ markedly from their counterparts in other justice systems. In continental Europe, the prosecutor typically is an appointed official who serves a centralized governmental authority (American Bar Association 1970). In England, the idea of a paid official whose job it is to prosecute offenses on behalf of the state has never taken hold. Prosecution has always been predominantly a private undertaking (Friedman 1993, 29). Only in America is the prosecutor an elected local official who functions as "the primary law enforcement official in a specific jurisdiction" (Jacoby 1980, 5).

The local prosecutor has been called the most powerful actor in local criminal justice (Cole 1988; Jacoby 1980). As an elected official, the prosecutor has an independent source of power—local voters—and constitutionally guaranteed grants of authority (Jacoby 1980). Except for the voters, to whom most prosecutors must submit in partisan elections every four years, there are virtually no public checks on the prosecutor's actions. Of course, like all American officials, the prosecutor works in a government of checks and balances. Judges, defense attorneys, the Bill of Rights, and the scrutiny of the press always loom as potential restraints on the prosecutor's power (Stewart 1987, 10). Nevertheless, in most states, the prosecutor is responsible only to the governor in cases of aggravated misfeasance or nonfeasance (Cole 1988). In theory the decision to prosecute or decline to prosecute can be reviewed by another official, such as a state attorney general or state appellate judge, but in practice this decision is rarely, if ever, subject to official review (Jacoby 1980, xxi). Thus, according to Jacoby, "the American prosecutor enjoys an independence and discretionary privileges unmatched in the world" (1980, 3).

Another reason why prosecutors are so powerful is that they occupy an intermediary, or linking, position in the justice process. Both the police and the courts depend on the prosecutor. By declining to prosecute, the prosecutor can effectively cancel arrest decisions made by the police. Similarly, if the prosecutor fails to bring wrongdoers to court, judges cannot convict and punish them. Of course, the prosecutor, in turn, also depends on the police and the courts—the former to apprehend perpetrators and gather evidence and the latter to convict and punish those charged by the prosecutor. But it is the prosecutor's decision to file or not to file charges that is key to the whole process. The prosecutor's actions "influence the operations of the police, coroner, grand jury, and judge" (Cole 1988, 150).

The position of prosecutor is also one of the most sensitive in the justice process. The prosecutor has the responsibility to convict criminals yet, at the same time, must uphold some of the most cherished rights of the American people. While prosecutors must vigorously pursue the guilty, they are also supposed to ensure that justice is accorded to all defendants. With one decision—to file criminal charges—a prosecutor may shatter the lives of individuals and bankrupt corporations, regardless of whether a conviction is ever secured or not. Thus, the prosecutor's decisions strongly influence the allocation of justice in the community (Cole 1988).

Because of the profound impact prosecutors have on individual suspects, it is easy to overlook the broader and more important symbolic effects of their daily decisions. These decisions set the moral boundaries of the community. Whether potentially criminal events will be officially defined as criminal or ignored is up to the prosecutor. When a prosecutor declines to prosecute, the event, in effect, is defined as noncriminal or as not worthy of official action. The scope of the law is narrowed and the range of acceptable behavior broadened. By their actions, local prosecutors signal those who look "to the criminal process for guidance on what is right and wrong, what laws will be enforced, and what limits will be imposed on the government" (Stewart 1987).

Local Prosecutors and Corporate Crime

Although prosecutors are powerful actors in local criminal justice, what do they have to do with corporate crime? Don't most local prosecutors concentrate on violent street crimes and drug-related offenses? Isn't corporate crime more the domain of federal regulators and prosecutors? Certainly, local prosecutors have their hands full dealing with violence and drugs. It is also true that, historically, the federal government has assumed primary responsibility for controlling corporate crime. The reasons for federal dominance include matters of politics, law, and resources, a full discussion of which is beyond the scope of this book. Nevertheless, over the past two decades, state attorneys general and local prosecutors have grown increasingly concerned with the problem of corporate crime (Cullen et al. 1987; Hammett and Epstein 1993a).

In the early 1970s, a national trend developed against white-collar and corporate crime, in which state attorneys general and local prosecutors played an important, though often overlooked, role (Abrams 1980; Katz 1980). In 1972, the state attorneys general singled out consumer fraud, a form of corporate crime, as a major concern (Skoler 1982, 67). The following year the National District Attorneys' Association (NDAA) established the Economic Crime Committee to promote local white-collar crime enforcement, to enhance the capabilities of local prosecutors to deal with white-collar crime, and to increase their professional commitment to doing so (Edelhertz and Rogovin 1982a, ix–x). This committee represented the first nationally coordinated effort to improve local white-collar crime control capabilities. By 1975 forty-three district attorneys' offices were participating in the committee's Economic Crime Project, which promoted specialization and networking as strategies for containing economic and corporate crime. To overcome their lack of expertise in prosecuting these new offenses, local prosecutors established special economic crime units. In theory, by concentrating on economic crimes, unit staff would develop necessary technical and legal skills. The special units then joined with other law enforcement and regulatory agencies to form control networks. Members of the control networks exchange information, share expertise and resources, and develop coordinated responses to local economic crimes.

Evaluations of exemplary units in the project indicated that the control network approach could work well at the local level (Whitcomb et al. 1979; Finn and Hoffman 1976). Throughout the 1970s, it was widely advocated by U.S. Department of Justice and NDAA officials (Abrams 1980; Edelhertz and Rogovin 1982b). Some saw evidence that local prosecutors were responding:

[By 1978] a clear recognition had developed, on the part of prosecutors in every part of the United States, that enforcement of laws against white-collar crime was the business of the local prosecutor as well as of federal prosecutors. Local prosecutors were more ready than ever before to commit resources of staff and dollars to this effort, even in the face of competing demands for resources to deal with violent crime and property crime. Cadres of local assistant district attorneys had been trained and battle hardened and were moving beyond simple cases to take on more sophisticated fraud schemes including state anti-trust offenses. Communication networks had developed among the assistant district attorneys staffing those economic crime units and some were coordinating actions across jurisdictional lines [sometimes across the continent]. (Edelhertz and Rogovin 1982c, 11)

Since this assessment, the political and prosecutorial environment has changed significantly. Whereas local prosecutors once concentrated almost exclusively on economic crimes such as consumer fraud, now they are prosecuting a broader variety of cases. Concerned with occupational safety violations and illegal dumping of toxic wastes, prosecutors in a number of states have sought criminal indictments against corporations for noneconomic offenses (Hammett and Epstein 1993a; Cullen et al. 1987, 312–19). With landmark cases, such as the Film Recovery Systems, Inc., case in Chicago, the *Twilight Zone* case in California, and the Ford Pinto case in Elkhart, Indiana, local prosecutors have broken new legal ground and have begun to set new moral boundaries around the conduct of business in America.[2]

The new focus of local prosecutors on noneconomic corporate crimes reflects both a change in law and changing federal-state relationships. Courts have broadened traditional notions of corporate criminal liability (Brickey 1984), and new regulatory initiatives at all levels of government have expanded the statutory tools available for prosecutors to use against harmful corporate behavior. Throughout the 1980s, the federal government shifted responsibility for many programs to state and local officials, cutting back on enforcement of environmental and workplace laws and regulations. The federal government's retreat challenged local officials to take the initiative against social problems such as corporate crime. And there is evidence that local prosecutors are aware of and are responding to this challenge. In a 1987 survey of California district attorneys on their handling of corporate offenses, nearly three-fourths reported receiving citizen complaints about corporate misconduct (Maakestad et al. 1987). A significant majority (75 percent) had conducted corporate prosecutions. More important, a sizeable minority (40 percent) believed that in the future their offices would devote more resources to corporate crime prosecution.

The study of California prosecutors, however, is one of only a handful of efforts to investigate what local prosecutors are doing about corporate crime. Although a few isolated studies of how individual offices handle certain types of corporate crime exist (e.g. Hammett and Epstein 1993b), no national studies on local prosecutors are available. The increasingly important efforts of local prosecutors against corporate crime have gone largely unnoticed and undocumented.

Corporate Crime as a Social Problem

In a free-enterprise system, the business corporation can be a remarkably efficient and productive form of organization. It also can be remarkably criminal. Driven by competition and self-interest, American business corporations produce a level of material wealth that is the envy of the world. But the goods and services that make up this wealth are not always produced legally or safely. In the name of profit, business corporations pollute air, land, and water; they poison, maim, and kill workers and consumers; they cheat, lie to, and simply steal from the government, consumers, and one another. The bureaucratic form of organization substantially increases efficiency and productivity, but it also generates new opportunities for criminal behavior (Wheeler and Rothman 1982). Like the Roman god *Janus,* the business corporation has two faces: producer of stupefying material wealth on one side, and wreaker of financial, physical, and environmental havoc on the other.

Illegal acts committed through and for the benefit of business corporations (or other types of business entities) are a form of white-collar crime known as "organizational" or "corporate" crime (Clinard and Yeager 1980, 18; Clinard and Quinney 1973, 188). Corporate crime often is distinguished from another form of white-collar crime known as "occupational crime," where the offense is committed for the personal gain of an individual or group of individuals. In corporate crime, the offense is committed with the support of and for the benefit of a corporation, organization, or other form of business enterprise. Although the distinction between corporate and occupational crime usually is conceptualized as a dichotomy, it probably makes more sense to think of it as a continuum (Coleman 1994, 11). At one end are offenses, such as embezzlement, which are committed strictly for personal gain and without any support from the organization. At the other end are offenses committed solely to advance the interests of the organization—for example, the corporate homicide that occurred during the Milwaukee tunnel project. In between are offenses in which both personal and organizational motives are served. In these cases, the individual and the organization benefit simultaneously. This model may be most appropriate for crimes involving small private businesses where the interests of the organization and those of individuals coincide closely. For example, in the case described in the introduction involving the metal-platers in Chicago who illegally dumped toxic chemicals, the interests of the individuals and those of the organization are virtually identical.

Over the past decade, corporate crime has emerged as a salient public issue and as an important area of criminological research. As part of a broad social movement against white-collar crime (Katz 1980), growing numbers of citizens, lawmakers, and law enforcers now recognize that the illegal conduct of business corporations exacts a heavy toll from its individual, corporate, and governmental victims (Cullen et al. 1987). Although we lack reliable data on the economic cost of corporate crime, many believe it dwarfs the total annual loss from street crime (Coleman 1989; Levi 1987). Official estimates of the economic costs of corporate crime have grown over the past few decades from a few billion dollars to hundreds of billions. In the late 1960s, the President's Commission on Law Enforcement and Administration of Justice estimated that securities fraud cost anywhere between $500 million and $1 billion per year. Another half billion was lost annually on worthless or misrepresented drugs and therapeutic devices. Fraud in the home repair and improvement industry cost an estimated $1 billion per year (President's Commission on Law Enforcement and Administration of Justice 1967a, 103–4). These impressive-sounding amounts pale in comparison to the 1972 estimate of the Senate Subcommittee on Antitrust and Monopoly which put the costs of corporate crime at between $174 and $231 billion per year (Coleman 1989, 6). In the most notorious recent example of corporate crime, the savings and loan crisis, the sums of money are mind-boggling, considering that they involve only a single industry. Official congressional sources put the cost of bailing out insolvent savings and loan institutions at $200 billion for the 1990s, with another $100 to $173 billion to be added on over the first two decades of the 21st century. Determining the exact proportion of these losses attributable to criminal activity is impossible, but government sources estimate that criminal activity was a central factor in 70 to 80 percent of savings and loan insolvencies (Calavita and Pontell 1990, 309–10). An inkling of the magnitude of the difference in costs between street crime and corporate crime can be gained by simply comparing the cost of some average street crimes with the cost of the average securities offense investigated by the Securities and Exchange Commission (SEC). According to Shapiro (1984, 9), the cost of the average securities offense is $400,000. According to the Federal Bureau of Investigation, in 1989 the average take for selected street crimes was as follows: bank robbery, $3,591; burglary, $1,061; theft, $462; and motor vehicle theft, $5,222 (U.S. Department of Justice 1990b, 160).

Sadly, in addition to its economic costs, corporate crime has a violent dimension. Corporate violence is rarely direct, rarely obvious, and corporate criminals do not physically confront their victims with guns and knives. Rather, they practice what has been called *quiet violence* (Frank 1985). Nevertheless, corporate violence traumatizes victims just as tragically and just as severely as street crime. Reliable statistics on the physical costs of corporate crime are even harder to come by than those for its economic costs. The National Safety Council estimates that ten thousand people are killed each year in work-related accidents and that another one hundred thousand die from occupationally related diseases (Coleman 1994, 9). Of course, not all of these deaths and injuries are caused by corporate criminal activity. In some cases, workers cause their own deaths and injuries by violating company safety rules. But according to one estimate, more than one-third of all on-the-job injuries result from illegal working conditions (Reasons et al. 1981), while about one-third are caused by unsafe acts committed by workers. Well-documented examples of employers intentionally or negligently creating hazardous working conditions for workers are not hard to find. For decades, companies in the asbestos industry, for example, lied to workers about the harmful effects of working with asbestos (Brodeur 1985). Rather than investing adequate time and money in safety equipment and training for workers, some corporations simply gamble with the lives and safety of their employees.

The quiet violence committed by corporations does not stop at the plant gate. Many consumers are injured or killed annually by consumer products. For example, according to the 1993 annual report of the National Product Safety Commission, between October 1, 1991, and September 30, 1992, 4,369 deaths were associated with use of consumer products. The National Electronic Injury Surveillance System (NEISS) estimates that in fiscal 1993 hospital emergency room–treated injuries associated with the use of consumer products totaled over 13,300,000 (National Product Safety Commission 1993).[3] As with workplace-related fatalities and injuries, not all consumer injuries and deaths result from illegally unsafe products. Consumers sometimes injure themselves by using products in wholly inappropriate ways. It is impossible to determine precisely how many of the injuries and deaths that consumers suffer result from corporate criminal activity, yet case studies in a variety of different industries have found that, to hold down the costs of production, business corporations often cut corners on product safety (Ermann and Lundman 1992; Cullen et al. 1987; Hills 1987; Braithwaite 1985a; Frank 1985; Hochstedler 1984). Rather than testing products to make sure they are safe, some corporations simply rush them out the door; sometimes, they even engage in cold-hearted calculations to determine whether the company can pay off anticipated claims by consumers or their survivors and still maintain an acceptable profit margin.[4]

The physical costs of corporate crime also occur via the subtle and long-term effects of environmental contamination and pollution. Estimating these costs is more art than science, but illegal environmental contamination clearly imposes heavy costs on health and property values (Stone 1987; Tallmer 1987). For example, hazardous wastes that are illegally disposed of can cause serious health problems by contaminating surface water or groundwater, polluting the air via evaporation, fires, or explosions, and contaminating the food chain. Exposure to many common industrial solvents—such as xylene, methyl ethyl ketone, ethylbenzene, and trichloroethane—can cause damage to nearly every human organ system. If pregnant women are exposed to these substances, their children may suffer birth defects (Hammett and Epstein 1993a, 7). These are not rare or exotic pollutants. They are used in manufacturing operations in every city and town across the country.

As with street crimes, concern for their immediate victims makes it easy to overlook the broader social and economic consequences of corporate crimes. They are thought to create distrust and undermine public confidence in the morality of big business (Shover et al. 1994; Kramer 1984; Sutherland 1940). Diminished faith in the fairness of the financial markets may cause potential investors to reduce their investments in the market, stifling economic growth (Clinard and Yeager 1980, 8; Conklin 1977, 7). By disregarding the rules of free and open competition, business organizations that engage in criminal behavior gain unfair advantage over their law-abiding competitors. The ability of the market to reduce the costs of goods and services and to improve efficiency through competition is, thus, threatened. In sum, corporate criminal behavior harms the American economy and free enterprise system (Clinard and Yeager 1980, 11–12; Edelhertz 1970, 9).

Despite the physical, economic, and social costs of corporate crime, prosecutors have reason to be chary of using the criminal process against corporate offenders. Corporations generally commit offenses that are incidental to, and in the furtherance of, legitimate business objectives. Harsh enforcement measures, no matter how well intended, may have deleterious effects on innocent parties (Bardach and Kagan 1982; Diver 1979). If criminal penalties disrupt business operations, employees may be thrown out of work. The spillover effects of criminal sanctions may harm investors, consumers, and the local community (Moore 1987). Thus, the control of crimes committed by businesses raises unique problems and may require different measures from those used to control other forms of crime (Clinard and Yeager 1980). The best method of controlling business misconduct is a matter of considerable dispute.

Corporate Crime as a Prosecutorial Problem

Most illegal corporate conduct does not result in criminal prosecution (Clinard and Yeager 1980; Sutherland 1949). Scholars differ over why this is so. One school of thought stresses the political and economic power of corporations; the other emphasizes the practical difficulties of applying the criminal law to corporate offenders. These views represent recurrent themes in research on corporate crime but are not necessarily mutually exclusive. Undoubtedly, both have merit.

According to those who favor the power view of corporations, corporate and other well-to-do offenders evade the criminal law because of their economic and political power (Reiman 1979, 139). Access to money and political pull enables corporations and the financial elites who run them to exert significant influence on local law enforcement agencies. Most local prosecutors are elected officials; this politicization significantly influences prosecutorial decision making in corporate cases (Bequai 1978, 147). The political nature of their position tends to make local prosecutors beholden to powerful local business interests and reluctant to offend potential supporters in the business community and their powerful political allies. Since most local prosecutors eventually leave their positions to enter private practice or to seek higher political office, their long-term economic or political success may hinge on their standing with local economic and political elites. Hence, according to this school of thought, local prosecutors are unwilling to antagonize potential future clients and campaign contributors by vigorously pursuing crime in high places.

In recent years, another less cynical and conspiratorial view of the social control of corporate crime has gradually emerged. According to this view, the special institutional features of business corporations make control of businesses a distinct problem from that of individuals in ordinary situations (Stone 1975, 7). Corporate offenses pose special investigatory and prosecutorial problems that make the successful application of the criminal law complicated and difficult (Shapiro 1990, 1984; Levi 1987; Rakoff 1985; Stone 1975). The failure of prosecutors to apply the criminal law to corporate delicta is caused by insufficient resources, legal constraints, and availability of alternative sanctions.

Insufficient Resources

Most organizations pursue multiple objectives with limited budgetary, personnel, and technical resources. Criminal justice organizations are no exception. Since they cannot meet all of the numerous, conflicting, and shifting demands placed on them, criminal justice administrators must make strategic decisions on the priority of objectives.

The difficult and time-consuming process of investigating, preparing, and prosecuting a case against a corporation often severely taxes prosecutors' resources (Bequai 1978). Detection of illegal acts committed in organizational settings is hindered by the ability of organizations to restrict access to their inner workings. Corporations often are able to control the investigator's and prosecutor's access to crucial information (Mann 1985). Gathering evidence buried in corporate files may exceed the investigatory capabilities of prosecutors. Simply determining whether a crime has occurred, let alone identifying the responsible parties, can be a major difficulty.

After a corporate crime is detected, prosecutors confront a determined and powerful adversary. Unlike most ordinary offenders, corporate lawbreakers possess substantial resources with which to legally delay investigation and prosecution. Their attorneys can raise time-consuming objections to legal procedures. Case studies of corporate crimes suggest that isolated local prosecutors often lack the necessary organizational resources to overcome such obstacles (Cullen et al. 1987; Schudson et al. 1984; Vaughan 1983).

Legal Constraints

Prosecutors also must contend with legal constraints. Legal constraints are features of the law that make it more or less difficult for legal actors to apply. For example, the legal standard of probable cause makes it harder for police to conduct legal searches than would be the case if only a reasonable suspicion were required. In corporate criminal cases, prosecutors frequently face legal constraints of a conceptual, constitutional, and evidentiary nature.

Conceptually, courts have encountered difficulties transferring traditional, individualistic notions of the criminal law to nontraditional, corporate settings. For example, indictments against corporations have been dismissed because of restrictive judicial interpretations of the legal meaning of *person,* the appropriateness of existing criminal sanctions for corporate actors, and the need to prove *mens rea* (Maakestad 1986, 1981; Fisse 1983; Coffee 1981). These concerns may limit the perceived options available to corporate criminal prosecutors.

Corporations may raise constitutional arguments that threaten the viability of prosecutors' cases. For example, in one case, a trial judge ruled that Occupational Safety and Health Administration regulations preempted state law, and he dismissed criminal indictments against a corporation and its officers (Cullen et al. 1987, 325). The belief that federal regulatory law preempts state law may reduce the number of options that prosecutors see as viable in corporate cases.

Prosecutors also must contend with evidentiary constraints. Seldom is it possible for a prosecutor to offer dramatic, "smoking-gun" proof of criminal knowledge or intent in a corporate context. Proof of such knowledge or intent is critical, for it is the element of *mens rea* that can turn what might have been a civil suit into a criminal proceeding. In today's complex and often labyrinthine corporate structures, it can be extremely difficult to pinpoint individual responsibility for specific decisions. In addition, large-scale organizations develop mechanisms for shielding their members from responsibility for corporate actions (Katz 1979, 1977; Gross 1978). These problems in developing evidence seriously complicate the prosecutor's decision-making calculus.

Alternative Remedies

Numerous federal and state regulatory agencies have jurisdiction over various aspects of corporate conduct. Prosecutors must depend on those agencies both for technical expertise and for the development of crucial evidence. Traditionally, regulatory agencies have been more concerned with encouraging compliance than with punishing wrongdoing. They do not see themselves as law enforcers and often are reluctant to use the criminal law in response to corporate misconduct (Levi 1987, 163; Braithwaite 1985b, 10). Given the difficulty of getting regulators to cooperate in criminal proceedings against corporations, prosecutors may opt for alternative, noncriminal rather than criminal sanctions.

The problem of deciding what type of remedy to pursue can be further complicated when the interests of victims conflict with broader social interests. Sometimes victims are more interested in restitution than retribution and may oppose the use of criminal proceedings. Yet, prosecutors may believe that failure to respond sternly to corporate crimes undermines belief in the notion of equal justice under law. The tension between community and victim interests may complicate the choice of remedy for prosecutors.

Both the power view and the special-institutional-features view illuminate some of the difficulties prosecutors face in controlling corporate crime, yet, they tell us little about the corporate crime prosecutions that do occur. They also fail to address variation in rates of corporate crime prosecutions over time and place. A growing body of evidence, which we review in more detail in chapter 3 suggests that prosecutors at all levels of government are taking a more active stance against corporate crime. In the decade preceding this project, unsystematic, largely anecdotal evidence from a variety of sources suggested that local prosecutors were becoming more aggressive toward corporate crime. Reports of innovative corporate prosecutions conducted by local prosecutors appeared in newspapers and law review articles (Magnuson and Leviton 1987). Seminars on white-collar crime prominently featured the role of the prosecutor (Edelhertz and Rogovin 1982a), and case studies of particularly egregious crimes were common (Cullen et al. 1987; Hills 1987; Hochstedler 1984). Yet, no systematic quantitative studies were available on how local prosecutors respond to corporate crime. While the 1980s witnessed an unprecedented explosion of high-quality research on responses to white-collar and corporate crime, most of it was focused on the federal system (Benson and Walker 1988; Simpson 1987; Hagan and Parker 1985; Shapiro 1984; Wheeler et al. 1982; Hagan et al. 1980). In this book, we present the first systematic national study of how local prosecutors handle corporate crime.

Notes

1. In Alaska, Connecticut, and Delaware, local prosecutors are appointed by the state attorney general, who has responsibility for criminal prosecutions in these states. Local prosecutors in New Jersey are appointed by the governor. In the District of Columbia, the U.S. Attorney for the District of Columbia prosecutes both local and federal crimes (Dawson 1992).

2. In *People v. Film Recovery Systems, Inc.*, a corporate president, plant manager, and plant foreman were convicted of murder and reckless conduct for their actions in exposing company employees to hydrogen cyanide. The exposure caused the death of one worker and serious injuries to several others. The corporation for which they worked also was found guilty of involuntary manslaughter and reckless conduct. In the *Twilight Zone* case, movie director John Landis was prosecuted for the deaths of Vic Morrow and a child actor who died during the filming of *Twilight Zone: The Movie*. Landis was eventually acquitted of the charge. In the Ford Pinto case, a local prosecutor charged the Ford Motor Company with reckless homicide.

3. The NEISS data indicate that a product was associated with an injury but not necessarily that the product caused the injury.

4. The most infamous example may be the memorandum produced by the Ford Motor Company in relation to the Pinto (Dowrie 1987). According to an internal company memorandum, Ford calculated that it was cheaper to pay off burn victims and their families than to make an eleven-dollar change in how the Pinto's gas tanks were installed.

3

STUDYING LOCAL PROSECUTORS

Overview

To carry out this project, we used a multimethod strategy that combined
survey, archival, and interview data. First, to learn about the extent of
the corporate crime problem as perceived by local prosecutors, we conducted a national mail survey of local prosecutors in spring 1988. We sup-
plemented the survey data by merging it with archival data on population,
employment, income, local government finances, and crime for each jurisdiction in the sample. These data permitted us to measure selected dimensions of the community context in which local prosecutors operate and to
provide a more informed empirical view of their actions. After the survey
and preliminary analysis were completed, we conducted field research in
four jurisdictions, with special units for white-collar, economic, or corporate crime, in fall 1988 and spring 1989. The offices were selected because
they handle relatively large numbers of corporate cases and concentrate on
different types of cases. We studied offices located in different regions of
the country: Cook County, Illinois, which includes Chicago; Los Angeles

County, California; Nassau County, New York, which is located on Long Island; and Duval County, Florida, which includes the city of Jacksonville.

By using both quantitative and qualitative research strategies, we hoped to provide both an empirical overview and an in-depth analysis of the themes and policy objectives that motivated this study. The survey data permit us to describe basic features of prosecutors' attitudes and activities in regard to corporate crime, such as the number and types of prosecutions they typically conduct, their attitudes toward corporate offenders, their views on the helpfulness of other agencies, and a host of other matters. With the archival data, we investigate how activity against corporate crime varies across communities and regions of the country. This contextual analysis focuses on how community characteristics influence the general level of activity against corporate crime and the use of the control network strategy.

Finally, the field studies give us insight into the world and culture of the local prosecutor. Here, we seek to understand the process of corporate crime prosecution from the perspective of those who handle such cases on a daily basis. We describe how prosecutors, investigators, and regulators think about corporate crime, how they interpret the nature of the offense and the character of the offender, how they view and interact with one another, what investigative and prosecutorial problems corporate crimes pose for them, and how those problems are handled. Our primary aims are to extend current thought about legal decision making and the operation of local legal systems.

The National Survey

The Sample

The sample of local prosecutors was drawn from a membership mailing list provided by the National District Attorneys' Association (NDAA). In most states, criminal prosecutions are conducted by locally elected officials representing a county or county-equivalent geographic area. But in some states, felony and misdemeanor prosecutions are handled by different officials. Both types of officials may be members of the NDAA. In drawing the sample of local prosecutors, we used state statutes to identify officials responsible for prosecuting locally committed felonies.[1] Officials responsible only for prosecuting misdemeanors were excluded from the sample.

We attempted to survey all prosecutors whose offices are located in or near large metropolitan areas and a 25-percent random sample of all nonmetropolitan, or rural, offices. To identify offices located in or near metropolitan areas, we consulted the *Statistical Abstract of the United States* (U.S. Bureau of the Census 1989b). Appendix II of the *Abstract* lists the counties included in three classes of metropolitan statistical areas: consolidated metropolitan statistical areas (CMSA), primary metropolitan statistical areas (PMSA), and metropolitan statistical areas (MSA). All counties located in either a MSA or a PMSA constituted the sampling frame for urban jurisdictions.[2] Most of the addresses on the NDAA membership list also identified the county in which the office was located. By comparing the NDAA list to the urban counties list, we were able to identify most offices located in counties in urban areas. For addresses that had no county identifier, we referred to the *Rand McNally Cosmopolitan World Atlas* (Rand McNally and Company 1971), which lists the county seat for all counties in the United States. Where a metropolitan county seat matched one of the city addresses on the NDAA mailing list, we included that office in the urban sample. A total of 617 offices on the NDAA mailing list were identified as being located in urban areas. The remaining approximately 1,665 offices on the NDAA mailing list constituted the sampling frame for rural offices. We selected a simple random sample of 425 offices, approximately 25 percent of the sampling frame. The total sample contains 1,042 offices.

In spring 1989, we mailed questionnaires and cover letters to our sample, following standard survey protocol (Dillman 1978). After we had sent a reminder postcard and two additional mailings, a total of 685 questionnaires were returned for an overall response rate of 66 percent. Of these, 420 (68 percent response rate) came from urban jurisdictions and 265 (62 percent response rate) from rural jurisdictions. Given the sampling design, the final sample is disproportionately composed of respondents located in urban districts. For this reason and because preliminary analyses revealed that rural districts have little corporate crime, we report only on the results for the urban districts.

The Questionnaire

In addition to the number and types of corporate criminal prosecutions, the questionnaire also addressed five other areas of concern. One set of questions focused on prosecutors' perceptions of and attitudes toward the problem of corporate crime. We asked how serious the problem was in their jurisdiction and whether they had seen or anticipated an increase in activity against corporate crime. Another series of questions addressed the organizational and fiscal resources of the prosecutor's office, focusing on the budget and the number of attorneys and investigators in the office and whether the office has a special unit devoted to white-collar or economic offenses. Next, we asked about the organization of local law enforcement networks—that is, other governmental agencies that local prosecutors work with on corporate cases or that serve as referral sources of corporate cases. To help us understand the decision-making process in corporate cases, we included a series of questions that focused on perceived constraints on prosecutorial decision making. Finally, we asked prosecutors about their views on the causes of and remedies for corporate crime and their goals in using the criminal law against corporate criminals.

The Archival Data

To measure selected dimensions of community context, aggregate data on population, employment, income, local government finances, and crime for each jurisdiction in the sample were abstracted from the *County and City Data Book, 1988, Files on Diskette* (U.S. Bureau of the Census 1988). In addition, data were taken from *County Business Patterns, 1987* (U.S. Bureau of the Census 1989a). These data were merged with the survey data. The data compiled in the *City and County Data Book* come from a variety of governmental sources and refer to different years. In general, though, the data reference the years 1984 through 1988. Hence, it is appropriate to use them as indicators of the community context in 1988, the reference year for our survey.

In most states, local prosecutors are county officials and their jurisdictions are contiguous with individual county boundaries. In a few states, however, prosecutors serve judicial districts that encompass multiple counties. In these cases, we combined the archival data from the constituent counties of the judicial district before merging the archival data with the survey data.

Sample Bias and Community Context

The possibility of sample bias is a persistent problem in all survey research. Sample bias refers to systematic differences between those who respond to a survey instrument and those who do not. Of course, some variability between respondents and nonrespondents is unavoidable in survey research. If present to a significant degree, sample bias can reduce the external validity of the findings and their generalizability to the population from which the sample was drawn. Our survey of local prosecutors is not immune to this potential weakness. Although our response rate of 68 percent is relatively good for a self-administered mail survey, it does not guarantee that the nonrespondents are the same as the respondents.

We are fortunate, therefore, to have some data on the nonrespondents which we could use to investigate the possibility of sample bias. Because we know the counties in which our nonrespondents are located, we were able to gather aggregate archival data on their social, crime, and economic characteristics. We compared the jurisdictions of the respondents and nonrespondents on these measures. The comparison does not tell us whether the attitudes and experiences of the nonrespondents differ from those of the respondents. Nevertheless, it does permit us to determine whether the respondents and nonrespondents are located in jurisdictions that differ systematically on aggregate demographic, crime, and economic characteristics. This check on sample bias is particularly important for this study, because we theorize that the community context influences prosecutorial activity against corporate crime.

As Table 3.1 shows, the respondent and nonrespondent jurisdictions are virtually identical in population size, but there is some evidence of greater variability among the nonrespondent jurisdictions. The standard deviation for the nonrespondent subsample is much larger than it is for the respondent subsample (740,373 compared to 361,868). Since the two largest jurisdictions in the sample, with populations over 5 and 8 million, respectively, did not respond to the survey, this may account for the large standard deviation for population size in the nonrespondent jurisdictions. Overall, though, for this important variable sample bias does not appear to be a problem. Table 3.1 also presents comparative data on a number of other social, demographic, and economic variables. These variables were selected for analysis because they tap potentially important dimensions of the community context in which prosecutors work, such as the size of the crime problem that confronts local law enforcement, the fiscal resources of the community devoted to the crime problem, and characteristics of the population which may influence the demands made on local law enforcement agencies.[3]

One dimension of the community context which may influence the resources local prosecutors have with which to respond to corporate crime is the amount of street crime in their jurisdictions. We use the official crime

Table 3.1. Comparison of Jurisdictions of Respondents and Nonrespondents
on Selected Characteristics

| Characteristic | Respondent | | Nonrespondent | | | |
	Mean	Std. Dev.	Mean	Std. Dev.	t	Prob.
Population	281,700	361,868	285,531	740,373	0.08	.94
Total crime rate	4,391	3,504	4,145	2,218	−1.43	.15
Violent crime rate	377	373	359	487	−0.44	.66
Expenditures*	48.63	65.54	47.54	46.96	−0.21	.84
Per capita income	12,361	2,495	12,226	2,119	−0.67	.50
Percentage nonwhite	10.08	11.53	10.18	11.51	0.11	.92
Unemployment rate	6.78	2.74	7.45	2.97	2.79	.01
Percent college educated	15.84	6.60	14.89	6.13	−1.68	.09

* Local government direct general expenditures for police protection per capita.

rate (serious crimes known to the police per 100,000) as an indicator of the local street crime problem. Since prosecuting street crimes takes time, personnel, and money, the availability of these limited resources for corporate crime prosecutions inevitably fluctuates with the size of the local street crime problem. Hence, it is important to determine whether our survey respondents are located in jurisdictions with atypically high or low crime rates. Because violent crime is the most threatening type of crime, we compare our respondent and nonrespondent jurisdictions on both the total and the violent crime rates.

Another community characteristic that may influence the availability of resources for corporate crime control is local governmental expenditures for law enforcement. Prosecutors located in communities that can afford, or that choose, to spend more money on crime control may have larger budgets and correspondingly larger staffs than their counterparts in less-well-off jurisdictions. Unfortunately, we do not have information on the local prosecutors' budget and staff for the nonrespondent jurisdictions, but we do know how much these jurisdictions spend on police protection generally. To investigate whether the respondent and nonrespondent jurisdictions devote similar resources to crime control, we compared them on per capita expenditures for police protection.

Finally, a large body of research has demonstrated that the demographic and economic characteristics of communities influence the enforcement styles of law enforcement agencies. Most of this research has focused on relationships between community characteristics and styles of policing or sentencing practices in courts. Nevertheless, it is reasonable to assume that community characteristics also influence the office of the local prosecutor. We compared the respondent and nonrespondent jurisdictions on percentage of nonwhite population, personal income per capita, the unemployment rate, and percentage of population with sixteen or more years of education. Previous research has shown that these variables influence law enforcement practices.

The respondent and nonrespondent jurisdictions are similar in crime rates, government expenditures for police protection, personal income per capita, and percentage of nonwhite population. The only statistically significant differences between the respondent and nonrespondent jurisdictions involve the unemployment rate and aggregate educational attainment. As measured by the percentage of the population with sixteen or more years of education, the respondents tend to be located in jurisdictions that are more highly educated. Their jurisdictions also tend to have a lower civilian labor force unemployment rate than do the jurisdictions in which the nonrespondents are located. Although these differences are statistically significant, it is doubtful that they are important substantively; the absolute differences are not large.

In addition to aggregate social, crime, and economic characteristics, another important contextual variable is regional location. As we will show later, prosecutors in some regions of the country are more active against corporate crime than are their counterparts in other regions. To assess whether the sample is geographically biased, we calculated response rates by region (see Table 3.2).[4] As with population size, there is no evidence of sample bias by region. Response rates for the four regions range from a low

Table 3.2. **Response Rates, by Region of the Country**

Region	Response Rate	N
South	67.4	162
West	74.0	54
Northeast	62.3	71
Midwest	70.0	133
Overall response rate	68.1	420

of 62 percent in the Northeast to a high of 74 percent in the West. These differences are not statistically significant.

Our investigation of sample bias suggests that the respondents are located in jurisdictions similar to those of the nonrespondents. In all likelihood, then, the survey results accurately represent the views and experiences of urban local prosecutors nationwide.

Limitations of the Survey

In the following chapters, we report extensively on the results of our survey of local prosecutors. We believe that our analysis of sample bias indicates that we can have some confidence in the generalizability of the findings. Yet, like all research methods, surveys have their weaknesses and limitations. Rather than remind the reader repeatedly as we go along, we present the limitations here and trust that the reader will keep them in mind for what follows.

One limitation has to do with our unit of observation versus our unit of analysis. Although the questionnaire was completed by the local prosecutor or an assistant, most of the information we sought pertained not to the prosecutor as an individual but rather to the office in which the prosecutor was located.[5] For example, one set of questions asked about the factors that increase or decrease the likelihood that a corporate prosecution would be undertaken. Our objective here was to uncover general office policies regarding prosecutorial decision making. We have no guarantee that the person filling out the questionnaire accurately represented office policy. In large offices, individual assistant prosecutors possibly interpret and implement policies in varying ways. Nevertheless, we are confident that in the vast majority of cases our questionnaire was completed by a person who has some influence on setting office policies. As we show in chapter 4, our surveys were completed by attorneys with substantial experience, who occupied supervisory positions in the local prosecutor's office. While we usually refer to the prosecutor's office as our unit of analysis, the reader should keep in mind that the data were actually gathered from an individual.

A second limitation of the survey method arises out of the difficulty of accurately measuring the intensity of prosecutorial activity against corporate crime. In general, we used the number of corporate prosecutions typically conducted in a year as our indicator of activity.[6] We believe that number of prosecutions is a defensible indicator of activity, but it is not a perfect one. Corporate cases are not all created equal. Prosecuting a case against a large corporation demands more resources than prosecuting one against a small mom-and-pop store. The decision to take on a large, resource-intensive case may mean that other cases cannot be pursued. Hence, a prosecutor who pursues a landmark environmental case against a large corporate offender may appear to be less active than counterparts who concentrate solely on the more numerous, garden-variety consumer fraud offenses. We suspect that most of the time number and quality are related and that the offices that handle the most cases also handle the biggest ones. Nevertheless, an office may be active, in the sense of devoting resources to corporate crime, even though it does not conduct many prosecutions.

The Field Studies

To supplement the national survey, we conducted a series of field studies in fall 1989 and spring 1990 in Cook County, Illinois, Los Angeles County, California, Duval County, Florida, and Nassau County, New York. These offices were selected because the survey results indicated that they handle relatively large numbers of corporate cases and concentrate on different types of cases. We also wanted to maximize cultural and social variation in community context in the field sites.

At each field site, we spent approximately ten working days. We interviewed attorneys in the local office, representatives from the state attorney general's office, state and federal regulatory officials, and local and state police personnel. The mix of agencies and officials varied from site to site. In general, we relied on the attorneys in the local office to identify the individuals in other agencies with whom they most often work on corporate cases.[7]

Most of the interviews were tape recorded and later transcribed for analysis. To facilitate analysis of the interviews, we used *Ethnograph* (Seidel et al. 1988), a computer program designed for qualitative data analysis which makes it easier to sort through textual material quickly and reliably. Although *Ethnograph* facilitates the management of interview data, the reliability and validity of the data analysis ultimately depend on careful coding of the interviews. To ensure that the interviews were accurately and reliably coded, we developed a coding scheme organized around major issues, such as networking with other agencies, constraints on prosecutorial discretion, or the purposes of prosecution. We also instituted a system of cross-checking coding work. To analyze the coded interviews, we used *Ethnograph* to abstract passages dealing with particular themes—say, for example, networking with federal agencies. We then reviewed those passages as a group to identify patterns.

A Concluding Note

In writing up the results of our study, we faced a problem inherent in all multimethod investigations—how to organize and integrate the presentation of qualitative and quantitative data. Because each type of data provides a different view of local prosecutors and permits us to address different questions, we decided that for the most part we would present the quantitative and qualitative results separately. Thus, chapters 4 through 7 focus primarily on the national survey data, but at times we draw upon our interviews and other case study materials to enrich our presentation of the quantitative results. The case studies are treated in greater detail and depth in chapters 8 through 10.

Notes

1. In Texas, district attorneys and criminal district attorneys were sampled; commonwealth attorneys in Kentucky, state attorneys in Connecticut, and district attorneys and county prosecuting attorneys in Wyoming were sampled.
2. CMSAs represent combinations of MSAs and PMSAs.
3. Previous research on the influence of community context on social control has demonstrated that all of these variables are related to control responses. In general, see Liska (1992) and the articles and citations therein.
4. States were grouped into regions according to the U.S. Bureau of the Census definition of regions (U.S. Bureau of the Census 1986).
5. More information on the respondents is presented in chapter 4.
6. See chapter 4 for a more complete description of our operationalization of the concept prosecutorial activity.
7. With a few exceptions, the interviews with attorneys were conducted by Professor William Maakestad of Western Illinois University. Professor Maakestad is an attorney and was a codirector on the original project. The interviews with regulatory and law enforcement personnel were conducted by Michael Benson.

PART II

*Social Context
and Local Crime
Control*

4

Social Context and the Scope of the Corporate Crime Problem

It takes a real malicious purpose, a mens rea in the old law school terminology, to commit some of the conduct that we deal with.

ASSISTANT DISTRICT ATTORNEY, DUVALL COUNTY, FLORIDA

Defining Corporate Crime and Measuring Prosecutorial Activity

A major objective of this project was to ascertain the number and types of corporate criminal cases handled by local prosecutors, which meant, of course, that we had to provide the prosecutors who received our survey with a definition of corporate crime. Unfortunately, the definition of corporate crime, like that of its conceptual ancestor, white-collar crime, is notoriously controversial. Researchers disagree as to whether the concept should be defined narrowly, to include only acts punishable under criminal law, or more broadly, to include acts punishable under civil or administrative law (Cullen et al. 1987). John Braithwaite has clearly articulated the arguments in favor of the broader definition: "To exclude civil violations from consideration of corporate crime is an arbitrary obfuscation because of the frequent provision in law for both civil and criminal prosecution of the same corporate conduct. In considerable measure, the power of corporations is manifested in the fact that their wrongs are so frequently punished only civilly" (Braithwaite 1982, 1466). Braithwaite undoubtedly is correct that the power of corporations often enables them to avoid criminal sanctions. To exclude conduct that is punished civilly from consideration as corporate crime reduces, and to some unknown degree misrepresents, the magnitude of corporate misconduct.

Despite the cogency of Braithwaite's arguments, we decided to use a narrow definition of corporate crime for methodological and substantive reasons. A basic principle of questionnaire design is that questionnaires should be as simple and brief as possible, particularly in the case of self-administered instruments. The presence of complex questions with ambiguous or debatable terms virtually invites methodological disaster in the form of low response rates and increased measurement error. After discussions with some local prosecutors and professors of law, we concluded that including civil violations in our definition of corporate crime would unnecessarily complicate the questionnaire and raise questions in the minds of many of our respondents. As attorneys, they are both notorious for and accustomed to making fine distinctions in the legal categorization of conduct. Hence, we deemed it more advisable to use the narrower, less debatable definition. On a substantive level, we noted that little is known about the use of criminal proceedings by local prosecutors against corporate entities. By using the narrower definition of corporate crime, we hoped to obtain a more accurate estimate of the prevalence of corporate criminal prosecutions. Thus, for the purposes of the national survey, corporate crime was defined as "a violation of a criminal statute either by a corporate entity or by its executives, employees, or agents acting on behalf of and for the benefit of the corporation, partnership, or other form of business entity." Directions on the questionnaire specified that "this definition excludes crimes committed by an employee against an employer for the purpose of personal gain, such as embezzlement or theft."

We were interested not only in the prevalence of corporate criminal prosecutions, generally, but also in how local prosecutors respond to different types of offenses. Since our respondents are located in different states, each with its own unique legal code, it was not possible for us to ask questions about specific offenses as defined by legal statutes. Rather, we had to define offenses more generically. The questionnaire focused on nine broad categories of corporate offenses: consumer fraud, securities fraud, insurance fraud, tax fraud, false claims and statements, workplace-related offenses (e.g., unsafe working conditions), environmental offenses (e.g., dumping toxic waste), illegal payments to government officials, and unfair trade practices (e.g., price-fixing, bid-rigging, or restraint of trade). Although this list is not exhaustive, it does represent a broad, heterogeneous collection of offenses. Of course, because our respondents operate under different legal codes, there is no guarantee that their answers to questions about these offenses refer to exactly the same forms of proscribed conduct. Nevertheless, with the possible exceptions of environmental and workplace offenses, we believe that the offenses are sufficiently common that it is safe to assume they are defined similarly in all states.

It is difficult to estimate accurately how active local prosecutors are against corporate crime. Both in the survey and in our interviews with prosecutors, we found that they often could not readily say exactly how many corporate prosecutions they initiated or concluded on an annual basis. We had hoped to be able to estimate how many local corporate crime prosecutions were conducted nationwide in our reference year of 1988. Apparently, however, local prosecutors do not keep easily accessed records on such matters.[1] Hence, we used two ordinal measures of the frequency of prosecutions. The first measure asked whether in 1988 the respondent's office had prosecuted any of the nine types of corporate crime. The second asked how often the selected corporate crimes typically were prosecuted ("never," "fewer than 1 case per year," "about 1 to 3 cases per year," or "more than 3 cases per year"). In the analyses reported hereafter, we rely on these measures of activity against corporate crime.

Respondent, Office, and Jurisdiction Characteristics

From the outset, we assumed that local prosecutors are very busy people and probably not ordinarily inclined to spend time filling out questionnaires. Therefore, instructions on the questionnaire directed that it be completed by "the district attorney or the attorney most knowledgeable about white-collar and corporate prosecutions in the office." By taking this approach, we hoped to increase the likelihood that our questionnaires would be filled out by knowledgeable attorneys. As Table 4.1 shows, these directions appear to have been followed. Only three questionnaires were completed by nonattorneys. On average, the respondents had about ten-and-a-half years of experience as prosecuting attorneys, and 75 percent of them had at least six years' experience. Thus, we have some confidence

Table 4.1   **Respondents' Titles**

Title	Number of Respondents	Percentage
Commonwealth attorney	27	6.5
County attorney[a]	29	7.0
District attorney[b]	127	30.7
Prosecutor	16	3.9
Prosecuting attorney	59	14.3
Solicitor	5	1.2
State's attorney	38	9.2
Assistants identified with a special unit	29	6.8
Assistants not identified with a special unit	82	19.8
Investigator	1	0.2
Other	2	0.5
No Answer	5	—
Total	420	100

[a] Also includes "county" and "prosecuting" attorney.

[b] Also includes "criminal district attorney" and "district attorney general."

that the surveys represent the views of experienced prosecutors, though in some cases questionnaires were completed by an assistant local prosecutor rather than by the local prosecutor personally.

The offices in which the respondents work vary considerably in size and budget. Table 4.2 presents descriptive statistics on the budget and the number of full- and part-time attorneys and investigators in the office. The range for these variables is considerable, and since the distributions are strongly skewed to the right, the median is a more appropriate indicator of central tendency than the mean. Judging by the median, the typical local prosecutor's office has nine full-time attorneys, one full-time investigator, and a budget of around $600,000 per year. The smallest office has no full-time attorneys; the largest has over two hundred. The largest office has a budget of over $30 million per year; one quarter of the districts have annual budgets of $1.8 million or more.

America is a land of extremes, and this fact is certainly illustrated in the demographic makeup of the jurisdictions in our sample. The jurisdictions in which the respondents are located vary greatly along a number of social and economic dimensions, such as population size, crime rates, unemployment, and personal income per capita. The smallest jurisdiction

Table 4.2 Characteristics of Respondents' Offices

Characteristic	Mean	Median	SD
Full-time prosecutors	22.0	9	34.8
Part-time prosecutors	1.9	1	3.5
Full-time investigators	6.6	1	14.1
Part-time investigators	0.2	0	0.7
Budget (in $1,000s)	2,115	636	3,897

included in the sample, Grand Isle County, Vermont, had a 1986 population of 5,300; the largest jurisdiction, Harris County, Texas (which includes Houston), had a population of 2,798,300.[2] The mean and median were 281,058 and 150,500, respectively. The total crime rate ranged from zero in several jurisdictions to a high of 12,794 in Multnomah County, Oregon, where the city of Portland is located. The average crime rate was 4,417. Substantial variation also exists in the violent crime rate, which ranges from a low of zero to a high of 4,295. On average, violent crime rates are higher in the South and West than in the Midwest and Northeast, but in all regions there is substantial variation in violent crime. Two indicators of economic wellbeing, the unemployment rate and personal income per capita, also had large ranges. In Hidalgo County, Texas, the official unemployment rate stood at 19.6 percent, compared to the lowest unemployment rate of 2.0 percent, in Merrimack County, New Hampshire. Personal income per capita ranged from a low of $6,030 in Webb County, Texas, to a high of $22,650 in Marin County, California, with a mean of $12,357.

Jurisdictional and office characteristics vary by region. As Table 4.3 shows, compared to prosecutors located in other regions, those in the Midwest tend to serve smaller jurisdictions and work in offices with correspondingly smaller budgets. Prosecutors from western states, on the other hand, serve in comparatively large districts and offices. (The relatively larger size of offices in western jurisdictions may account for the slightly higher response rate from prosecutors located in this region.) Particularly noteworthy is the finding that the median number of full-time prosecutors in western jurisdictions is twenty-six, two to three times more than in any other region. Not surprisingly, the median office budget in western districts is also comparatively large. Prosecutors in southern states appear to serve

Table 4.3   Office and Jurisdictional Characteristics, by Region

Region	Mean	Median	SD
Midwest, N = 133			
Population, 1986	211,510	123,100	281,645
Violent crime rate	336	191	471
Total crime rate	4,075	3,684	1,989
Personal income per capita	12,438	12,165	1,776
Unemployment rate	6.85	6.60	2.36
Full-time prosecutors	13.83	7.00	20.02
Budget (in $1,000s)	943	500	1,465
Northeast, N = 71			
Population, 1986	353,859	228,100	353,345
Violent crime rate	270	190	283
Total crime rate	3,553	3,422	1,709
Personal income per capita	13,216	12,689	2,829
Unemployment rate	5.77	5.30	2.33
Full-time prosecutors	25.28	11.00	38.03
Budget (in $1,000s)	2,801	1,000	4,023
South, N = 162			
Population, 1986	237,000	131,500	328,325
Violent crime rate	428	340	329
Total crime rate	4,495	4,121	2,210
Personal income per capita	11,691	11,316	2,564
Unemployment rate	6.94	6.40	3.18
Full-time prosecutors	18.53	7.50	31.66
Budget (in $1,000s)	1,571	500	3,097
West, N = 54			
Population, 1986	487,985	248,700	521,057
Violent crime rate	459	354	280
Total crime rate	6,164	5,832	1,664
Personal income per capita	13,012	12,574	2,845
Unemployment rate	7.27	6.35	2.44
Full-time prosecutors	47.19	26.00	51.47
Budget (in $1,000s)	5,557	2,850	6,689

jurisdictions that are economically less well off than their counterparts in other regions. Their jurisdictions have the lowest average personal income per capita and the second highest average unemployment rate. These results suggest that significant regional variation occurs in resources available to district attorneys.

Perceptions of the Corporate Crime Problem

In chapter 2, we showed that corporate crime exacts a serious toll from its individual, business, and governmental victims. Billions of dollars are lost to corporate crime every year, and it is more than just the amount of money involved that makes corporate crime a serious problem. In the pursuit of increased profits, unscrupulous corporations and businesses threaten the safety and health of workers and consumers every day. The objective costs of corporate crime cannot be denied.

Despite the financial and physical costs of corporate crime, it is by no means clear that corporate crime is regarded as a serious social problem by either law enforcement officials or the general public. Indeed, it is sometimes contended that corporate crime is not a high priority for law enforcement officials (Reiman 1995; Conklin 1977). A variety of factors, including the alleged moral neutrality of corporate offenses, the elevated social position of the offenders, and the overwhelming press of violent street crimes, have been offered to explain this neglect (Conklin 1977). In this section, we examine our survey data to see how prosecutors view the corporate crime problem in their jurisdictions. First, though, we review what we know about public attitudes toward corporate crime.

Despite the supposed moral neutrality of white-collar and corporate crimes and the great attention given to violent street crime in the media, the public ranks some corporate crimes as similar in seriousness to traditional street crimes (Braithwaite 1985b; Cullen et al. 1982; Schrager and Short 1980). In particular, crimes committed by businesses which cause injury or death, such as manufacturing dangerous products, are regarded as equal in seriousness to violent street crimes (Schrager and Short 1980). In general, the public ranks crimes by corporations as more serious than crimes against corporations (Levi 1987, 60).

One might expect that business executives would view the matter differently than the general public. However, with some exceptions business executives may be more like the general public than not. Understandably, business executives tend to rank offenses in which they may be potential offenders as less serious than those in which they may be potential victims (Levi 1987). Nevertheless, like the general public, executives evaluate many white-collar and corporate crimes as serious offenses. Early research by Aubert (1952) found that Norwegian businessmen condemned violations of wartime price and rationing regulations. A survey of one hundred executives in Australia suggested that their responses to various sorts of fraud paralleled those one might expect to find in the general public. The executives ranked corporate offenses involving injury or risk of injury as more serious than simple credit card frauds by lone individuals (Cole 1983, cited in Levi 1987). A survey of American executives found that they endorsed criminal sanctioning for corporate offenses perceived as harmful, though to a lesser degree than did the general public (Frank et al. 1989). According to research by Levi (1987, 70), senior executives in Britain rank some types of fraud as more serious than street crimes such as burglary or vandalism. The idea, then, that business executives have a tolerant or permissive view of white-collar types of crime is mistaken.

The implications of research on crime seriousness for criminal justice policy must be treated cautiously. That people regard some corporate crimes as equal in seriousness to violent street crimes does not mean corporate and street crimes pose equal threats in the average citizen's day-to-day life. People may be outraged in an abstract sense at the thought of defective products that maim and kill but more worried at a visceral level about personal victimization by street criminals. Nor does research on crime seriousness tell us whether the public wants white-collar types of crime more heavily policed (Levi 1987, 73). These matters warrant further empirical investigation. Nevertheless, evidence suggests that white-collar crime is a matter of some concern to the public.

But what about prosecutors? How do they view the corporate crime problem? To answer this question, we began by asking prosecutors about the seriousness of the corporate crime in their jurisdictions. Only 3.6 percent of the respondents reported that corporate crime was a "very serious" problem in their jurisdictions. Another 30 percent considered it a "somewhat serious" problem. Just under half of the respondents (49.6 percent) saw corporate crime as "not at all serious." The remainder (16.7 percent) responded that they "didn't know" about the seriousness. Of those expressing an opinion, then, about 60 percent feel that the corporate crime problem is "not at all serious" versus about 40 percent who feel that it is at least "somewhat serious."

Whether 40 percent represents a large or small amount of concern is difficult to say. Unfortunately, our survey data, gathered at only one point in time, do not permit us to determine whether the level of concern over corporate crime is increasing, decreasing, or remaining the same. The prosecutors' responses to two questions about trends in corporate crime prosecutions lead us to suspect that concern is increasing. Over one-quarter (27.9 percent) of the respondents reported that corporate prosecutions have increased during their tenure in office, and a similar number (29 percent) say that they anticipate conducting more corporate prosecutions in the future. Less than one percent have observed or anticipate a decrease in corporate prosecutions.

As is true of all social problems, the corporate crime problem is perceived to be more serious in some types of communities than in others. The problem of street crime, for example, is generally regarded as more acute in large cities than in less populous suburban and rural areas. The same appears to be true for corporate crime. Of the 40 percent of prosecutors who regard corporate crime as a very or a somewhat serious problem, most are located in large jurisdictions. As Table 4.4 shows, prosecutors located in jurisdictions in the upper quartile in population size (over 328,000) are much more likely to see corporate crime as a serious problem than are their counterparts in smaller districts. About one out of eight (11.8 percent) of the prosecutors in large jurisdictions regard corporate crime as a very serious problem, and 63.7 percent see it as somewhat serious. Prosecutors located in medium-sized jurisdictions do not regard the local corporate crime problem to be quite as serious as do their counterparts in large jurisdictions; just under a third (29.1 percent) see it as a somewhat serious problem. In smaller jurisdictions, a majority of prosecutors see corporate crime as not at all serious.

Population size is not the only community characteristic that influ-

Table 4.4 Perceived Seriousness of the Corporate Crime Problem, by Population Size of Jurisdiction

Perceived Seriousness[a]	Size of Jurisdiction[b]			
	Medium-Small (%)	Small(%)	Medium-Large(%)	Large(%)
Very serious	1.9	1.0	0.0	11.8
Somewhat serious	10.5	17.6	29.1	63.7
Not at all serious	73.3	55.9	51.5	16.7
Don't know	14.3	25.5	19.4	7.8

[a]In response to the question, "In your opinion, how serious is the corporate crime problem in your jurisdiction?"

[b]Districts are grouped by quartiles: small $\leq$ 75,500; medium-small $\leq$ 150,000; medium-large $\leq$ 328,100; large $>$ 328,100.

ences perceptions of corporate crime. Region of the country also makes a difference. A majority of prosecutors in western jurisdictions (68.5 percent) say that corporate crime is a somewhat or a very serious problem. In contrast, in all other regions more than half of the respondents regard corporate crime as not at all serious. Since western prosecutors tend to serve districts with larger populations than do other prosecutors, it is possible that this factor accounts for their view of the corporate crime problem as being more serious. To investigate this possibility, we divided the sample at the 75th percentile, creating subsamples of large versus other jurisdictions, and cross-tabulated region and perceived seriousness in each subsample. The results, shown in Table 4.5, indicate that regional variation in perceived seriousness remains even after size of jurisdiction is controlled. Compared to their counterparts in other regions, western prosecutors who serve small jurisdictions are about twice as likely to regard corporate crime as somewhat serious. Nearly half (46.7 percent) of the western prosecutors in small jurisdictions regard corporate crime as somewhat serious, compared to less than one quarter of their counterparts in other regions. In the large jurisdiction subsample, 95 percent of western prosecutors regard

Table 4.5 Perceived Seriousness of the Corporate Crime Problem, by Region in Large versus Small to Medium-Sized Jurisdictions

Perceived Seriousness[a]	Midwest (%)	Northeast (%)	South (%)	West (%)
	Large Jurisdictions[b]			
Very serious	4.6	0.0	16.7	25.0
Somewhat serious	63.6	73.1	50.0	70.8
Not at all serious	22.7	19.2	23.3	0.0
Don't know	9.1	7.7	10.0	4.2
N	22	26	30	24
	Small and Medium-Sized Jurisdictions[b]			
Very serious	1.0	0.0	1.6	0.0
Somewhat serious	17.3	23.3	12.6	46.7
Not at all serious	68.2	62.8	58.3	36.7
Don't know	13.6	14.0	27.6	16.7
N	110	43	127	30

[a]In response to the question, "In your opinion, how serious is the corporate crime problem in your jurisdiction?"

[b]Large jurisdictions are all those in the upper quartile of the population distribution (above 328,100 in population size). Small and medium-sized jurisdictions are those of 328,100 or less in population size.

corporate crime as at least somewhat serious, compared to between 68 and 83 percent of prosecutors in the other three regions.[3]

Just as they view corporate crime as being more serious than do their counterparts in smaller jurisdictions, prosecutors located in large jurisdictions are more likely to report an upward trend in corporate crime prosecutions. Over half of the respondents located in large jurisdictions have noted an increase in prosecutions during their tenure in office, and a majority (52.9 percent) expect this trend to continue (see Table 4.6). Although proportionately fewer of the prosecutors located in smaller jurisdictions report these trends, it is noteworthy that between one-fifth and one-quarter expect to prosecute more corporate cases in the future than in the past, and almost no one expects to do less.

In summary, community context influences perceptions of the corporate crime problem. Corporate crime is seen as a more serious and growing problem in large jurisdictions than in small ones, but a sizable minority of prosecutors located in jurisdictions with relatively small populations expect to prosecute more corporate crime cases in the future. Prosecutors

Table 4.6 Perceived Trends in Corporate Crime Prosecutions, by Population Size of Jurisdiction

	Size of Jurisdiction[a]			
Trends	Small (%)	Medium-Small (%)	Medium-Large (%)	Large (%)
Past[b]				
Increasing	10.6	16.5	25.7	58.3
About the same	76.0	71.8	64.4	38.8
Decreasing	0.0	0.0	1.0	1.9
Don't know	13.5	11.7	8.9	1.0
Future[c]				
More	14.3	20.6	27.9	52.9
About the same	68.6	55.9	51.0	44.1
Fewer	1.0	0.0	1.0	0.0
Don't know	16.2	23.5	20.2	2.9

[a]Districts are grouped by quartiles: small ≤ 75,500; medium-small ≤ 150,000; medium-large ≤ 328,100; large > 328,100.

[b]In response to the question, "During your tenure as a prosecuting attorney, has the number of corporate crimes prosecuted annually by your office been increasing, remaining about the same, or decreasing?"

[c]In response to the question, "In the future, do you expect that your office will prosecute more, about the same, or fewer corporate criminal cases than in the past?"

located in western states regard corporate crime as a more serious problem than do prosecutors located in other regions.

Responsibility and Jurisdiction for Corporate Crime

It is tempting to think that serious problems are met with serious treatment, but often this is not the case. Even though most prosecutors located in large jurisdictions regard corporate crime as a serious or somewhat serious problem, they may not be doing anything to control it. Prosecutors may feel that the responsibility for corporate crime belongs to someone else or that they do not have jurisdiction over crimes committed by corporations. As a prelude to investigating local prosecutors' actions against corporate crime, we first address the questions of responsibility and jurisdiction. Do local prosecutors believe that they have jurisdiction over corporate crimes, and who do they think conducts most prosecutions in their area?

Traditionally, the federal government has been thought to take primary responsibility for the control of corporate conduct, primarily through its regulatory agencies and commissions. Federal corporate criminal prosecutions are conducted by the ninety-six U.S. Attorneys' offices located throughout the country. Given the dominant role of federal agencies in regulating corporate conduct, one might expect that local prosecutors would perceive the U.S. Attorney's office as the agency most active against corporate crime. But when we asked the respondents who conducts most of the prosecutions of corporate crime in their jurisdictions, only 16 percent named the local U.S. Attorney's office. Slightly less than one-third said that their office conducts most local corporate crime prosecutions. The largest percentage (43 percent) said that the state attorney general's office conducted most corporate crime prosecutions in their area. We cannot assess the accuracy of prosecutors' perceptions of the activities of U.S. Attorneys against corporate crime. Perhaps local and state prosecutors really are doing more against corporate crime than the various U.S. Attorneys' offices. Alternatively, this finding may mean that local prosecutors simply do not know much about what the local U.S. Attorney is doing. We return to this issue below, when we discuss local prosecutors' communication and cooperation with other law enforcement and regulatory agencies.

The willingness of prosecutors to take an active role against corporate crime is influenced by their perceptions of the seriousness of the local problem. Not surprisingly, prosecutors who feel strongly about the seriousness of the corporate crime problem are more likely to report that they are leading the fight against it. Roughly half of those who regard corporate crime as a serious problem said that their office conducts most local corporate crime prosecutions, compared to only 20 percent of those who think that corporate crime is not a serious problem (see Table 4.7).

Presumably, local prosecutors have a clear understanding of their jurisdiction with respect to ordinary street crimes, but corporate crimes are less common than street crimes (at least insofar as the former are discovered). The opportunity to prosecute unlawful corporate conduct does not arise every day in most local jurisdictions. Prosecutors tend to be less experienced in recognizing and responding to corporate crimes than to street crimes. When potentially illegal corporate behavior does occur, prosecutors often find that applying the criminal law raises difficult questions of jurisdiction. Local action against a corporate crime, no matter how serious the transgression, is unlikely if the local prosecutor does not believe that he or she has jurisdiction over the offense in question. It is important, therefore, to understand the views of local prosecutors on their jurisdiction over corporate crimes.

We asked the respondents whether it is within the jurisdiction of their office to prosecute business entities for the nine corporate crimes discussed above. As Table 4.8 shows, the percentage of prosecutors reporting that they have jurisdiction varies considerably from crime to crime. Almost 95 percent of the prosecutors report jurisdiction over illegal payments to gov-

Table 4.7   Perceptions of Who Conducts Most Local Corporate Prosecutions, by Perceived Seriousness of Corporate Crime Locally

	Perceived Seriousness of Corporate Crime Problem			
Who Conducts Most Corporate Crime Prosecutions?	Very Serious (%)	Somewhat Serious (%)	Not At All Serious (%)	Don't Know (%)
District attorney	53.3	43.6	19.9	20.0
State attorney general	20.0	36.3	50.8	38.8
U.S. attorney	13.3	9.7	18.9	17.9
Don't know	13.3	10.5	10.5	22.4
N	15	124	201	67

Table 4.8 Jurisdiction over Selected Corporate Crimes

	Responses to Question[a]	
Corporate Crime	Yes (%)	No (%)
Consumer fraud	85.3	14.7
Securities fraud	64.3	35.7
Insurance fraud	89.2	10.8
Tax fraud	58.9	41.1
False claims and statements	87.4	12.6
Workplace offenses (e.g., unsafe working conditions)	38.7	61.3
Environmental offenses (e.g., dumping toxic wastes)	72.9	27.1
Illegal payments to government officials	94.1	5.9
Unfair trade practices (e.g., price-fixing, bid-rigging, restraint of trade)	46.6	53.4

[a]"Keeping in mind the working definition of corporate crime—that is, crime by or on behalf of a corporation—is it within the jurisdiction of your office to prosecute business entities for any of the corporate offenses listed below?"

ernment officials, but fewer than half say that they have jurisdiction over workplace offenses and unfair trade practices (39 percent and 47 percent, respectively).

Somewhat surprisingly, prosecutors located in the same state often do not agree on whether they have jurisdiction over particular crimes. Indeed, considerable lack of agreement is reported among respondents located in the same state over their jurisdiction in corporate cases. In every state, respondents differ over whether they, as local prosecutors, have jurisdiction over particular corporate crimes. For example, of the thirteen respondents from Alabama, eight report that they can prosecute consumer fraud crimes; four say that they cannot. (One Alabama respondent did not answer this question.) In Illinois, seventeen respondents report jurisdiction over business entities that make false claims or statements, but ten do not. Similar examples of disagreement were found in all states.

One possible explanation for this result is that some respondents may not have received any complaints about particular types of corporate crime and, hence, have had no reason to research the relevant state law. Not well informed about the law, these prosecutors may think that they do not have jurisdiction over particular offenses, when in fact they do. In support of this explanation, we note that prosecutors located in jurisdictions with large populations are more likely to report that they have jurisdiction over particular offenses. For example, 94 percent of the respondents located in large jurisdictions report they can prosecute consumer fraud cases, compared to 79 percent of their counterparts in small jurisdictions.[4] Similarly, 59 percent of prosecutors located in large jurisdictions say that they have authority over unfair trade practices versus 41 percent of prosecutors in small jurisdictions.

Alternatively, some prosecutors may be more aggressive than others about applying traditional law in innovative ways. For example, some states do not have consumer fraud statutes. Nevertheless, consumer fraud–like offenses in these states may be prosecutable under theft by deception statutes. Similarly, other areas of corporate misconduct, such as environmental and workplace-related offenses, may be reachable with innovative use of traditional laws. If this latter interpretation is correct, the results shown in Table 4.8 suggest that considerable variation exists in the ability and willingness of local prosecutors to use the criminal law against corporate crime.

The results on the question of jurisdiction have both negative and positive implications for local corporate crime control. The extent of disagreement over such relatively straightforward crimes as consumer fraud and false claims is worrying. Because prosecutors in some jurisdictions do not realize that they have authority over these crimes, corporate offenders may operate with impunity. However, the sizable number who report that they do have jurisdiction over such relatively new crimes as environmental and workplace-related offenses may mean that local prosecutors are looking beyond traditional street crimes and recognizing the serious threat posed by offenses committed in corporate settings.

Prevalence of Corporate Crime Prosecutions

In 1988, fully two-thirds of the offices responding to the survey prosecuted at least one corporate crime, and the crime most likely to be prosecuted was consumer fraud. As Table 4.9 shows, just over 40 percent of the respondents reported handling at least one such case. In contrast, only eight percent reported prosecuting an unfair trade practices case. Somewhat surprisingly, environmental crimes were prosecuted by over 30 percent of the respondents. This equaled the numbers for false claims and

Table 4.9 Prosecution of Selected Corporate
Crimes in 1988

	Responses to Question[a]	
Corporate Crime	Yes (%)	No (%)
Consumer fraud	40.8	59.2
Securities fraud	22.4	77.6
Insurance fraud	30.7	69.3
Tax fraud	16.0	84.0
False claims	31.0	69.0
Workplace offenses	11.0	89.0
Environmental offenses	30.6	69.4
Illegal payments	15.9	84.1
Unfair trade practices	7.8	92.2

[a]"In 1988, did your office *actually prosecute* any of the following corporate offenses?"

insurance fraud offenses. Consumer fraud also had the highest rate of prosecution compared to the other crimes. Table 4.10 shows that about 15 percent of the respondents say they "typically" prosecute more than three such cases per year and that another 20 percent handle one to three cases per year. The next most frequently prosecuted crimes are false claims, insurance fraud, and environmental offenses. Approximately 10 percent of the districts typically prosecute more than three of these offenses per year.

We observe the influence of community context on prosecutorial activity against corporate crime by noting the regional variations in rates of prosecution. In general, consistent with their view of corporate crime as a more serious problem, the most active local prosecutors are located in the West. Table 4.11 reports the percentage of prosecutors in each region who typically handle more than three cases per year of the selected corporate crimes. With two exceptions (workplace-related offenses and illegal payments), a greater percentage of prosecutors located in western states achieve this rate than do those in other regions. The West stands out as being particularly active against consumer fraud, false claims, and environmental and unfair trade offenses.

The greater level of activity against corporate crime among western prosecutors may be due to the size of districts they serve. The average west-

Table 4.10   Frequency of Prosecutions in a Typical Year

Corporate Crime	Responses to Question[a]			
	Never (%)	< 1 Case per Year (%)	1–3 Cases per Year (%)	> 3 Cases per Year (%)
Consumer fraud	31.5	33.4	20.2	14.9
Securities fraud	56.5	28.0	12.0	3.4
Insurance fraud	37.5	39.0	14.5	9.1
Tax fraud	61.4	25.3	7.6	5.7
False claims	40.2	33.6	14.8	11.4
Workplace offenses	68.3	25.4	5.0	1.2
Environmental offenses	45.1	33.8	12.7	8.3
Illegal payments	50.9	37.4	9.5	2.2
Unfair trade practices	74.9	17.7	3.0	4.5

[a]"Typically, how often does your office prosecute the corporate criminal offenses listed below?"

Table 4.11   Prosecutions of More Than Three Cases per Year, by Region

Crime	Region			
	South (%)	West (%)	Northeast (%)	Midwest (%)
Consumer fraud	10.6	41.5	15.9	8.6
Securities fraud	2.5	9.3	1.5	3.2
Insurance fraud	8.2	15.4	13.0	5.5
Tax fraud	7.0	9.4	1.5	4.7
False claims	8.8	30.0	11.8	7.0
Workplace offenses	2.6	2.0	0.0	0.0
Environmental offenses	2.5	33.3	8.6	5.5
Illegal payments	1.9	2.0	4.5	1.6
Unfair trade practices	1.3	27.5	0.0	1.6

ern district has a population of 487,985 versus 237,000 in the South, 353,859 in the Northeast, and 211,510 in the Midwest. As Tables 4.12a and 4.12b show, however, controlling for population size reduces but does not eliminate regional differences. Compared to their counterparts in other regions, prosecutors located in both large and small western districts still report the highest levels of activity against almost all forms of corporate crime.[5]

Table 4.12a   Prosecutions of More Than Three Cases per Year in Small Districts, by Region

	Small Districts[a]			
Crime	South (%)	West (%)	Northeast (%)	Midwest (%)
Consumer fraud	3.9	30.0	6.7	4.5
Securities fraud	0.8	0.0	0.0	0.0
Insurance fraud	3.9	10.0	2.2	2.7
Tax fraud	3.9	6.7	0.0	3.6
False claims	6.0	20.0	8.9	3.6
Workplace offenses	3.1	3.3	0.0	0.0
Environmental offenses	0.8	20.0	2.2	3.6
Illegal payments	0.8	0.0	2.2	0.0
Unfair trade practices	0.8	13.3	0.0	0.0

[a]Small districts ≤ 328,100 in population size.

Table 4.12b   Prosecutions of More Than Three Cases per Year in Large Districts, by Region

	Large Districts[a]			
Crime	South (%)	West (%)	Northeast (%)	Midwest (%)
Consumer fraud	37.5	54.2	30.8	27.3
Securities fraud	9.4	20.8	3.9	18.2
Insurance fraud	25.0	20.8	30.8	18.2
Tax fraud	18.6	12.5	3.9	9.1
False claims	18.6	37.5	15.4	22.7
Workplace offenses	0.0	0.0	0.0	0.0
Environmental offenses	9.4	45.8	19.2	13.6
Illegal payments	6.3	4.2	7.7	9.1
Unfair trade practices	3.1	41.7	0.0	9.1

[a]Large districts > 328,100 in population size.

Conclusions

The literature on corporate crime is famous, perhaps infamous, for its often hyperbolic rhetoric about the evils of corporate crime. This stridency is not surprising. Corporate crime is serious. It imposes many profound and varied costs on its victims. Nevertheless, for those in the law enforcement business, the seriousness of any particular type of crime must always be judged in relative terms. Relative to other forms of crime, corporate crime appears not to rank as the most serious problem for most local prosecutors. We did not ask the respondents to rank the seriousness of corporate crime relative to drug abuse and violent crime. We suspect, though, that it would have been ranked as less serious than both of these more highly publicized and well-known problems.

Evidence gathered during our field studies supports this speculation. In our interviews, we often heard that drug and violent crime cases take top priority and, accordingly, get the lion's share of resources. For example, in Chicago, a deputy district attorney, dismayed at the devastating effect that the war on drugs has had on other areas of prosecution, argued that no progress had been made against drugs. In his view, the tremendous and wasted infusion of resources into drug enforcement came at the expense of corporate crime and other areas of enforcement.

It's kaput. It's over. The game, the war, there is no war. We've filed them to the max on these drug things. We have allocated all our resources for drug things . . . Basically, we're not going to get a dime from anybody for any other area except drugs . . . After eight years of this approach the problem is ten times worse and it has hurt every other area of prosecution. By and large, when you're talking about corporate prosecutions, the judge is going to say, "I don't have time. I got thirty drug dealers."

Another prosecutor in Los Angeles expanded on this sentiment, noting that drug and street crime constitute only one element in a constellation of problems that compete with white-collar crime enforcement for money and manpower.

There are a tremendous number of people who have come into the state recently, either illegally or coming in on the various types of programs, which has increased health needs. Tuberculosis for example, which is quite prevalent in many parts of the world, and so there's increased needs there; schools suddenly burgeoning in certain areas; there are educational programs, bilingual programs which become more expensive; there are a lot of additional expenses that come in initially. Crime has increased. Los Angeles is now the national center for local gang participation in cocaine. I mean you find Los Angeles gangs operating in Kansas City and Chicago, elsewhere. So you have increased gangs, increased narcotics problems . . . Almost every area there is something that costs money. Now with the earthquake there is going to be additional money on the highway system; they just are going to raise the tax one fourth of a percent to pay for that. So there's going to be additional expenses there. There are a whole host of expenses which occur in this state which cut the total budget and because that total budget is cut, law enforcement is cut; prisons . . . federal courts now have said you can't send any more people to these prisons. There're already three times as many as there should be, so what do you have to do? You have to build prisons. Well, there's some problem. People love prisons but not in their neighborhood. So you gotta have prisons out who knows where which leads to greater expense for communication, [so it's] very difficult where you're going to put them; the expense is dramatic; the expense of care is dramatic; so all of this is money, and because the money is such a major aspect, it hits on law enforcement . . . particularly in regard to white collar crime, because the excitement is on crimes of violence and narcotics. And those are certainly big issues of the day, and the other sometimes gets lost.

Local prosecutors in California, of course, face their own unique set of problems. Their counterparts in most other states probably do not have to compete with earthquakes and immigrants for tax dollars, but in other states there are other problems. The amount of attention and resources that local prosecutors can allocate to corporate crime is always determined relative to the demands of other problems.

The data presented in this chapter indicate that, while corporate crime is not the most pressing problem confronting local prosecutors, it has, nevertheless, emerged from its previous obscurity. In our reference year, a substantial majority of offices (66 percent) prosecuted at least one corporate offense. Fewer than 15 percent of the respondents reported that their offices never prosecute any of the selected corporate crimes. It is fair to say, then, that the typical local prosecutor handles corporate crime cases every year.

Whether this level of local activity against corporate crime should be regarded as surprisingly large or depressingly small is, of course, a matter of opinion. We strongly suspect that, had this survey been conducted at any time prior to the mid-1970s, we would have observed virtually no local corporate crime prosecutions. It is also highly likely that whatever local corporate crime prosecutions there were then would have been restricted to consumer fraud and other financial crimes. We doubt that prior to the 1980s local prosecutors paid any attention to environmental or workplace-related offenses. Yet, our survey reveals that prosecutions of these nonfinancial crimes take place on a regular basis in a sizable number of local jurisdictions, confirming the trend, noted in the early 1980s, that local prosecutors were moving beyond simple fraud cases to take on more sophisticated forms of corporate crime (Edelhertz and Rogovin 1982b, 11). Given that corporate crime prosecutions can consume many more resources than street crime prosecutions, the willingness of local prosecutors to be involved in even a few cases should not be seen as insignificant. For many local prosecutors, corporate crime is now a matter of continuing concern.

Given the cross-sectional data at our disposal, we cannot determine whether the concern over corporate crime is continuing to grow or remaining stable. Some evidence suggests that the trend is upward, particularly in large cities. A majority of prosecutors located in large jurisdictions report an increase in corporate prosecutions during their tenure in office, and most expect that this trend will continue. Like so many other social problems, corporate crime seems to be a more serious concern in big cities than in small ones. Whether the rate of corporate crime is actually higher in big cities cannot be determined from our data. Prosecutors in large jurisdictions have more personnel and financial resources than their counterparts in small jurisdictions. The former can afford to set up mechanisms for receiving and responding to complaints about corporate misconduct, leading to more complaints from the victims of corporate crime. In large jurisdictions, corporate crime may have a higher salience for local prosecutors simply because they hear about it more often.

There are several reasons for viewing local prosecutors' present level of activity against corporate crime as significant. Even though most prosecutors handle only a few cases a year, when spread across the entire nation, this translates into several thousand corporate prosecutions each year. And the number of prosecutions must be viewed in relation to the number of offenders potentially available to commit crimes and to be prosecuted. There are far fewer corporations than individuals. So, even a few prosecutions per year may actually represent a more substantial rate of prosecutions of corporate offenders than the raw numbers indicate.

A qualitative difference exists between no prosecutions, as we might have expected to find in the 1960s, and even a few prosecutions per year per jurisdiction today. Even a few cases in a local jurisdiction sends an important message to the local business community. The general deterrent effect of corporate prosecutions, regardless of how few, should not be underestimated. As we will show, this assumption of deterrence is certainly held by the majority of local prosecutors. They strongly believe that even a small number of corporate prosecutions serves notice that illegal activity in the business community will not be tolerated. Use of criminal proceedings against corporations, even though they may be activated infrequently, also can reinforce other types of sanctions (Braithwaite 1985a). They can serve, therefore, as an important back-up to regulatory and other administrative controls on corporate conduct. Each case that occurs creates a precedent for prosecution, both in the office that conducted it and in other offices. These precedents strengthen society's control over corporate conduct generally.

Finally, some offices conduct corporate prosecutions at a much higher rate than do others. We need to learn more about these high-rate offices and about what makes for more, rather than fewer, prosecutions. Some local jurisdictions may be better protected against corporate predators than others.

Notes

1. We did ask respondents to tell us the number of corporate prosecutions that their office initiated in 1988 or, if they did not know the exact number, to provide an estimate. About one-half of the respondents could not tell us the exact number of prosecutions in 1988, but most were at least able to provide an estimate. Unfortunately, we have some reservations about the validity of these estimates. The mean for the estimated number of corporate crime prosecutions is substantially larger than the mean for the reported number of prosecutions (16.12 and 2.68, respectively). In at least two cases, the estimates are clearly too high. Two districts of less than half a million in population size reported conducting five hundred or more corporate prosecutions in 1988, which is several times larger than the number reported by much larger jurisdictions. In light of the large proportion of nonresponses to the question on the number of prosecutions and the validity of the estimated number of prosecutions, we decided to use the frequency measures described in the text.

2. That some of the urban districts are so small may seem surprising. However, these relatively small districts are located in either an MSA or PMSA. They were included in the sample on the theory that, because they are part of large metropolitan areas, they will experience similar problems with corporate misconduct to those of more populous jurisdictions.

3. As a further check, we collapsed the perceived seriousness variable into two categories (very serious and somewhat serious versus not at all serious). We then logistically regressed perceived seriousness on population size and region. The regression analysis found that region of the country makes a statistically significant contribution to the equation in both subsamples and in the sample as a whole. Western prosecutors view the corporate crime problem as being more serious than do prosecutors in other jurisdictions.

4. As above, large jurisdictions are defined as those in the upper quartile of the population distribution—that is, with populations greater than 328,100. Small jurisdictions are those in the lower quartile, with populations less than 75,500.

5. We also used multiple regression analysis to investigate the relative effects of population size and region on prosecutorial activity against corporate crime. As described in chapter 7, we constructed a scale of prosecutorial activity by combining responses to the questions on typical prosecutions per year. We then regressed this scale on region and population size. Region was operationalized as a set of three dummy variables with the West as the reference category. The results showed that, controlling for population size, western prosecutors are more active against corporate crime than are prosecutors in other regions.

5

SOCIAL CONTEXT
AND THE PROCESS OF
PROSECUTION

We all like to get in there with a good murder case or an armed
robbery where the guy's a real bad ass or a drug case or something.
But corporate cases, they're very dry and boring, and they're tedious,
and they're hard to win, and they're tough.

ASSISTANT DISTRICT ATTORNEY, DUVALL COUNTY, FLORIDA

Because corporate crimes are committed in organizational settings, they can be troublesome to detect, investigate, and prosecute (Stone 1975). Investigations and prosecutions tend to be long and costly affairs. Prosecutors often must contend with skilled defense attorneys who take full advantage of the procedural safeguards afforded by the law to criminal defendants. These attorneys actively seek to restrict prosecutors' access to evidence that frequently involves voluminous and complex technical or financial data (Mann 1985). Prevailing in such complicated cases is difficult even for experienced, well-funded federal prosecutors. For local prosecutors, it is an even more uncertain undertaking. Because most local prosecutors lack the technical expertise and financial resources of federal prosecutors, they often are thought to be ill-equipped to pursue corporate crime cases.

Despite obstacles and uncertainties, local prosecutors take on corporate crime cases every day. How do they discover and investigate these cases? Do they cooperate with federal law enforcement officials and with regulatory agencies in joint investigations, or do they tend to rely solely on the local police to investigate corporate crime? What constraints do local prosecutors face when deciding whether to proceed criminally or civilly against an alleged corporate offender? And are these constraints shaped by the community context in which prosecutors are located? This chapter focuses on the process of prosecution in corporate criminal cases.

We begin by investigating how corporate crimes are discovered and what investigative techniques local prosecutors favor in these cases. Next, we address the important topic of special units and networking with other agencies, paying particular attention to cooperation between local and federal authorities and to the influence of community context on networking. Finally, we focus on perhaps the most important decision in the prosecution process: whether to undertake a corporate criminal prosecution. What are the factors that local prosecutors consider when making this crucial decision?

Discovery and Investigation

In a famous scene in Clint Eastwood's movie *Dirty Harry*, Detective "Dirty" Harry Callahan, while getting a cup of coffee at a diner, observes a robbery in progress and springs into action. After shooting several of the would-be robbers, Dirty Harry challenges the one left standing to take a shot at him, with the immortal line "Go ahead. Make my day." The robber wisely decides that discretion is the better part of valor and surrenders to Harry. While this fictional episode certainly makes for thrilling movie-watching, it bears little resemblence to actual police work.

One of the most widely known, well-documented, and stable findings in criminal justice is that police work is largely reactive (Bittner 1980; Reiss 1971). The police rarely personally observe or discover instances of serious criminal conduct on their own. In the vast majority of cases, someone complains and the police react. Unlike Dirty Harry, real-world police officers do not stumble across many robberies in progress; rather, they are called on to handle crimes discovered by others or, more accurately, to clean up after crimes suffered all too keenly by the victims. Some exceptions to this general pattern exist. Most notably, illegal narcotics and vice crimes often are investigated proactively.

Proactive crime control strategies call for enforcers to seek out potential or ongoing criminal activity on their own initiative, as opposed to waiting for someone to complain before acting. These strategies are thought to be especially useful and necessary in cases where the putative victims participate in their own victimization, as in vice crimes, or where victims may not be aware of their own victimization, as in some white-collar and corporate crimes. A distinguishing feature of many corporate crimes is that they are integrated into routine, legitimate activities, making their discovery especially problematic (Benson 1985). Hence, many recommend adopting proactive approaches to corporate crime control. However, our survey data suggest that they are not the main source of corporate crime cases for local prosecutors. Table 5.1 shows how often local prosecutors receive referrals on corporate cases from different sources. Most often, cases come to their attention via complaints by business and citizen victims or referrals from the local police, who it is probably safe to assume are passing on complaints received from victims. The next most common sources are state regulatory agencies, followed by the state police and state attorney general's office. Federal law enforcement and regulatory agencies apparently do not refer many cases to local prosecutors and neither do public interest groups. Like street crimes, then, corporate crimes come to the attention of local prosecutors mainly by means of individual or business victim complaints.

That the most common source of corporate cases is complaints by victims suggests that local corporate crime control is more reactive than pro-

Table 5.1 Frequency of Referrals from Selected Sources

	Responses to Question[a]			
Referral Source	Never (%)	< 1 Case per Year (%)	1–3 Cases per Year (%)	> 3 Cases per Year (%)
Local police	25.3	39.5	20.3	14.9
State police	41.4	37.2	15.9	5.5
State attorney general	40.0	37.4	16.2	6.4
State regulatory agency	27.5	39.1	19.7	13.6
Federal regulatory agency	71.4	21.8	6.0	0.8
U.S. attorney's office	71.6	23.2	4.9	0.3
FBI	63.4	28.8	6.5	1.3
Business victims	22.4	36.8	19.4	21.4
Citizen victims	18.3	37.1	22.6	22.1
Public interest groups	59.2	28.1	8.8	3.9

[a]"In general, how often do the sources listed below refer potential corporate criminal cases to your office for investigation or prosecution?"

active. This result does not mean, though, that the best cases are discovered in this manner, nor does it mean that proactive strategies are completely ignored by local officials. The relatively few cases forwarded to local prosecutors by regulatory agencies may be more substantial and serious than those received from victims. Evaluations of the units participating in the National District Attorneys' Association's (NDAA's) Economic Crime Project found that many complaints from victims were either unfounded or trivial; the more important cases tended to come from other sources (Whitcomb et al. 1979; Finn and Hoffman 1976). Unfortunately, our survey data do not permit us to assess the quality of the cases that local prosecutors receive from different sources.

After an offense is brought to the attention of authorities, the next step in the process is investigation. In the case of the typical street crime, investigations are conducted primarily by the police; usually prosecutors are not extensively involved. Their role in the investigative process is confined primarily to evaluating the quality of the case brought to them by the police. In contrast, corporate crimes often are thought to require a more active role by the prosecutor and special investigative techniques (Katz 1977). In his research on federal prosecutors, Jack Katz found that they take a more active part in white-collar crime investigations than they do in street-crime investigations. In the typical white-collar case, federal prosecutors direct investigators about what to look for rather than simply evaluating whether the evidence investigators have gathered is legally sufficient to win in court. The prosecutor takes a more active role in the investigation by advising investigators as to the type of evidence needed to make the case or by negotiating with the individuals allegedly involved in the offense to see if one or more will testify against the others. This pattern of early and active involvement in the investigation of corporate cases also is found among local prosecutors. According to a local prosecutor in Duval County, Florida, who handles environmental violations, if he does not personally take charge of the investigation, it would not get done at all. In his view, having to investigate as well as prosecute cases was inappropriate for a prosecutor:

I went to law school to be a lawyer, not to be an investigator; and I shouldn't have to be out there snooping around in the middle of the woods and fields and all that to catch these people. There ought to be somebody that's doing that . . . Our role is to be prosecutors. We're trained in the rules of evidence. Our role is to go in there like Perry Mason and win the damn case in front of a jury and that's what I enjoy doing. I don't think it really should be incumbent upon our office to go out and discover all these environmental crimes. I think there ought to be an agency somewhere that does it. But unfortunately, there isn't.

We asked respondents to rate the usefulness of seven investigative methods. Table 5.2 shows the results. The most useful method appears to be a search of financial records, as 70 percent of those using this method rated it very useful. Over 50 percent rated interviews, grand jury subpoenas, document examination, and search warrants as very useful. In contrast, only 29 percent rated confidential informants as very useful, and even fewer (23 percent) rated computers as a very useful method of investigating corporate crimes. However, nearly half (47 percent) have never used computers as a method of investigation. These results may suggest that, in conducting corporate investigations, prosecutors are more comfortable using standard investigative techniques, such as interviews and search warrants, than they are using special techniques, like confidential informants and computer surveillance. A similar point was made by many of the investigators interviewed during the field studies. When asked how they went about investigating corporate crimes, many commented that the basic techniques used for corporate and street crimes are the same. They involve talking to people, trying to get the full picture of what happened, and looking for inconsistencies in what suspects and informants tell them. We will return

Table 5.2   Usefulness of Selected Investigative Methods

Investigative Method	Response to Question[a]			
	Very Useful (%)	Somewhat Useful (%)	Not Very Useful (%)	Never Used (%)
Interviews	58.3	39.3	2.5	17.3
Financial records search	70.8	26.7	2.5	19.8
Grand jury subpoena	54.1	31.2	14.7	41.1
Document examination	55.1	40.1	4.8	20.1
Confidential information	28.6	47.7	23.7	31.4
Computers	22.9	49.8	27.3	47.0
Search warrants	56.0	36.8	7.3	23.4

Note: Percentages in rows do not sum to 100. Percentages in the first three columns are based on the number of respondents who have used a method; percentages in column 4 are based on the total responding.

[a]"In your experience, have the following methods of investigating corporate crimes been very useful, somewhat useful, or not very useful?"

to a more detailed discussion of the investigative process in chapter 9, when we present the results of our field interviews with investigators.

Special Units and Networking

A decade ago, Edelhertz and Rogovin (1982c, 11) argued that local prosecutors were beginning to see white-collar law enforcement as part of their job. No longer willing to cede the federal government exclusive jurisdiction over corporate crimes, local prosecutors were beginning to pursue these cases themselves. Unfortunately, without baseline data, we cannot determine whether this trend has continued, but some evidence suggests that it has.

As of 1978, district attorneys in sixty-six jurisdictions were participating in the NDAA's Economic Crime Project (Edelhertz and Rogovin 1982c, 11). The survey which does not include information from the two hundred or so nonresponding urban districts—indicates that close to one hundred jurisdictions, representing nearly one quarter of urban districts, have a special unit. A smaller, but still notable, number of urban prosecutors' offices are involved in multiagency task forces on white-collar or corporate crime. The growing use of special control procedures may mean that corporate and other white-collar crimes have permanently emerged from their pre-1970 levels of obscurity in local law enforcement.

Because crimes committed in organizational settings raise difficult investigative and prosecutorial problems, many observers have called for local prosecutors to use special strategies to combat corporate and other white-collar crimes. One strategy is to establish special units for these crimes. Ideally, by concentrating on corporate crimes, the prosecutors in the units develop the technical and legal expertise necessary to handle these complex cases. Another strategy is to develop interagency control networks that permit prosecutors and other agencies to share information, resources, and expertise. The feasibility of both strategies was demonstrated by the NDAA's Economic Crime Project, but how widely they are used by local prosecutors is unknown.

Just under 23 percent of the respondents in our survey indicated that their office had a special "in-house unit for investigating and prosecuting economic or white-collar crimes" ($n = 97$). About 8 percent ($n = 32$) reported being involved in an "interagency task force or strike group that focuses on economic or white-collar crimes." There is considerable overlap between the two groups, as three-quarters of those involved in an interagency task force also had a special unit. Overall, a total of one hundred and three (24.4 percent) of the respondents appeared to be using one or more of the special control strategies suggested by the NDAA's Economic Crime Project. Hereafter, we refer to these as *special control districts.*

The use of special control arrangements varies by size of district and region of the country. As expected, it is much more prevalent in large than in small jurisdictions. Although just over 70 percent of the respondents located in large jurisdictions reported having made special arrangements, fewer than one in ten of their counterparts located in small districts have done so. Special units and networks are also more common in western and, to a lesser degree, northeastern districts than in midwestern or southern districts (see Table 5.3).

Networking—that is, working collaboratively with other agencies—is an integral part of the special control strategies available to local prosecutors. To find out how extensively local prosecutors work with other agencies, we asked the respondents how often they cooperated with selected agencies on corporate crime investigations. Table 5.4 shows the results. Local prosecutors collaborate most often with the local police and state regulatory agencies. Almost 40 percent of the respondents said that they work with the local police on at least one corporate case per year, and 28 percent work with state regulatory agencies that often. The relatively high levels of cooperation with local police suggest that many prosecutors deal with corporate crimes as they do with traditional street crime. They wait

Table 5.3   Special Control Districts, by Region and Population Size

	Region				Population size[b]		
Control District[a]	Midwest (%)	Northeast (%)	South (%)	West (%)	Small (%)	Large (%)	Total (%)
No	84.2	63.4	83.2	48.2	90.8	29.8	76.0
	(112)	(45)	(134)	(26)	(286)	(31)	(317)
Yes	15.8	36.6	16.8	51.9	9.2	70.2	24.0
	(21)	(26)	(27)	(28)	(29)	(73)	(102)

[a]Special control districts are those that answered yes to at least one of the following questions. "Does your office have a special in-house unit for investigating and prosecuting economic or white-collar crimes?" or "Is your office a member of an interagency task force or strike group which focuses on economic or other white-collar crimes?"

[b]Small district ≤ 328,100 in population size; large districts >328,100 in population size.

Table 5.4 Frequency of Joint Investigations with Selected Agencies

| | Responses to Question[a] | | | |
Agency	Never (%)	< 1 Case per Year (%)	1–3 Cases per Year (%)	> 3 Cases per Year (%)
Local police	29.3	33.2	21.5	16.0
State police	45.2	32.7	15.5	6.6
State attorney general	39.4	39.4	16.1	5.2
State regulatory agency	35.4	36.4	15.9	12.4
Federal regulatory agency	70.3	22.7	5.9	1.0
U.S. attorney's office	66.8	25.8	5.9	1.5
FBI	60.9	29.2	7.4	2.5
Another prosecutor	44.4	35.1	17.7	2.8

[a]"How often does your office cooperate on joint investigations of corporate crimes with the agencies listed below?"

for the police to bring them cases. It also may mean that the crimes involved are rather routine, garden-variety consumer frauds, as these are the offenses police are most likely to hear about (Stotland 1982). A smaller, but still notable, percentage of respondents (21.3 percent) work with the state attorney general's office and state police at least once a year. Cooperation among prosecutors in different jurisdictions appears to occur at about the same rate: 20.5 percent of the respondents report working with another prosecutor's office on at least one corporate case per year. Joint investigations with federal agencies are rare; fewer than ten percent of the respondents said that they work with the FBI, U.S. Attorney's office, or federal regulatory agencies as often as once a year. Indeed, in three out of five offices, prosecutors never work with these agencies.

Membership in a control network influences the frequency of joint investigations, as cooperation is more prevalent among control network districts. Extensive cooperation with federal agencies, however, is still relatively uncommon. Fewer than one in four of the special control districts cooperated at least once a year with the FBI, U.S. Attorney, or federal regulatory agencies. In contrast, three out of four districts cooperated at least once a year with the local police on a corporate crime case, and 40 percent cooperated with the police more than three times a year.

One explanation for the rarity of cooperative investigations involving federal agencies may be that local prosecutors do not find them to be very helpful. Table 5.5 shows how prosecutors rated the helpfulness of various

Table 5.5   Helpfulness of Other Agencies

	Among Those Asking for Help[a]			
	Very Helpful (%)	Somewhat Helpful (%)	Not Very Helpful (%)	Those Who Never Asked (%)
State attorney general	47.1	37.5	15.4	29.3
State regulatory agency	48.3	44.2	7.5	26.1
Federal regulatory agency	18.8	45.5	35.8	54.6
U.S. Attorney's office	26.7	42.8	30.5	52.1
FBI	31.3	46.0	22.7	46.2

Note: Values in rows do not sum to 100. Percentages in the first three columns are based on the number of respondents who asked for help. Percentages in column 4 are based on the total responding.

[a]In response to the question, "In the past, when your office has asked for assistance on technical matters in corporate cases, how helpful have the agencies listed below been in assisting your office to make the case?"

agencies that they asked for technical assistance. A large majority of prosecutors (over 70 percent) has asked for technical assistance from the state attorney general and state regulatory agencies. Of those asking for help, about one-half found these agencies to be very helpful. Fewer than 20 percent found them to be not very helpful. In contrast, local prosecutors are much less likely to approach federal agencies for technical assistance. Over one-half have never asked for assistance from the U.S. Attorney's office or a federal regulatory agency. Just under one-half have never approached the FBI. Of those asking federal regulatory agencies for help, only 18.8 percent found them to be very helpful. Twice as many prosecutors (35.8 percent) rated them as not very helpful. U.S. Attorneys and the FBI fared better than federal regulatory agencies, but they were regarded as being less helpful than state agencies.

Overall, integration between local prosecutors and other levels of government, especially federal agencies, does not appear to be widespread. More prosecutors worked with the local police than with any other agency on corporate cases. Their lack of cooperation with, and less-than-ringing-endorsement of the helpfulness of, federal agencies is troublesome. This same pattern was observed over a decade ago (Edelhertz and Rogovin 1982c, 108). It would appear, therefore, that calls for greater local and federal cooperation have met with only partial success.

Regional Variation in Interagency Relationships

Since prosecutors located in western districts are more active than their counterparts in other regions, we investigated whether regional differences also exist in interagency working relationships. If western prosecutors employ interagency networks more than do other prosecutors, it helps explain their comparatively high levels of activity against corporate crime. It also suggests that promoting interagency networking may be a good way to enhance the effectiveness of prosecutors located in other regions.

Prosecutors located in western states cooperate with other agencies in joint investigations of corporate crime cases more often than do other prosecutors (see Table 5.6). Particularly notable are the comparatively large percentages of western prosecutors who cooperate regularly with the local police, state regulatory agencies, and other prosecutors. For example, over one-half of the western respondents report that they engage in cooperative investigations with state regulatory agencies at least once per year. In all other regions, fewer than one-quarter of the respondents report a similar level of activity. Four out of ten of the western respondents report working on joint investigations with other prosecutors regularly. Fewer than two out of ten prosecutors in other regions do so. The only agency with which western prosecutors apparently interact less frequently than do other prosecutors is the state police. We are unsure as to why this is the case. Possibly,

Table 5.6 Districts Conducting at Least One Joint Investigation per Year with Selected Agencies, by Region

	Responses to Question[a]			
Agency	Midwest (%)	Northeast (%)	South (%)	West (%)
Local police	30.7	34.8	35.8	62.3
State police	19.5	37.1	22.5	6.0
State attorney general	18.8	23.2	19.5	30.2
State regulatory agency	24.8	22.9	23.8	55.6
Federal regulatory agency	4.9	4.6	6.1	17.3
U.S. attorney	6.5	5.9	6.8	13.2
FBI	8.1	11.8	7.4	18.9
Another prosecutor	17.6	20.3	14.8	43.4

[a]"How often does your office cooperate on joint investigations of corporate crimes with the agencies listed below?"

state police agencies may emphasize different law enforcement functions in the west, such as highway traffic patrol.

We cannot determine if the amount of interagency cooperation in western districts is a cause or a consequence of their high levels of activity against corporate crime. It may be that western prosecutors work with other agencies often because they have more corporate crime. Alternatively, their apparent ability to establish good working relationships with other agencies may permit them to take on more cases against corporate offenders. Since the differences between the West and other regions remain even with population size controlled, we are inclined toward the latter interpretation.

Special Control Arrangements and Activity

Special units and task forces are thought to increase the capabilities of local prosecutors to take on corporate crimes. But do they have this effect? As Tables 5.7a and 5.7b show, using these strategies does make a difference. Prosecutors in special control districts are considerably more active than are their counterparts in noncontrol districts.

The significance of these findings for evaluating the effectiveness of the special control strategies is not clear. Do prosecutors located in control network districts handle more corporate crimes because of greater ability to do so or because corporate crimes occur more often in their jurisdictions? This question is difficult to answer because we do not have an independent measure of the number of corporate crimes in our sample districts. Hence, we cannot assess whether prosecutors located in special control districts prosecute more of the available offenses than do their counterparts in regular districts. If we assume that population size correlates roughly with business activity and, hence, with the amount of corporate crime, we can use population as a proxy control for corporate crime and investigate whether special control arrangements influence activity against corporate crime independent of population size. Accordingly, we divided the sample into two groups based on population: medium-sized districts (between 150,000 and 328,100) and large-sized districts (over 328,100). We then examined prosecution rates in each group, comparing special control districts with regular districts. Table 5.8 shows the results.

Controlling for population size reduces but does not eliminate the association between special control arrangements and prosecution rates. Respondents from medium-sized special control districts reported prosecut-

Table 5.7a   Frequency of Prosecutions in Special Control Districts

Corporate Crime	*Frequency*			
	Never (%)	*< 1 Case per Year* (%)	*1–3 Cases per Year* (%)	*> 3 Cases per Year* (%)
Consumer fraud	7.9	19.8	30.7	41.6
Securities fraud	26.5	27.5	32.4	13.7
Insurance fraud	15.0	33.0	27.0	25.0
Tax fraud	48.5	26.7	12.9	11.9
False claims	20.4	28.6	23.5	27.6
Workplace offenses	59.6	28.3	11.1	1.0
Environmental offenses	24.8	34.7	19.8	20.8
Illegal payments	25.5	43.9	24.5	6.1
Unfair trade practices	53.0	24.0	8.0	15.0

Note: N = 102. Special control districts are those that answered "yes" to at least one of the following questions: "Does your office have a special in-house unit for investigating and prosecuting economic or white-collar crimes? Is your office a member of an interagency task force or strike group that focuses on economic or other white-collar crimes?"

Table 5.7b   Frequency of Prosecutions in Other Districts

Corporate Crime	*Frequency*			
	Never (%)	*< 1 Case per Year* (%)	*1–3 Cases per Year* (%)	*> 3 Cases per Year* (%)
Consumer fraud	39.2	37.9	16.8	6.8
Securities fraud	66.6	28.2	5.3	0.0
Insurance fraud	44.8	40.9	10.4	3.9
Tax fraud	65.7	24.8	5.9	3.6
False claims	46.6	35.2	12.1	6.2
Workplace offenses	71.2	24.5	3.0	1.2
Environmental offenses	51.8	33.6	10.4	4.2
Illegal payments	59.1	35.3	4.6	1.0
Unfair trade	82.1	15.6	1.3	1.0

Note: N = 317.

ing six types of offenses more often than their counterparts in large districts without such arrangements. For example, 67 percent of the medium-sized special control districts prosecuted one or more consumer frauds per year, but only 47 percent of the large districts without special arrangements did so. If we are correct that the amount of corporate crime varies with population size, then special arrangements increase prosecutorial activity inde-

Table 5.8   Special Control and Other Districts That Prosecute One or More Selected
Corporate Crimes in Medium- and Large-Sized Jurisdictions

Corporate Crimes	Medium-Sized Jurisdictions[a]		Large-Sized Jurisdictions[a]	
	Special Controls			
	No (%)	Yes (%)	No (%)	Yes (%)
Consumer fraud	30.4	66.7	46.7	72.2
Securities fraud	9.0	16.7	20.0	53.4
Insurance fraud	21.5	37.5	38.7	59.2
Tax fraud	16.4	20.8	13.8	27.8
False claims	19.2	54.2	27.6	48.6
Workplace offenses	6.6	25.0	10.3	7.1
Environmental offenses	13.9	25.0	32.2	45.8
Illegal payments	6.6	25.0	20.0	34.8
Unfair trade practices	2.6	16.7	10.4	25.4
N	82	24	31	73

[a]Medium-sized districts are between 150,000 and 328,100 in population size.
[b]Large-sized districts are greater than 328,100 in population size.

pendent of the level of corporate crime in a district.[1] The number of corporate crime prosecutions in a district is determined by more than just the number of such crimes committed there.

What causes the relatively high level of corporate crime prosecutions in special control districts? One explanation may be that prosecutors located in special control districts define corporate crime as a more serious problem than do their counterparts in regular districts. The survey data support this speculation. When they are compared to their counterparts, significantly higher percentages of prosecutors in offices with special units rated corporate crime as a somewhat (65.1 percent versus 18.1 percent) or very serious (10.6 percent versus 1.3 percent) problem.

Discretion, Constraints, and Context

Although it is tempting to think of criminal laws as clear and precise proscriptions with unambiguous behavioral referents, those who must apply them to events of everyday life know otherwise. The demarcation between lawful and unlawful conduct often is not obvious. When does a public altercation between two acquaintances become disorderly? At what point does communication between two companies about prices or markets become a criminal conspiracy? These questions cannot be answered without careful scrutiny of situational elements of individual cases. The lesson is clear: legal actors must exercise judgment as they apply the law to ambiguous and ever-changing events. Discretion is an unavoidable component of "law in action" (Friedman 1975).

The decision to prosecute a corporate crime is rarely automatic. Like other legal actors, prosecutors make decisions under constraints. Viewed abstractly, *constraints* are forces that shape individual decision making. They mold the exercise of discretion by legal actors, determining when and how laws are enforced. For example, insufficient time and personnel make it impossible for police officers to arrest all who violate the law (LaFave 1965). Prosecutors are no different. Some constraints encourage them to seek indictments and prosecution; others militate against use of the criminal process, perhaps in favor of other remedial measures. Before deciding to proceed with a corporate crime prosecution, prosecutors must consider a number of factors related to the offense, the resources available to them, the actions of other agencies, the preferences of victims, the potential impact of the prosecution on the local community, and community expectations. The unique combination of factors involved in a given case determines whether a corporate prosecution will take place.

To assess how important various constraints are for prosecutorial decision making, we asked the respondents to indicate the likelihood that certain factors would limit their willingness to prosecute a corporate crime in their jurisdiction. We also asked them to indicate the likelihood that another set of factors would increase their willingness to prosecute a corporate crime.

Constraints That Limit Prosecutions

Table 5.9 lists the factors that may limit a prosecutor's willingness to prosecute a corporate criminal case. The factors are organized into four categories: resource constraints, legal or investigative constraints, availability of alternative remedies, and community expectations or impacts. Not surprisingly, inadequate personnel resources constrain many prosecutors' offices from undertaking corporate crime cases. Between 50 and 60 percent of the respondents reported that insufficient investigative or prosecutorial personnel "definitely" or "probably" would limit their willingness to prosecute.

Table 5.9   Factors Limiting Willingness to Prosecute Corporate Criminal Offenses

	Responses to Question[a]			
Limiting Factor	Definitely Would Not Limit (%)	Probably Would Not Limit (%)	Probably Would Limit (%)	Definitely Would Limit (%)
Lack of cooperation from victim(s)	3.7	19.8	50.1	26.4
Actual or pending action by a federal regulatory agency	4.4	21.2	49.3	25.1
Actual or pending action by a state regulatory agency	4.9	25.2	48.9	21.0
Insufficient investigatory personnel	11.8	27.9	39.7	20.6
Difficulty of establishing mens rea in a corporate criminal context	7.9	36.1	44.7	11.3
Insufficient prosecutorial personnel	17.6	31.5	35.5	15.4
Insufficient cooperation from other agencies	15.0	37.7	42.1	5.2
Insufficient expertise in corporate crime cases	18.8	45.4	27.1	8.8
Actual or pending private civil suit(s)	20.3	45.8	27.2	6.6
Insufficient public support for prosecuting corporate criminal cases	51.1	39.9	6.6	2.4
Potential negative impact that a corporate prosecution might have on local economy	57.3	37.6	3.4	1.7

[a]"To what extent would the factors listed below limit your willingness to prosecute a corporate criminal offense committed in your jurisdiction?"

The legal and investigative difficulties that corporate crimes pose also strongly influence the willingness of prosecutors to undertake such cases. Strong majorities noted factors that make it difficult to win corporate criminal cases. Lack of cooperation from victims and the difficulty of establishing mens rea in a corporate context pose particularly important obstacles for local prosecutors. Other legal or investigative difficulties, such as lack of cooperation from other agencies and insufficient expertise in corporate crime cases, appear to be less important as limiting factors.

Local prosecutors recognize that corporate crimes often fall under the jurisdictions of multiple agencies and that criminal prosecution may not be the only remedy available for corporate offenders. The availability of alternative remedies appears to exert a strong influence on the willingness of local prosecutors to invest their own resources in corporate cases. Seven out of ten respondents indicated that they would be less willing to prosecute if state or federal regulatory agencies acted. Although many prosecutors deem regulatory sanctions as adequate substitutes for criminal proceedings, they do not feel the same way about private civil suits. About one-third of the prosecutors reported that an actual or pending private civil suit against a corporate offender would limit their willingness to proceed on their own.

The least important limiting factors appear to be those related to community expectations and the potential impact that a corporate prosecution might have on the local community. Only a few prosecutors said that insufficient public support or the potential negative impact of a prosecution on the local economy would limit their willingness to proceed.

Factors That Encourage Prosecutions

In contrast to the constraints that limit the willingness of local prosecutors to take on corporate cases, some factors act to encourage prosecutions. In Table 5.10 the factors that prosecutors said would increase their

Table 5.10 Factors Increasing Willingness to Prosecute Corporate Criminal Offenses

	Responses to Question[a]			
Increasing Factor	Definitely Would Not Increase (%)	Probably Would Not Increase (%)	Probably Would Increase (%)	Definitely Would Increase (%)
Physical harm to victim(s)	0.5	4.9	25.4	69.1
Substantial economic harm caused by the offense	1.5	5.9	41.9	50.7
Large number of victims	1.0	6.4	40.1	52.5
Evidence of multiple offenses rather than a single offense	1.7	3.7	36.5	58.1
The need to demonstrate publicly that the law applied equally to all offenders	2.7	23.4	52.2	21.7
The need to deter other potential corporate offenders	1.5	12.8	58.3	27.4
Failure of regulatory agencies to act	4.7	41.9	41.9	11.6
Victim preference for prosecution	4.2	25.2	58.6	12.0
Public concern over the corporate criminal offense	2.2	18.4	64.4	15.0
Media attention on the case	9.9	43.1	39.9	7.2

[a]"To what extent would the factors listed below increase your willingness to prosecute a corporate criminal offense committed in your jurisdiction?"

willingness to prosecute are grouped into categories: the nature of the offense, deterrent and educational functions, community concerns, and other factors. The most important factors involve the nature of the offense. Over 90 percent of the respondents indicated that they would be more willing to prosecute in cases that involve physical harm to victims, evidence of multiple offenses, large numbers of victims, or substantial economic harm. Slightly less important are factors related to the deterrent and educational functions of prosecution. Over 85 percent said that the need to deter other potential corporate offenders would increase their willingness to prosecute. About 75 percent felt the same way regarding the need to demonstrate publicly that the law applies equally to all offenders. While community expectations do not appear to limit prosecutorial resolve in corporate cases, they may increase it. Almost eight out of ten respondents said that public concern over a corporate criminal offense would probably or definitely increase their willingness to prosecute. Just under half (47.1 percent) said that media attention on a case would increase their willingness. The preferences of victims exert a strong influence on prosecutorial discretion. Over 70 percent of the respondents said that, if a victim prefers prosecution, their willingness to prosecute would be increased. This percentage is virtually identical to the number that said lack of cooperation from victims would limit their willingness to prosecute. Finally, just as the availability of alternative remedies appears to deter local prosecutors from taking on corporate cases, the lack of alternative remedies appears to spur them forward, though not quite as strongly. Just over one-half of the respondents (53.5 percent) reported that their willingness to prosecute would be increased if regulatory agencies failed to act. Recall that over 70 percent said that actual or pending action by regulatory agencies would limit their willingness to prosecute.

Taken together, Tables 5.9 and 5.10 present a complex picture of prosecutorial discretion. The role of community context in influencing prosecutorial discretion is especially complicated. While fewer than 10 percent of prosecutors say that insufficient public support would limit their willingness to prosecute, 79.4 percent report that public concern over an offense would increase it. Similarly, just 5 percent say that a potential negative impact on the local economy would limit their willingness to prosecute, but almost 50 percent say that media attention on the case would increase their willingness. With respect to the influence of community context on corporate crime prosecutions, these results appear inconsistent and difficult to reconcile.

One interpretation is that, in selecting cases, local prosecutors are guided both by community expectations and by a sense of professional obligation to apply the law equally. When the general public or media focus attention on a case, prosecutors may decide to take an interest in it because they feel a responsibility to be responsive to community concerns. Where prosecutors independently decide that an offense warrants action, their professional obligation to apply the law without favor would make them less inclined to bow to outside pressure to forego prosecution. Thus, community expectations may have a greater influence on how cases are selected than on how they are treated after they enter the system.

Community Context and Constraints

As the results presented in Tables 5.9 and 5.10 show, not all constraints are equally important. Some factors are more likely than others to limit or to increase the prosecutor's willingness to prosecute. An important question for our contextual theory of corporate crime prosecution is whether the salience of constraints for prosecutors is influenced by the contexts in which they are located. If we are correct that community context shapes prosecutorial decision making, then context should be related to the salience of constraints. For example, a study of California district attorneys found that the importance of adequate resources and alternative remedies varied with jurisdictional population size (Benson et al. 1988). In contrast to their counterparts in large districts, prosecutors in small districts were more likely to be constrained by these factors and by the potential impact of corporate prosecutions on the local economy. Hence, we expect that prosecutors located in large jurisdictions will feel differently about constraints than will their counterparts in small jurisdictions. Likewise, those who handle corporate cases routinely probably take a different view of these offenses than do those who encounter such cases rarely, if at all.

To see how context influences the salience of constraints, we began by analyzing the influence of population size and regional location on perceived constraints. We divided jurisdictions into large and small groups at the seventy-fifth percentile. Those in the large group (the upper quartile) have populations of 328,000 or more. To assess the effect of regional location, we contrasted prosecutors located in the West to those located in other regions. The results are shown in Tables 5.11a and 5.11b: Table 5.11a shows the effects of size and location on factors that limit prosecutors' willingness to undertake corporate cases; Table 5.11b does the same for the factors that increase willingness.

Beginning with the limiting factors and focusing on general patterns, it is apparent from Table 5.11a that the major difference between prosecutors located in large versus small jurisdictions involves the limiting effects of alternative remedies. Although a majority of all prosecutors say they would be limited by regulatory actions, those located in large jurisdictions are less likely to forego prosecution. Similarly, they are less likely to be limited by the presence of private civil suits. These results suggest that, compared to their counterparts in small jurisdictions, prosecutors in large jurisdictions are less likely to view criminal and regulatory proceedings as interchangeable forms of control. They are more likely to proceed independently against corporate offenders, regardless of whether other control agencies are also applying sanctions.

Other statistically significant differences between large and small jurisdictions in responses to constraints involve the level of cooperation from other agencies, insufficient expertise, and potential, negative economic impacts on the community. As expected, prosecutors located in large jurisdictions are less likely to be limited by insufficient cooperation from other agencies, insufficient expertise, or negative economic impacts. Particularly for the potential, negative economic impact of prosecution, the difference between large and small jurisdictions is diminutive. Regardless of the size of the jurisdiction they are located in, the vast majority of prosecutors say that the potential economic impact of a prosecution on the community is not a matter of great concern.

Contrary to our expectations, population size does not have a statistically significant effect on either of our measures of personnel resources (prosecutorial and investigative staffs), but regional location does. Prosecutors located in the West are more likely to be limited by insufficient prosecutorial or investigative personnel than are their counterparts in the nonwestern regions. Western prosecutors are also more likely to be limited by the difficulty of proving *mens rea* in a corporate criminal context. We speculate that the differences between western and other prosecutors on these issues may be related to their levels of experience with corporate cases. Prosecutors from the West generally report higher rates of prosecution than

Table 5.11a   Factors Limiting Willingness to Prosecute, by Population Size and Regional Location

	Population Size		Regional Location	
Factor[a]	Small (%)	Large (%)	Non-West (%)	West (%)
Resource Constraints				
Insufficient prosecutorial personnel	48.7	57.7	48.9	64.8**
Insufficient investigatory personnel	64.2	66.7	62.5	81.3***
Legal or investigative constraints				
Difficulty of proving *mens rea* in a corporate criminal context	56.1	55.3	54.2	66.7*
Lack of cooperation from victim(s)	76.4	77.1	76.4	77.8
Insufficient cooperation from other agencies	49.8	40.4*	46.3	54.7
Insufficient expertise in corporate crime cases	38.2	28.6*	35.0	40.7
Alternative remedies				
Actual or pending action by a federal regulatory agency	76.8	67.6*	75.6	66.7
Actual or pending action by a state regulatory agency	72.8	61.9**	71.4	61.1
Actual or pending private civil suit(s)	37.2	23.8***	34.7	27.8
Community effects				
Insufficient public support for prosecuting corporate criminal cases	9.8	6.7	9.8	3.7
Potential negative impact that a corporate prosecution might have on the local economy	6.5	1.0**	5.6	1.9

*Chi-square *p*-value < .10
**Chi-square *p*-value < .05
***Chi-square *p*-value < .01
[a]Percentage of respondents who said that the selected factors "probably" or "definitely" would limit their willingness to prosecute a corporate case.

Table 5.11b   Factors Increasing Willingness to Prosecute, by Population Size and Regional Location

| | Population Size | | Regional Location | |
| | Small | Large | Non-West | West |
Factor[a]	(%)	(%)	(%)	(%)
Nature of offense				
Physical harm to victim(s)	94.4	95.1	94.1	98.1
Substantial economic harm caused				
by the offense	90.8	98.1**	91.8	98.2*
Large number of victims	91.5	96.1	91.5	100.0**
Evidence of multiple offenses rather				
than a single offense	94.1	96.1	94.1	98.2
Deterrent and educational functions of prosecution				
Need to demonstrate publicly that				
the law applies equally to all				
offenders	74.8	71.6	73.1	79.6
Need to deter other potential				
corporate offenders	83.9	91.2*	84.1	96.3**
Community concerns				
Media attention on the case	73.3	87.3**	74.9	87.1
Public concern over the corporate				
criminal offense	77.7	84.5	78.5	85.2
Other factors				
Victim preference for prosecution	72.7	64.7	70.8	69.8
Failure of regulatory agencies to act	51.0	61.2*	51.8	64.8*

*Chi-square *p*-value < .10

**Chi-square *p*-value < .05

[a]Percentage of respondents who said that the selected factors "probably" or "definitely" would increase their willingness to prosecute a corporate case.

do prosecutors in other regions. Perhaps their more extensive experience with corporate cases has sensitized them to the difficult legal obstacles that these cases raise and to the drain that they can impose on resources. Western prosecutors understand that it is difficult to prove *mens rea* in corporate cases without a significant investment of prosecutorial and investigative resources. Hence, they are more likely to be limited by these factors than are less experienced and less knowledgeable prosecutors in other regions. We explore this interpretation below by examining the influence of level of activity on perceived constraints.

Turning to the factors that increase prosecutors' willingness to undertake corporate cases (see Table 5.11b), we find few sizable differences between large and small or western and nonwestern jurisdictions. This similarity in outlook among prosecutors is especially true with respect to the nature of the offense. Regardless of the size of the jurisdiction they serve or its regional location, virtually all prosecutors are more likely to pursue corporate offenders who cause physical or substantial economic harm to victims and those who commit multiple offenses affecting large numbers of victims.

Size of jurisdiction and location do affect how prosecutors view what might be characterized as the symbolic aspects of corporate cases. Media attention on a case is more important to prosecutors located in large jurisdictions. Almost nine out of ten of our respondents (87.3 percent) located in large jurisdictions said that media attention would increase the likelihood that they would prosecute a corporate case. Just over seven out of ten prosecutors (73.3 percent) in small jurisdictions felt this way. The need to deter other potential corporate offenders was also cited as a motivating factor more often by prosecutors in large as opposed to small jurisdictions (91.2 versus 83.9 percent, respectively) and by prosecutors located in the West as opposed to other regions (96.3 versus 84.1 percent, respectively). These findings may mean that cases which become *causes célèbres* in the local media may be viewed by prosecutors in large jurisdictions as particularly good opportunities to warn other potential corporate offenders. In smaller jurisdictions, with their lower rates of corporate crime, the potential deterrent effects of media attention may not be regarded as important by local prosecutors. Similarly, given their higher rates of prosecution, western prosecutors may be more attuned to the need for deterrence than are their less experienced counterparts in other regions.

Our interpretation, thus far, of the influence of community context on perceived constraints has implicitly assumed that resources and experience are particularly important influences on how local prosecutors view constraints. To more directly investigate this interpretation, we examined whether office size and level of activity are related to perceived constraints. Office size is measured by the number of full-time prosecuting attorneys; level of activity is measured by an index of the number of corporate crimes that the office typically handles in a year. The number of attorneys is an indicator of the resources available in the office to handle corporate cases.

The number of cases typically handled indicates the level of experience the office has with corporate cases. We expect that both the availability of resources and the level of prior experience will be related to prosecutors' views on constraints.[2]

To investigate the effect of office size on perceived constraints, we began by dividing the sample into large and small offices based on the number of full-time attorneys in the office. Since the distribution of full-time attorneys is highly skewed, we used the 75th percentile as the cutoff point.[3] Offices with twenty-three or more full-time attorneys were categorized as large; those with fewer than twenty-three as small. Then, we compared their responses to our questions on factors that limit or increase willingness to prosecute.

We used a similar procedure to investigate the effect of prior experience on perceived constraints. We divided the sample into high and low groups based on an index of level of activity. This index is formed by combining responses to the questions on how often the prosecutor's office typically prosecuted the nine types of offenses. Assigned ordinal ranks and summed, the item responses (never, less than 1 per year, 1 to three times per year, more than 3 times per year) form an index of *level of activity*. The index has an alpha reliability of .85 and ranges from 9 to 36. Since it is symmetrically distributed, we use the median (15 on the scale) as our cutoff point.[4]

As we expected, in large offices the availability of alternative remedies is significantly less likely to limit prosecutors' willingness to undertake corporate cases (see Table 5.12a). Similarly large offices are also less likely to be limited by a lack of public support for a corporate prosecution or by the potential negative impact that a prosecution might have on the local economy. The overall pattern of results is virtually identical to that observed for size of jurisdiction and alternative remedies, but the relationships are stronger.

The results on level of activity, however, are not exactly as we thought they would be. Because we found that regional location affects perceptions of resource constraints and because we know that offices located in the West tend to be larger and more active than offices in other regions, we had speculated that more active offices would be more likely to be constrained by insufficient personnel resources. That does not appear to be so. Comparing prosecutors with high versus low levels of activity, we find

Table 5.12a   Factors Limiting Willingness to Prosecute, by Size of Office and Level of Activity

	Size of Office		Level of Activity	
	Small	Large	Low	High
Factor[a]	(%)	(%)	(%)	(%)
Resource constraints				
Insufficient prosecutorial personnel	49.0	57.3	49.0	53.9
Insufficient investigatory personnel	64.5	66.0	64.6	65.2
Legal or investigative constraints				
Difficulty of proving *mens rea* in a corporate criminal context	55.5	57.3	51.5	62.1**
Insufficient cooperation from other agencies	49.2	41.7	48.2	46.9
Insufficient expertise in corporate crime cases	37.3	30.9	37.3	33.5
Lack of cooperation from victim(s)	76.4	77.3	76.7	76.5
Alternative remedies				
Actual or pending action by a federal regulatory agency	77.4	65.0**	78.0	69.4**
Actual or pending action by a state regulatory agency	73.5	58.8***	74.6	63.5**
Actual or pending private civil suit(s)	37.5	21.7***	34.3	32.9
Community effects				
Insufficient public support for prosecuting corporate criminal cases	10.5	4.1**	8.3	10.0
Potential negative impact that a corporate prosecution might have on the local economy	6.7	0.0***	5.0	5.3

*Chi-square *p*-value < .10

**Chi-square *p*-value < .05

***Chi-square *p*-value < .01

[a]Percentage of respondents who said that the selected factors would "probably" or "definitely" limit their willingness to prosecute a corporate case.

virtually no difference in the limiting effects of resource constraints. Some support for our interpretation is found, though, in the relationship between activity and perceptions of legal constraints. As predicted, prosecutors with high levels of activity report being more likely to be limited by the difficulty of proving *mens rea* in a corporate criminal context. We also note that active prosecutors are less likely to be limited by the actions of regulatory agencies.

Finally, we examined the influence of office size and level of activity on factors that increase prosecutors' willingness to prosecute (see Table 5.12b). As we found with size of jurisdiction, size of office mainly influences perceptions of the deterrent functions of prosecution and the importance of community concerns. Prosecutors with large staffs are notably more likely to prosecute if there is media attention on and public concern over a corporate case. Similarly, they are more likely to endorse the importance of the need to deter other offenders. Consistent with our expectations, offices with high levels of activity are also more likely to see the need to deter other offenders as an important increasing factor.

Overall, on the basis of Tables 5.12a and 5.12b, office size appears to be a more important influence on the perceived salience of contraints than is prior experience. Size significantly influences perception of five of the limiting factors and four of the increasing factors. Prior experience significantly affects only three of the limiting factors and one of the increasing factors. Although the observed differences in perceived constraints are statistically significant, substantively they are not large. For example, only about 10 percent of the prosecutors located in small offices say that they would be less willing to prosecute a corporate case if public support were lacking compared to about 4 percent of prosecutors in large offices. This finding indicates that the differences between prosecutors in large and small offices are matters of degree, not kind. They hold basically similar views on the factors that limit their willingness to prosecute corporate cases.

Conclusions

This chapter elaborates and extends the theme introduced in chapter 1—that community context is important for prosecutors. It affects how they view other agencies and how they approach decision making in corporate cases. Context also is related to the size and organization of local pros-

Table 5.12b Factors Increasing Willingness to Prosecute, by Size of Office
and Level of Activity

	Size of Office		Level of Activity	
Factor[a]	Small (%)	Large (%)	Low (%)	High (%)
Nature of offense				
Physical harm to victim(s)	93.9	96.8	94.1	95.3
Substantial economic harm caused				
by the offense	91.0	97.9**	91.1	94.7
Large number of victims	91.6	95.8	92.0	93.5
Evidence of multiple offenses rather				
than a single offense	93.9	96.9	93.3	96.5
Deterrent and educational functions of prosecution				
Need to demonstrate publicly that				
the law applies equally to all				
offenders	74.7	71.6	73.1	75.2
Need to deter other potential				
corporate offenders	83.3	93.7***	81.9	91.1***
Community concerns				
Media attention on the case	73.7	86.5**	74.0	80.0
Public concern over the corporate				
criminal offense	77.4	86.5**	78.6	81.0
Other factors				
Victim preference for prosecution	71.7	67.4	70.8	70.4
Failure of regulatory agencies to act	50.8	62.5**	51.9	55.9

*Chi-square p-value < .10

**Chi-square p-value < .05

***Chi-square p-value < .01

[a]Percentage of respondents who said that the selected factors "probably" or "definitely" would increase their willingness to prosecute a corporate case.

ecutors' offices. And these office characteristics, in turn, exert particularly strong influences on decision making. Thus, our results so far suggest that we should think of the relationship between context and corporate crime prosecution as a chain of causation. Context influences office characteristics, which, in turn, influence rates of prosecution.

We continue to elaborate on this theme in the next two chapters. Chapter 6 examines prosecutors' views on the causes of corporate crime and the problem of correcting it. In chapter 7 we develop and test a more sophisticated, multivariate model of prosecutorial activity against corporate crime in which context is linked to activity via the intervening dimension of the office structure.

Notes

1. As a further check, we conducted additional analyses of the effects of population size and special units on prosecutorial activity against corporate crime. First, we created a *prosecutorial activity scale* based on responses to the questions regarding how often the respondents' offices typically prosecuted the nine types of offenses. We assigned ordinal ranks and summed the item responses (never, less than 1 per year, 1 to 3 times per year, more than 3 per year) to form the scale of prosecutorial activity. The scale ranges from 9 to 36 and has an alpha reliability of .85. We then regressed the scale on population and special units. Both variables were statistically significant at the .0001 level, and their standardized coefficients were .35 and .32, respectively.

Next, we examined prosecution rates for the individual crimes separately. We dichotomized responses to the items on frequency of prosecution for the nine selected offenses (never and less than 1 per year = 0; 1 to 3 times per year and more than 3 times per year = 1). We then logistically regressed the dichotomized responses for each offense type on population size and special units. With only one exception, both variables made statistically significant contributions to the various equations. The exception involved workplace-related offenses. For this type of offense, population size did not have a significant effect, but special units did. Results of the logistic regressions are presented below.

Logistic Regression Analysis of the Frequency of Prosecution for Selected Corporate Crimes

Corporate Crime	Independent Variable Standardized Coefficients		Chi-Square Probability	
	Population	Units	Population	Units
Consumer fraud	.28	.37	.0028	.0001
Securities fraud	.57	.39	.0001	.0001
Insurance fraud	.43	.22	.0001	.0052
Tax fraud	.15	.18	.0516	.0348
False claims	.26	.26	.0281	.0002
Workplace offenses	.03	.25	.8215	.0341
Environmental offenses	.31	.16	.0002	.0461
Illegal payments	.33	.28	.0002	.0035
Unfair trade practices	.23	.46	.0090	.0001

2. We use the euphemistic construction "related to" at this point, because the causal order of the relationship between activity against corporate crime and perceived constraints

is ambiguous. Does one's perceptions of constraints influence one's level of activity or vice versa? Does one's level of activity influence one's perceptions of constraints? On the one hand, prosecutors who, for whatever reason, are more active against corporate crime may come to disregard some of the constraints that their less active counterparts perceive in these cases. On the other hand, perceptions of constraints may precede level of activity. Unfortunately, because our data are not longitudinal, we cannot settle this issue empirically at this time. In reality, it is probably most likely that the relationship is reciprocal, with perceptions influencing willingness to prosecute in one case and the experience of prosecution influencing how constraints in subsequent cases are viewed.

3. The coefficient of skewness for full-time attorneys is 3.08. The range for this variable is from 0 to 220, with a mean of 22 and a median of 9.

4. Although a direct count of the actual number of corporate prosecutions would perhaps be a more valid indicator of prosecutorial activity, such information unfortunately is not readily available. As we discussed in chapter 3, a question on the survey asking about the exact number of corporate prosecutions conducted by the respondents' offices in 1988 produced a sizable number of nonresponses. However, for those who did answer this question, reported prosecutions in 1988 correlate strongly with the prosecutorial activity index. Hence, we have some confidence that the index does provide a valid measure of variation in the level of prosecutorial efforts against corporate crime.

6

SOCIAL CONTEXT AND CORRECTING CORPORATE CRIME

In corporate criminal cases, the process of prosecution is complicated, and the decision to prosecute depends upon many factors. Prosecutors consider the seriousness of the crime, availability of resources, their relations with other agencies, and the potential impact of prosecution on the community. Additionally, the decision to use criminal sanctions against corporate offenders depends on the prosecutor's overall goals or objectives.

In imposing criminal sanctions on those who break the law, criminal justice officials pursue multiple, sometimes conflicting, goals. Traditionally, six goals for criminal punishment are identified.

—*Specific deterrence:* the use of punishment to deter the person being punished from committing other crimes.

—*General deterrence:* the use of punishment to deter other potential offenders from committing similar crimes.

—*Retribution:* the use of punishment to pay back offenders for the harm they caused to their victims and to society.

—*Boundary maintenance:* the use of punishment to make a public statement that certain kinds of behavior will not be tolerated.

—*Rehabilitation:* the use of punishment to reform offenders so that they may become constructive members of society, or, in the case of corporations, to restructure internal operations.

—*Incapacitation:* the use of punishment, either imprisonment or death, to protect society by incapacitating offenders so they cannot victimize others.

Presumably, prosecutors and other criminal justice officials try to achieve one or more of these goals, but the priority they assign to individual goals may vary from one type of offender or offense to another. For example, federal judges regard general deterrence as an especially important goal in sentencing white-collar offenders (Mann et al. 1980; Wheeler et al. 1988). However, for those who commit crimes of interpersonal violence, punishment or incapacitation rather than general deterrence may be regarded as the primary goal. Priorities may vary also depending on where the official is located in the justice process. That is to say, the goals and priorities of prosecutors may not be the same as those of judges. Recent research has expanded our understanding of the goals that judges pursue when sentencing white-collar offenders, but little is known about prosecutors in this regard. This chapter focuses on the goals that prosecutors pursue in the case of corporate wrongdoing and their views on the related issues of the causes of and remedies for corporate crime.

Prosecutors' Goals

To better understand how prosecutors view the traditional goals of the criminal law, we asked the survey respondents to rank their most important prosecutorial goals in three different situations: individuals who commit traditional street crimes; individual businesspeople who commit corporate crimes; and corporations or other business entities that commit corporate crimes. A question of particular importance is whether prosecutors, like judges, pursue different goals when confronted with street criminals as opposed to individual corporate executives or corporate entities.

As Table 6.1 shows, prosecutors pursue different punishment objectives depending on the type of offense and the type of offender. In cases involving individuals who commit traditional street crimes, over 60 per-

Table 6.1 First and Second Most Important Objectives of Prosecution, by Type of Offender and Offense

	Individual Street Crime[a]		Individual Corporate Crime[b]		Corporation Corporate Crime[c]	
Objective	First (%)	Second (%)	First (%)	Second (%)	First (%)	Second (%)
Special deterrence	35.5	15.8	31.3	14.6	24.7	11.5
General deterrence	16.7	32.0	39.1	30.1	39.8	32.8
Retribution	9.4	13.3	10.0	18.7	15.9	19.6
Boundary maintenance	4.4	10.8	11.0	25.3	17.6	29.5
Rehabilitation	2.2	7.1	2.8	5.3	2.0	6.4
Incapacitation	31.8	20.9	5.8	6.1	—[d]	—

[a]In general, which of the above objectives would you rank as the two most important objectives of prosecuting individuals who commit traditional street crimes, for example burglary, robbery, or battery?

[b]In general, which of the objectives would you rank as the two most important objectives of prosecuting individual businesspersons who commit corporate crimes?

[c]Recognizing that corporations cannot be incapacitated, which of the objectives would you rank as the two most important objectives of prosecuting corporations or other business entities that commit corporate crimes?

[d]Incapacitation was not listed as a potential objective of prosecution of corporate crimes committed by business entities. See note c.

cent of prosecutors chose either special deterrence or incapacitation as their most important objective. General deterrence ran a distant third. In contrast, for individual businesspeople who commit corporate crimes, general deterrence was the modal category, with 39.1 percent ranking it as the most important objective of prosecution. Special deterrence was the next most frequently cited objective. Nearly one-third of prosecutors (31.3 percent) think that it is the most important objective for punishing individual corporate executives. Only 6 percent of the respondents ranked incapacitation as the most important objective for individual executives.

Prosecutors appear to pursue broader objectives in handling corporate crimes than they do when dealing with street criminals. Their focus is less on the impact of punishment on the offender and more on the impact of punishment on the community as a whole. This broader view is reflected not only by how they rank general deterrence but also by their views on punishment as a means of boundary maintenance. Although relatively few prosecutors rank boundary maintenance as the most important objective for individual offenders, it is clearly more likely to be a rationale for punishment if the offender is a corporate executive rather than a street criminal. Over twice as many prosecutors regard boundary maintenance as the most important objective in punishing corporate executives as compared to individual street criminals (11.0 percent versus 4.4 percent, respectively).

The focus on the broader effects of punishment becomes even more pronounced if the offender is a corporation rather than an individual. General deterrence was ranked as either the most (39.8 percent) or second most (32.8 percent) important objective by over seven out of ten prosecutors (for a total of 72.6 percent). Nearly one-half of the prosecutors (47.1 percent) ranked boundary maintenance as the most (17.6 percent) or second most (29.5 percent) important objective in corporate cases. The large percentages ranking general deterrence and boundary maintenance as important objectives in corporate cases suggest that prosecutors regard these cases as opportunities to educate the business community. Surprisingly, one out of six prosecutors (15.9 percent) ranked retribution as the most important objective in prosecuting crimes by business entities. In street crime cases, only one out of ten prosecutors (9.4 percent) ranked retribution as most important.

Although there is some evidence that social context influences the goals prosecutors pursue, by and large prosecutors appear to share a consistent viewpoint on corporate crime. Table 6.2 shows the percentage, by type of offense, of prosecutors in different-sized jurisdictions who ranked special deterrence, general deterrence, incapacitation, or boundary maintenance as the most important objective. Prosecutors in smaller jurisdictions appear somewhat more likely to endorse general deterrence than do their counterparts in larger jurisdictions. Interestingly, comparable percentages of prosecutors in larger jurisdictions rank special deterrence as their most important objective for both street criminals and corporate criminals. In contrast, prosecutors in smaller jurisdictions see special deterrence as much more important for street criminals than for corporate criminals.

We speculate that this difference in perspective between prosecutors located in larger versus those in smaller jurisdictions may stem from the former's greater experience with corporate offenders. Prosecutors in small jurisdictions, who have little experience with corporate crime, may hold stereotypical views about the rationality and criminality of corporate criminals. These prosecutors may think of corporate offenders as typically well-to-do business executives or large corporations who are first-time offenders. Prosecutors in large jurisdictions, who have had more experience with garden-variety corporate criminals, may know otherwise; many corporate

Table 6.2   Most Important Objective of Criminal Prosecution, by Type of Offense
and Size of Jurisdiction

		Size of Jurisdiction		
Objective	Small (%)	Medium-Small (%)	Medium-Large (%)	Large (%)
Individual Street Criminal				
Special deterrence	39.8	28.6	37.3	35.9
General deterrence	17.5	22.5	15.7	11.7
Incapacitation	26.2	28.6	28.4	43.7
Boundary maintenance	3.9	12.2	1.0	1.0
Individual Corporate Executive				
Special deterrence	29.7	29.5	36.0	30.1
General deterrence	43.6	42.1	34.0	36.9
Incapacitation	5.0	5.3	4.0	8.7
Boundary maintenance	8.9	15.8	9.0	10.7
Corporate Criminal				
Special deterrence	24.0	13.8	26.0	34.0
General deterrence	44.0	47.9	34.0	34.0
Incapacitation[a]	—	—	—	—
Boundary maintenance	15.0	24.5	15.0	16.5

Note: Percentages do not sum to 100 because not all response categories are shown.

[a]Incapacitation was not given as a response option in the case of offenses by corporate entities.

criminals are small-time business proprietors who, if not deterred sharply, will be repeat offenders.

There are few regional differences among prosecutors in how they rank the various objectives (see Table 6.3). Regardless of regional location, most prosecutors rank special deterrence and incapacitation as the most important objective in the case of individual street criminals. In the case of individual executives who commit corporate crimes, both general and special deterrence were rated as about equally important. For crimes committed by corporations, prosecutors located in the South, Northeast, and Midwest were most likely to rank general deterrence as the most important objective. Their counterparts in the West ranked special deterrence more often as the most important objective.

Overall, the survey findings suggest strong parallels between how federal judges look at white-collar criminals and how local prosecutors look

Table 6.3   Most Important Objective of Criminal Prosecution, by Type of Offense
and Region

	Region			
Objective	South (%)	West (%)	Northeast (%)	Midwest (%)
Individual Street Criminal				
Special deterrence	40.8	37.7	26.5	32.8
General deterrence	12.1	13.2	23.5	20.3
Incapacitation	32.5	37.7	32.5	28.1
Boundary maintenance	5.1	3.8	2.9	4.7
Individual Corporate Executive				
Special deterrence	35.5	38.5	31.3	23.2
General deterrence	35.5	30.8	37.3	48.0
Incapacitation	4.5	7.7	7.5	5.6
Boundary maintenance	11.0	13.5	11.9	9.6
Corporate Criminal				
Special Deterrence	26.3	38.5	27.3	15.8
General deterrence	30.9	28.9	39.4	55.1
Incapacitation[a]	—	—	—	—
Boundary maintenance	18.4	21.2	16.7	15.8

Note: Percentages do not sum to 100 because not all response categories are shown.

[a]Incapacitation was not given as a response option in the case of offenses by corporate entities.

at corporate offenders. In both cases, general deterrence is the primary purpose for invoking the criminal law, but recognition of the importance of retribution also shapes reactions. Wheeler et al. (1988) report that federal judges express a strong sense of moral outrage over crimes of greed committed by well-to-do people. Prosecutors, investigators, law enforcement personnel, and regulatory officials report a similar sense of outrage in their work. In our interviews with prosecutors and other enforcement officials, we found repeated expressions of this moral outrage directed against corporate offenders, especially those who endanger health and safety.

In the field interviews, the theme of general deterrence emerged frequently. Prosecutors, investigators, and regulatory officials at all levels of government clearly regarded general deterrence as the primary purpose of criminal law enforcement against corporate wrongdoing. This belief in the general deterrent effectiveness of criminal law enforcement is based on two assumptions about the temperament of the individuals involved in corporate and white-collar offenses. First, white-collar and corporate offenders are assumed to be rational planners; second, they are thought to be averse to formal punishment by the justice system. Unlike ordinary street criminals, then, they may be especially sensitive to the threat of punishment because of their elevated social positions in the community. For example, one local prosecutor had this to say about the deterrent effects of prosecution on corporate offenders:

We take very seriously the impact on a human being's life of being charged with a felony and then convicted of it. The opprobrium associated with the criminal process falls very heavily on someone who views himself or herself as a pillar of the community and outstanding businessperson—the "I am not a crook" kind of thing. We take very seriously that impact. We're not at all flippant about the use of the criminal tool. Still, it's a major policy of this office to have that jail time. The threat of jail time or the exposure to substantial jail time is the best single deterrent we have to change corporate behavior in the white-collar crime area.

Similar views were expressed almost universally by other prosecutors and by many investigators and regulatory officials. Prosecutors' perceptions of the impact that criminal sanctions have on corporate executives is borne out by recent research. Corporate executives consistently have been found to have a strong aversion to criminal punishment (Clinard 1983, 158; Cullen and Dubeck 1985; Frank and Lombness 1988; Lynxwiler et al. 1984).

General deterrence is an important objective for local prosecutors in corporate cases, but they also recognize and pursue a range of other goals. The most important of these are education, punishment, and problem-solving. The educational effects of corporate crime prosecutions on the business community and the public at large can be profound. As prosecutors see it, use of the criminal tool is one way to impress on the business community that white-collar crime is not just a sort of regulatory function. This approach can be especially important in communicating with smaller, less well-established business concerns. Unlike large corporate enterprises, smaller firms may not keep close track of changing regulations and laws. Because corporate prosecutions often receive considerable publicity in the news media, they can make smaller firms aware of their legal responsibilities in, for example, environmental matters.

The publicity generated by a few corporate prosecutions also may serve to educate and to activate the public at large. One respondent argued that an active local prosecutor can educate the public on the wrongfulness and potential harmfulness of some business practices. As citizens become more attuned to these practices, the likelihood increases that they will report them to authorities. An active prosecutor also can give citizens more leverage in their disputes with businesses. If local businesses know that the local prosecutor or state attorney general is active against business crime, they are more likely to respond personally to complaints from consumers to avoid negative publicity and resulting loss of business. In effect, a prosecutor who is active against corporate crime empowers citizens and enlists them in the fight against corporate wrongdoing.

Local prosecutors sometimes use their powers not so much to curb or punish the behavior of a particular offender as to attack more general problems. In these cases, the prosecutor takes a broader view of his or her role in the justice system and tries to achieve broader goals than deterrence or education. For example, in a case involving a prosecutable environmental violation by a large, generally law-abiding corporation, one prosecutor elected not to pursue a criminal indictment. In return for not being indicted, the company agreed to pay a large civil fine. The money from the fine then was used to fund environmental awareness and education workshops for local law enforcers.

Moral rather than utilitarian concerns sometimes motivate local prosecutors to take action against corporate offenders. The interviews revealed that prosecutors sometimes are more interested in punishment than in deterrence or education. Prosecutors, investigators, and, to a lesser degree, regulatory officials expressed a strong sense of moral outrage at some corporate offenses and offenders. One investigator, for example, argued that, in the case of environmental crime, incarceration is a "punishment that really does fit the crime." Since environmental crimes jeopardize lives and health, it is appropriate for the perpetrators to be incarcerated. This view was most strongly held regarding environmental and workplace-safety–related offenses, which often have direct and clear effects on individual health and wellbeing. The same view was expressed by officials who handle financial frauds. After describing a case involving a fraudulent employment service that bilked approximately 850 people out of ninety-five dollars each, one investigator exclaimed, "Would it be sufficient to say that the organizers of this scheme should do sixty days in the county jail? To

me that would be ludicrous. These people should be sent to the penitentiary, because . . . the aggregate impact that they have is certainly [of] a
felony nature."

Local law enforcement long has been accused of taking an overly tolerant view of white-collar and corporate crime. Certainly it is still the case
that the vast bulk of local attention and resources is directed against street
crime. Nevertheless, the interviews suggest that, like federal judges, local
prosecutors are morally outraged by many corporate offenses and are no
longer willing to tolerate them. We asked a prosecutor in Jacksonville,
Florida, what he thought about the argument that monetary fines are more
appropriate than the criminal law to use in controlling economic crimes.
He responded this way:

I would be surprised anyone could with a straight face make that argument, but
I'm sure they do. For one thing, those who commit those kinds of crimes are criminals, and they tend to have a real souring effect on our faith in our government,
on our government officials, and our business institutions if they can do it and get
away with it, and there's no ability to curb that type of thing through punishment.
And they tend to assemble in states and jurisdictions where they do have that attitude because they can easily set that up as a cost of doing business, but you can't
set up incarceration as a cost of doing business . . . So to deter in the future, you
have to punish those that commit that type of crime.

Perceptions of Causes and Remedies of Corporate Crime

As with other forms of crime, the causes of corporate crime are complex and involve multiple factors. Although this study was not designed
specifically to investigate these factors, we wanted, nevertheless, to take
advantage of our access to prosecutors to explore their views on the causes
of corporate crime and on how best to control it. Prosecutors are on the
front lines in the effort against corporate crime. They handle cases on a
regular basis and, through their repeated contact with corporate offenders,
no doubt have learned much about the motives and methods of the corporate criminal. As first-hand observers of the corporate criminal in action,
prosecutors are an important source of information about the causes of and
potential remedies for their behavior.

Prosecutors' views on how to control corporate crime also deserve attention because of the key role prosecutors play in implementing social

control policies. Many remedies have been suggested for reducing corporate crime, ranging from tougher criminal penalties to more emphasis on ethics in college business schools. The impact of any particular policy, however, depends in part on whether prosecutors are willing to commit to it. For example, some have called for prosecutors to make greater efforts to educate the business community about its legal responsibilities. But this approach is likely to have only limited success if prosecutors think that ignorance of the law is not the root cause of corporate misconduct. Prosecutors will ignore calls to educate the business community if they think that the root cause of corporate crime is weak criminal penalties. Those who make policy must take into account the views of those who execute policy.

Causes of Corporate Crime

The causes of corporate crime are not well understood. Indeed, we know less about corporate crime than about other forms of crime (Braithwaite 1985b). In the decades following Sutherland's original use of differential association theory, few scholars attempted to apply standard criminological theories to white-collar and corporate crime (Clinard 1946; Cressey 1953; Hirschi and Gottfredson 1987; Lasley 1988). Even fewer attempted to develop theories specifically for these forms of crime (Braithwaite 1989; Coleman 1987; Shover and Bryant 1993). Nevertheless, even though theories of corporate crime are neither numerous nor well articulated, prior research suggests that a variety of structural and individual factors are involved.

The structural causes of corporate crime refer to external conditions that influence the organization's survival or growth. Often these conditions are related to the market or industry within which the organization competes for survival. To illustrate, severe competition within an industry pressures corporations to find new ways to ensure their survival and growth. In some cases, the new ways involve criminal behavior. The structure of an industry may influence opportunities for particular types of offenses. Antitrust offenses, such as price-fixing, for example, require coordination and cooperation among competitors. Organizing a price-fixing scheme is easier in industries in which there are only a few large operators as opposed to industries where many small companies operate. From a structural perspective, the root cause of corporate crime lies not with the individual but with the pressures and opportunites associated with working in business organizations. The pressure toward law-breaking is an inherent and un-avoidable feature of competitive economies (Coleman 1987).

In contrast to structural explanations, individualistic explanations focus on individual causes of behavior. Typically, individualistic explanations cite such factors as low moral standards among businesspeople, weak detection and regulation, or simple greed in the business world. From this perspective, crime is the result of a failing or weakness in the individual. Crime happens either because criminals cannot control themselves or because there is no credible threat deterring them. Crime is not the result of external, situationally induced pressures.

We asked prosecutors to rate the importance of eight selected factors as causes of corporate crime. The items combined a mix of structural and individual factors. As Table 6.4 shows, prosecutors tend to rank individual-level factors, such as ineffective control, as more important than structural factors, such as inadequate profits. The "low rate of detection" was rated by more prosecutors (42.7 percent) as a very important cause of corporate crime than any other cause. The second most important cause was "ineffective regulation by administrative agencies." The moral standards of businesspeople also were seen as important. Just over one-quarter of prosecutors ranked as very important causes "low ethical standards among businesspeople" and "the belief that illegal practices are a necessary and

Table 6.4 **Importance of Selected Causes of Corporate Criminal Offenses**

	Response to Question[a]			
Cause	Very Important (%)	Somewhat Important (%)	Not Too Important (%)	Don't Know (%)
Inadequate company profits	12.3	38.1	27.3	22.3
Severe market competition	10.8	43.0	26.4	19.8
Belief among businesspeople that illegal practices are a necessary and accepted way of doing business	27.7	43.8	13.1	15.3
Low ethical standards among businesspeople	29.4	36.6	15.9	18.2
Low rate of detection for corporate offenses	42.7	42.0	3.7	11.5
Weak criminal penalties	22.5	37.5	26.0	14.0
Ineffective regulation by administrative agencies	33.9	41.4	9.0	15.7
Vague and unclear state and federal legislation	17.9	39.8	22.1	20.1

[a]"In your opinion, how important are each of the following as causes of corporate criminal offenses?"

accepted way of doing business." In contrast, notably lower percentages of prosecutors rank inadequate profits (12.3%) or market competition (10.8%) as very important causes.

Prosecutors favor individualistic explanations over structural explanations of corporate criminal involvement. They emphasize weak detection or regulation, poor individual morality, and a lack of self-control, while they de-emphasize structural sources of crime, such as inadequate profits and severe market competition. In the view of some prosecutors, corporate executives demonstrate no more self-control than do ordinary criminals or children. A prosecutor in Chicago, commenting on how business responds to environmental regulation, noted that,

The problem is that a lot of industries are like little children. They push for a limit and they will go until you set the limit for them. And so, they are constantly pushing, "Oh, please just give me a little longer. Just give me six more months." And the agency keeps trying to work with them instead of saying "this is where you've gotta move. You've gotta do it now." And maybe for a lot of marginal businesses it will mean shutting down production, but that could be the cost of having things safe.

Corporate crime is seen by prosecutors as largely the result of individual moral weaknesses and the failure of the regulatory and criminal justice systems to detect and punish offenses adequately. But prosecutors recognize the power of organizations to shape individual choice and behavior. Indeed, some are both outraged and dismayed by the willingness of corporate executives to pursue corporate profitability at the expense of community health and safety. As prosecutors see it, corporate executives all too often check their integrity and morality at the door when they go to work. They hide behind the shield of business necessity to justify patently harmful decisions. An assistant district attorney in Chicago found himself baffled by businesspeople's ability to ignore the consequences of their business decisions:

Why individuals will do in the name of a corporate entity something they would never do as individuals is beyond me. I mean, Grace and Company will pollute wells in Woburn, Massachusetts, without a second thought, but individually those executives would never go out there to somebody's well and pour poison in it. But somehow they get behind this corporate thing and it's perfectly OK. It's a business decision then. The Chamber of Commerce complains that the criminal law is replacing reasoned business decisions. In other words, if I pour poison in the well for no good reason, I'm a criminal, but if I do it for a profit, that's a reasoned business decision.

The tendency of prosecutors to see corporate crime in individualistic rather than structural terms follows from a general perspective on human behavior which they hold because of their position in the justice system. To win in court, prosecutors must show that criminal behavior was voluntary and intentional. They must defeat any suggestion that the actor's behavior was somehow beyond his or her control. Failure to show that the defendant's behavior was voluntary and intentional would raise questions about appropriateness of criminal sanctions. Thus, it is natural for prosecutors to define crime as a matter of individual responsibility rather than as a product of structural factors.

To investigate how context influences views on the causes of corporate crime, we again subdivided the sample by population size and regional location. Table 6.5 reports the percentage of prosecutors in the different-sized

Table 6.5   Importance of Selected Factors as Causes of Corporate Crime, by Size of Jurisdiction

	Size of Jurisdiction			
Cause[a]	Small (%)	Medium-Small (%)	Medium-Large (%)	Large (%)
Inadequate company profits	52.9	44.2	56.1	48.0
Severe market competition	51.9	58.0	50.5	54.9
Belief among businesspeople that illegal practices are a necessary and accepted way of doing business	65.4	67.0	72.0	81.6
Low ethical standards among businesspeople	61.5	58.3	68.0	75.5
Low rate of detection for corporate offenses	79.6	80.2	85.7	93.2
Weak criminal penalties	55.8	55.8	57.1	70.9
Ineffective regulation by administrative agencies	65.4	74.0	73.7	88.2
Vague and unclear state and federal regulation	54.8	62.5	59.6	54.4

[a]Each cause was ranked by respondents as either very important or somewhat important.

jurisdictions who ranked the selected factors as either very important or somewhat important causes. As was the case with the objectives of prosecution, regardless of the size of jurisdiction served, prosecutors share roughly similar views on the causes of corporate crime. What differences exist are matters of emphasis. For example, most prosecutors regard low ethical standards and a culture of illegality as important causes, but this view is more strongly held by prosecutors from large jurisdictions than those from smaller ones. Over 80 percent of prosecutors located in large jurisdictions ranked as an important cause a belief among businesspeople that illegal practices are an accepted way of doing business. About 66 percent of their counterparts in small and medium jurisdictions ranked this cause as important. Similarly, low ethical standards were ranked as an important cause by 75 percent of prosecutors from large jurisdictions versus approximately 60 percent of their counterparts from smaller jurisdictions. Table 6.5 also shows that prosecutors from large jurisdictions are more likely to see the low rate of detection, weak criminal penalties, and ineffective regulation by administrative agencies as important causes. In contrast, there are no systematic differences between prosecutors in large versus those in small jurisdictions in their views on the structural factors of inadequate profits and severe competition.

Like population size, regional location does not exert a strong or consistent influence on how prosecutors view the causes of corporate crime. As Table 6.6 shows, few large differences are found between prosecutors located in different regions. Prosecutors located in the West regard ineffective regulation by administrative agencies as a more important cause than do prosecutors located elsewhere. But overall, western prosecutors hold views generally similar to those held by other prosecutors on most of the causes of corporate crime.

Remedies for Corporate Crime

The causes of a social problem influence the potential usefulness of methods for its control or elimination. That is, causes imply remedies. We asked prosecutors to evaluate the usefulness of selected methods of improving corporate compliance with the law. As shown in Table 6.7, the results on remedies correspond with those on causes. More prosecutors ranked ineffective regulation as a very important cause of corporate crime (33 percent) than weak criminal penalties (22.5 percent). Consistent with this view, prosecutors were more likely to endorse tougher civil penalties

Table 6.6   Importance of Selected Factors as Causes of Corporate Crime, by Region

Cause[a]	Region			
	South (%)	West (%)	Northeast (%)	Midwest (%)
Inadequate company profits	45.8	53.9	50.0	54.8
Severe market competition	54.2	57.7	43.1	57.1
Belief among businesspeople that illegal practices are a necessary and accepted way of doing business	68.0	80.8	76.5	69.5
Low ethical standards among businesspeople	68.6	55.8	70.6	64.3
Low rate of detection for corporate offenses	79.4	88.5	88.1	88.1
Weak criminal penalties	60.9	65.4	66.2	53.5
Ineffective regulation by administrative agencies	74.4	88.5	77.3	70.1
Vague and unclear state and federal regulation	61.5	63.5	55.2	52.0

[a]Each cause was ranked by respondents as either very important or somewhat important.

over tougher criminal penalties as a useful method of securing greater compliance with the law.

Nearly one-half of the sample (48.2 percent) thought that more training for police on investigating corporate crime would be very useful. This is not surprising, given the large number of respondents who work mainly with the local police. Recall that over 40 percent said that the low rate of detection was a very important cause of corporate crime and that another 42 percent stated that this factor was somewhat important in fostering business violations. Over eight out of ten prosecutors (84.7 percent) think that detection is a major problem in controlling corporate crime.

Prosecutors appear to believe that better detection and regulation of corporate misbehavior are more important than tougher criminal penalties to secure more compliance with the law. Tougher civil penalties were ranked as a potentially very useful method of improving compliance by just under one-half of prosecutors (46.2 percent). Fewer than one-third (29.1 percent) of the respondents said that tougher criminal penalties would be very useful. Nearly three times as many prosecutors said that tougher criminal penalties would be not very useful as compared to those who thought tougher civil penalties would not help (17.5 percent versus 6.7 percent, respectively). The severity of punishment, then, does not ap-

Table 6.7 Usefulness of Selected Methods for Improving Corporate Compliance
with the Law

| Method | Response to Question[a] | | | |
	Very Useful (%)	Somewhat Useful (%)	Not Very Useful (%)	Don't Know (%)
Tougher criminal penalties	29.1	44.0	17.5	9.4
Tougher civil penalties	46.2	37.8	6.7	9.4
Educational programs for local prosecutors on corporate crime	36.4	46.8	10.1	6.7
More training for police on investigating corporate crime	48.2	36.9	8.6	6.4
More emphasis on ethics in business schools	23.9	31.3	30.0	14.8

[a]"In your opinion, how useful would the following methods be for improving corporate compliance with the law in your state?"

pear to be as important as the certainty of punishment. Prosecutors' emphasis on certainty over severity may arise out of their belief that corporate offenders are exquisitely sensitive to punishment. However, when asked which single method would be most useful, one-quarter of the respondents (26.5 percent) chose tougher criminal penalties (see Table 6.8). Only slightly more (31.1 percent) chose tougher civil penalties as the most useful means.

Social context does not appear to exert much influence on how prosecutors evaluate methods for improving corporate compliance with the law. Neither size of jurisdiction nor regional location is significantly related to prosecutors' views on the usefulness of the selected methods (see Tables 6.9a and 6.9b). Regardless of the size of the jurisdiction served, substantial majorities of prosecutors, ranging from 67 to 85 percent, regard tougher criminal and civil penalties as very useful or somewhat useful methods of improving corporate compliance with the law. Prosecutors in large jurisdictions are especially likely to feel that tougher criminal penalties are needed. Prosecutors are equally positive about the usefulness of educational programs for themselves and the police. In contrast, they are less likely to think that emphasizing ethics in college business schools would be a useful method of reducing corporate crime, though a majority see some value in this approach.

Turning to regional location, we note a similar pattern (see Table 6.9b).

Table 6.8 Most Useful Method for Improving Corporate
Compliance with the Law

Method	Responses to Question[a] (%)
Tougher criminal penalties	26.5
Tougher civil penalties	31.1
Educational programs for local prosecutors on corporate crime	9.5
More training for police on investigating corporate crime	16.5
More emphasis on ethics in business schools	9.0
Other	7.5

[a]"Of the methods listed in the previous question, which do you feel would
be the most useful means of improving corporate compliance with the law?"

Regardless of their regional location, prosecutors give roughly equal importance to the usefulness of most of these selected methods. The only notable
exception to this pattern is found among prosecutors located in the Northeast, where two-thirds of prosecutors said that more emphasis on ethics in
college business schools would be a useful approach. In contrast, only
about one-half of prosecutors located in other regions of the country feel
this way. As with size of jurisdiction, then, regional location does not appear to be an important social context shaping prosecutors' views about
corporate crime control policies.

Conclusions

In this chapter and part of the preceding chapter, we have investigated
the factors that shape how local prosecutors respond to corporate crime.
The factors shaping responses include constraints on decision making in
specific cases as well as the goals that prosecutors pursue in corporate cases
generally. We found relatively strong agreement among prosecutors in a
number of areas. They agree on the sorts of corporate cases that deserve to
be prosecuted criminally: those involving harm and those indicative of a
pattern of offending. A relatively strong consensus exists among prosecutors on the general goals of prosecution in corporate cases, the underlying
causes of corporate crime, and the methods for improving corporate com-

Table 6.9a   Usefulness of Selected Methods for Improving Corporate Compliance with the Law, by Size of Jurisdiction

	Size of Jurisdiction			
Method[a]	Small (%)	Medium-Small (%)	Medium-Large (%)	Large (%)
Tougher criminal penalties	70.9	67.0	69.3	84.6
Tougher civil penalties	85.4	78.6	85.0	86.5
Educational programs for local prosecutors	74.0	85.1	87.3	86.5
More training for police on investigations	78.9	86.6	86.3	88.5
More emphasis on ethics in college business schools	49.5	56.7	56.9	57.7

[a]Each method was ranked by respondents as either very useful or somewhat useful.

Table 6.9b   Usefulness of Selected Methods for Improving Corporate Compliance with the Law, by Region

	Region			
Method[a]	South (%)	West (%)	Northeast (%)	Midwest (%)
Tougher criminal penalties	71.7	77.8	80.0	70.5
Tougher civil penalties	80.4	90.7	82.8	86.1
Educational programs for local prosecutors	85.5	83.3	84.4	79.5
More training for police on investigations	85.5	88.9	76.9	86.8
More emphasis on ethics in college business schools	56.1	49.1	66.2	50.8

[a]Each method was ranked by respondents as either very useful or somewhat useful.

pliance with the law. Although social context, at least as operationalized by size of jurisdiction and regional location, is not entirely insignificant, it is certainly not a major influence on how prosecutors think about corporate crime and corporate crime prosecutions. This is not to say that context is unrelated to what prosecutors actually do about corporate crime. As we demonstrated in chapter 4, context is important in shaping the level of activity against corporate crime.

The level of unanimity among prosecutors in their views on goals, causes, and remedies is surprising and deserves further consideration. In later chapters, we undertake this consideration through an analysis of our interviews with prosecutors and regulators in the field sites. But at this point, we can introduce the idea of a *common legal culture of prosecution:* that is, a set of norms, values, and beliefs about the causes of corporate crime and the role of the criminal justice system in responding to it. This culture of prosecution is part of a broader cultural pattern that permeates American society. It involves notions of harm, blameworthiness, fairness, and responsibility, and it guides how prosecutors and others involved in the control of corporate crime view these offenses.

7

TOWARD A CONTEXTUAL THEORY OF PROSECUTORIAL ACTIVITY AGAINST CORPORATE CRIME

In previous chapters, our aim was to provide a detailed picture of what prosecutors nationwide are thinking and doing about corporate crime. Aside from noting the influence of population size and regional location, we did not investigate in depth the influence of social context on local responses to corporate crime. In this chapter, our aim is different. We want to focus directly on the relationship between social context and local prosecution of corporate crime.

We are particularly interested in understanding how aspects of the social context, besides size and region, are related to the attitudes that local prosecutors have on corporate crime and their responses to it. Macrosociological research has shown that official reactions to street crime are conditioned by the social context in which they occur.[1] We believe that the same is true of responses to corporate crime. They, too, are conditioned by social context. Indeed, the contextual factors that shape reactions to ordinary street crime are intimately related to reactions to corporate crime, though in ways not previously considered. The influence of community context on law enforcement reactions to ordinary street crime is well known. For example, some police agencies employ a legalistic approach to law enforcement; others use a watchman or service style (Wilson 1968). Judges in rural communities sentence black citizens differently than do judges in urban areas (Myers and Talarico 1987; Hagan 1977; Pope 1975). These styles of enforcement are largely shaped by the norms, concerns, demands, and activities of local communities (Wilson 1968).

A major thesis of this book is that community context also influences the agencies and organizations that respond to white-collar and corporate crime (Hagan et al. 1982). Evidence from a variety of studies supports this thesis. For example, the caseloads, enforcement priorities, and investigative strategies of regional offices of the Securities and Exchange Commission vary significantly (Shapiro 1984). Shover et al. (1986) show that the Federal Office of Surface Mining adopted more stringent enforcement strategies in Appalachian states than in western states. Others have shown how contextual factors influence the selection and processing of cases by regulatory agencies (Bardach and Kagan 1982; Feldman and Zeckhauser 1978). Studies of the sentencing of white-collar offenders also reveal substantial geographic and temporal variation in sentence severity (Benson and Walker 1988; Hagan and Palloni 1986; Hagan and Parker 1985; Nagel and Hagan 1982; Wheeler et al. 1982; Hagan et al. 1980). In response to local conditions, regulatory and criminal justice agencies develop different enforcement styles to combat white-collar and corporate crimes.

In this chapter, we present a more detailed analysis of the local conditions that influence prosecutorial responses to corporate crime. We begin by discussing the nature of contextual explanations, then develop and test a contextual model of prosecutorial activity. Finally, we address the implications of our results for macrosociological theories of crime control.

Contextual Explanations and Corporate Crime Control

Contextual or environmental explanations of behavior are commonplace in the social sciences, particularly in sociology. The logic underlying such explanations is straightforward. The behavior of some unit of analysis, for example a person or an organization, is explained, at least in part, by reference to the characteristics of its environment (Stinchcombe 1987, 201). For example, characteristics of communities, such as the level of social disorganization, have been used successfully to explain variation in rates of crime and victimization among community members (Sampson and Groves 1989; Taylor and Covington 1988; Simcha-Fagan and Schwartz 1986; Bursik 1988). This logic has been applied to understanding the behavior of organizations that react to crime, such as police departments, judicial systems, and prisons. For example, investigators have studied the effect of minority group size on police-per-capita rates, municipal expenditures for police protection, and police use of deadly force (Jackson 1989; Liska et al. 1981; Liska and Yu 1992). Another prominent line of research focuses on covariation between economic conditions and imprisonment rates. Although the precise mechanisms by which economic conditions such as unemployment influence imprisonment rates are debated, broad agreement exists that the two are inversely related (Inverarity 1992; Hochstetler and Shover 1997). As economic conditions decline, imprisonment rates increase.

The same approach can be applied to the local prosecutor's office and corporate crime control. To do so requires that we identify the features of local prosecutors' environments which we think influence activity against corporate crime and then investigate whether they actually are related to variation in rates of corporate crime prosecutions. From results presented earlier, we know that local prosecutors' offices vary in size, organizational structure, and attitudes about corporate crime. And we have evidence that these organizational characteristics are related to variation in activity against corporate crime. For example, in chapter 5, we showed that corporate crime prosecutions are more common in offices that have an in-house unit on white-collar crimes or that belong to an interagency task force on these crimes. We called the offices that have made these arrangements special control districts. Before we build our contextual model of activity against corporate crime, we first identify the characteristics of local prosecutors' offices that directly determine corporate crime prosecution rates. Important characteristics include the resources available to prosecute corporate crimes and the general office culture regarding the control of corporate crime. The impact that social context has on the overall rate of prosecutions is mediated, we suspect, by these office characteristics.

Prosecutorial Resources

In chapter 5, we learned from prosecutors that the availability of prosecutorial resources and expertise is important in the decision to undertake corporate cases. Fully one-half of our respondents indicated that insufficient prosecutorial and investigative resources would limit their willingness to prosecute corporate criminal offenses, and over one-third said that insufficient expertise would limit them. These survey results confirm what white-collar crime and legal scholars have often argued—successful application of the criminal law in corporate cases is difficult (Levi 1987; Rakoff 1985; Shapiro 1984; Stone 1975). The detection and investigation of corporate crimes pose special obstacles for prosecutors. Because of their technical and legal complexity, prosecution of corporate crimes requires more investigative and prosecutorial resources and greater technical expertise than does prosecution of street crimes. Case studies of corporate crime have found that local prosecutors often have inadequate organizational resources and expertise to overcome these obstacles (Cullen et al. 1987; Schudson et al. 1984; Vaughan 1983). Thus, it is clear that resources and expertise are potentially important determinants of prosecutorial activity and must be included in our model.

To measure the availability of prosecutorial resources, we used the number of full-time attorneys in the office. Expertise is a more difficult concept to operationalize, involving as it does intangibles such as experience and skill. As a crude measure, we operationalized expertise with a dummy variable indicating whether or not the office has a special unit devoted to white-collar or economic crime prosecutions or is involved in an interagency task force focused on these types of crimes. For our contextual theory, it is important to know whether community context influences the likelihood that prosecutors make these special organizational arrangements to fight corporate crime.

Most organizations pursue multiple objectives with limited budgetary, personnel, and technical resources. Criminal justice organizations, such as the local prosecutor's office, are no exception. Since they cannot meet all of the numerous, conflicting, and shifting demands made on them, prosecutors, like other criminal justice administrators, must make strategic decisions on the priority of objectives. High-priority objectives, of course, are more likely to be allocated scarce resources than are low-priority objectives. Prosecutors who establish an in-house unit or who join an interagency task force for investigating and prosecuting corporate crimes demonstrate in concrete terms that corporate crime is a high-priority objective.

Office Culture

While prosecutorial resources and expertise are likely to be important determinants of activity against corporate crime, they are not self-activating. Unless a prosecutor is motivated to use them against corporate crime, neither will lead to more corporate prosecutions. Certain attitudes toward corporate crime may keep prosecutors from conducting such prosecutions. If prosecutors regard alternative civil or administrative remedies as appropriate in cases of corporate wrongdoing, they may be less inclined to expend resources on corporate prosecutions. Our contextual theory assumes that the office culture influences the overall level of activity against corporate crime. We expect that activity will be higher in offices in which cultural support for corporate criminal prosecutions is present.

To measure office culture on alternative remedies, we used three items introduced in chapter 5 as factors that limit the prosecutor's willingness to undertake a corporate case. The items ask to what extent the respondent's willingness to prosecute would be limited if federal or state regulatory agencies or private parties initiated action against a corporate offender. Assigned ordinal ranks and summed, the item responses ("definitely would be limited," "probably would be limited," "probably would not be limited," "and definitely would not be limited") form an "alternative remedy" scale.[2] This scale taps the prosecutor's willingness to forego criminal prosecution if other remedies are likely to be imposed by regulatory agencies or private parties.

Community Context

Our attention now turns to the community context in which the prosecutor's office is situated. In earlier chapters, we examined only two dimensions of the community context: population size and regional location. Here, we develop a multidimensional conceptualization of community context by examining three other important dimensions: crime, economic conditions, and legal culture. To control for the amount of corporate crime, we include a measure of the number of potential offenders in a jurisdiction. We hypothesize that, along with regional location, these dimensions of the community context influence both what prosecutors think about corporate crime and what they do about it.

Potential Offenders. It makes sense to assume that the number of prosecutions in an area is, at least in part, a function of the number of offenses available to be prosecuted. For example, cities plagued by violent crimes probably tend to arrest and prosecute violent offenders more frequently than do cities blessed with few violent crimes. This fact complicates the investigation of how community context influences crime control responses.

To show that community context exerts an independent influence on crime control, one must first control for the amount of crime. Researchers interested in the relationship between community context and responses to ordinary street crime long have recognized this problem (Liska et al. 1981; Liska and Chamlin 1984). To control for it, researchers first factor out the effects of the crime rate on criminal justice responses and then determine how much of the remaining variation in responses is associated with community context. For example, Hochstetler and Shover (1997) hypothesized that economic conditions, specifically the size of the labor surplus, influence prison commitments independent of crime rates. To investigate this hypothesis, the researchers had to control for reported crime rates and then determine whether changes in unemployment rates influence changes in prison commitments. In this case, the hypothesis was confirmed: Hochstetler and Shover found that changes in unemployment affect prison commitment rates, independent of reported crime rates.

Investigators who study the effects of community context on official reactions to street crime have an advantage over those who study corporate crime. Isolating the effects of community context on official reactions is more difficult in the case of corporate crime. Unlike those for ordinary street crimes, independent indicators of the amount of corporate crime in a community are not available. Therefore, it is difficult to tell whether observed correlations between community context and prosecution rates are due to the effects of community context or simply to variation in the amount of corporate crime. Nevertheless, since our theory predicts that community context influences prosecutorial activity independent of the number of offenses available for prosecution, we must control for the level of corporate crime.

Presumably the number of corporate offenses in an area is, in part, a function of the number of businesses located there. By definition, corporate crime can be committed only by business entities. Thus, the number of businesses can be considered a proxy indicator for the level of corporate crime. We constructed an index of *potential business offenders* by summing the number of manufacturing, service, retail, and wholesale trade establishments located in each jurisdiction.[3] The items making up this index are highly correlated with one another (r's $> .90$), and the index has an alpha reliability of .88. Not surprisingly, the index is strongly correlated with population size ($r = .97$) and thus may also be considered a control for the general size of the jurisdiction.[4]

Local Legal Culture. Communities establish the legal culture within which law enforcement agencies operate. Because most local prosecutors are locally elected officials, their day-to-day approaches to enforcement largely reflect the concerns and priorities of their constituencies and local communities (Cole 1988, 149; 1970). As elected officials, prosecutors must be sensitive to local legal culture as it relates to the control of corporate crime. Legal culture may be roughly defined as a set of community-based norms, values, beliefs, and understandings about when and how legal actors should carry out their official responsibilities (Friedman 1975; Galanter 1986). This culture influences the priorities and practices of law enforcement agencies because these agencies need external justification (Friedman 1975). With respect to corporate crime, we hypothesize that in some communities the legal culture more vigorously supports the use of criminal penalties as a means of controlling corporate wrongdoing than it does in others. Unfortunately, we do not have direct indicators of the local legal culture on corporate crime control. Hence, we must rely on less direct, proxy indicators of legal culture.

One of the most stable and consistent findings in empirical social research is the relationship between education and social and political liberalism (Weil 1985). As a complex, multifaceted ideology, liberalism is difficult to define concisely. Nevertheless, it encompasses certain core values that distinguish it from conservative political ideologies. One of the distinguishing features of liberalism is acceptance of the legitimacy and need for state intervention in the economy and for state-administered controls on economic and business conduct. Empirical research has consistently found college-educated individuals to be generally less trusting of business leaders and more favorable toward state intervention in the economy than those with less than a college education (Brint 1984; McAdams 1987). Based on this research, we hypothesize that the proportion of college-educated people in a community directly affects the local legal culture on corporate crime control. Communities with highly educated populations are skeptical of business leaders and unwilling to tolerate business misconduct. One manifestation of this intolerance toward business misconduct is support for corporate criminal prosecutions. As an indicator of the college-educated population, we used the percentage of the population with sixteen or more years of education.

Economic Conditions. Unlike ordinary crimes, corporate crimes often are committed by organizations that may make valuable economic contributions to communities. Communities vary in the degree to which they can be harmed by the loss or reduction of these economic contributions. If enforcement action causes a corporate perpetrator to relocate to another community, it may have significant negative effects for local tax revenues and employment (Moore 1987). In her analysis of antitrust enforcement, Simpson (1986, 1987) found that enforcement of federal antitrust law tends to decrease during recessions and economic downturns and increase during economic booms. In corporate crime cases more than in other criminal cases, legal actors are sensitive to the potential impact of their decisions on local economic conditions (Jowell 1986).

Two important dimensions of local economies are strength and specialization. Strength of economy refers to a community's general level of wealth. Specialization refers to the extent to which a community is dependent on a particular employer or type of employer for its economic well-being. We expect that, where the local economy is weak or dominated by a few large employers, corporate prosecutions will be less likely. In communities with weak local economies, prosecutorial resources will be lower, and those that are available will be more likely allocated to controlling ordinary street crime. In addition, communities with weak local economies should be more willing to tolerate corporate misconduct out of fear of losing jobs and tax revenues if enforcement is too stiff.

Overall strength of economy can be measured as the local per capita income. To assess economic specialization, we use a measure developed by economists called the Location Quotient (LQ). LQ can be used to measure whether an area's employment is over- or under-represented in a particular industry relative to the national industrial distribution of employment (Isard 1960, 123–26). The formula for LQ is

$$LQ_{ij} = 100 \times (E_{ij}/E_{usi})/(E_j/E_{us})$$

where

E_{ij} = employment in industry "i" in county "j"
E_j = total employment in county "j"
E_{usi} = total employment in industry "i" in the U.S.
E_{us} = total employment in the U.S.

If LQ is greater than 100, then industry "i"—for example, manufacturing—is over-represented in county "j" relative to the national industrial distribution of employment.

The LQ can be computed for a number of different industries (financial, manufacturing, retail, service, and other). We use the LQ for manufacturing employment as our measure of economic specialization. Our decision to focus on manufacturing employment was based on the rationale that the manufacturing sector of the United States economy generally is in a state of decline (McGarrah 1990; Eckstein et al. 1984). We hypothesized that communities that are economically dependent on weak industries will be less willing to control business activity tightly. By using the LQ for manufacturing to measure economic specialization, we can investigate this prediction.

Crime. In chapter 4 we found that the prosecutors in our sample are located in jurisdictions with dramatically varying rates of street crime. It hardly needs to be added that, in response to community concern, violent street crime has become an especially high-priority item for virtually every local prosecutor. Prosecutorial resources that are allocated toward controlling violent crime cannot simultaneously be used against corporate crime. Thus, we suspect that prosecutors located in communities with high rates of violent crime will be less willing and less able to devote significant resources to corporate crime control. To measure this dimension of the community context, we use the official violent crime rate, defined by the FBI's Uniform Crime Report as the number of violent crimes known to the police per 100,000 people.

Region. In previous chapters we presented evidence of strong regional variation in prosecutors' attitudes and activities toward corporate crime. To control for these regional effects, our contextual model includes a dummy variable for region. Prosecutors located in western states are contrasted against their counterparts in the northern, midwestern, and southern regions.

Prosecutorial Activity

The dependent variable is the level of prosecutorial activity against corporate crime. To measure level of activity, respondents were asked how often their office typically prosecuted the nine offenses described earlier. We assigned ordinal ranks and summed the item responses ("never," "less than 1 per year," "1 to three times per year," "more than 3 times per year") to form an index of *prosecutorial activity*. The index has an alpha reliability of .85 and ranges from 9 to 36.

Although a direct count of the actual number of corporate prosecutions would perhaps be a more valid indicator of prosecutorial activity, such information unfortunately is not readily available. We asked respondents about the exact number of corporate prosecutions that their office conducted in 1988. But this question produced a sizable number of nonresponses. Apparently, local prosecutors do not keep easily accessed records on corporate cases. For those who did answer this question, reported prosecutions in 1988 correlated strongly with the prosecutorial activity index. Hence, we have some confidence that the index does provide a valid measure of variation in prosecutorial efforts against corporate crime.

Figure 7.1 shows the full model of community context and prosecutorial activity. In this model, community context influences office characteristics and office culture on corporate crime. Taken together, context, characteristics, and culture determine the overall level of prosecutorial activity against corporate crime. Table 7.1 summarizes the variables in the model.

Because our model includes a mix of both dichotomous and continuous dependent variables, we use both logistic and ordinary least squares regression to analyze the data. Our theory is essentially exploratory and not sufficiently developed to permit a deductive model-testing approach. Thus, we estimate a series of equations to determine inductively the impor-

Figure 7.1 Contextual Model of Activity Against Corporate Crime

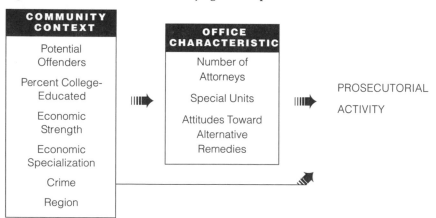

Table 7.1 Variables in the Contextual Model of Activity against Corporate Crime

Variables	Measure	Mean	Standard Deviation
INDEPENDENT			
Office characteristics			
Number of attorneys in office	Number of full-time attorneys	21.67	34.90
Special units	Presence of unit devoted to white-collar crime	1.24	.43
Alternative remedies	Ordinal scale	8.05	2.04
Community context			
Potential offenders	Natural log of number of business establishments	7.81	1.73
College education	Percentage with 16 years' or more education	16.17	6.73
Economic strength	Personal income per capita	12,461.54	2,473.23
Economic specialization	Location quotient for manufacturing employment	106.58	51.06
Crime	Violent crime rate	382.42	386.17
Region	Western region vs. all others	.12	.32
DEPENDENT			
Prosecutorial activity	Ordinal scale	15.47	5.24

tant causal linkages. Because this is an exploratory study, we use a probability level of .10 for assessing statistical significance.[5]

Testing the Model

Community Context and Office Characteristics

We begin our analysis by first examining the effects of community context on office characteristics. Table 7.2 shows the results of our ordinary least squares regression analyses of number of attorneys and the alternative remedy index. To reduce the complexity of this table and to ease comparison across equations, we present only the standardized coefficients. Comparison of these coefficients permits us to assess the relative importance of the independent variables on the various dependent variables in the model. The next table (7.3) shows the logit regression analysis for the dichotomous special units variable.

Number of Attorneys. In column 2 of Table 7.2, we observe that the size of the office (as measured by the number of attorneys) is strongly influ-

Table 7.2   OLS Regression Models of Number of Attorneys and
Alternative Remedies Scale

	Office Characteristic	
Variable	Number of Attorneys	Alternative Remedies
Potential offenders	.64***	−.09
Violent crime rate	.07*	.06
Specialization in manufacturing	−.13***	.07
Percentage with 16 or more years of education	−.17***	.04
Per capita income	.12**	−.11
Western region	.13***	−.02
Intercept	−129.07	9.76
R^2	.55	.03
F	78.62***	2.08*

*p < .10
**p < .05
***p < .01

enced by a number of contextual factors. Indeed, all of the contextual measures are significantly related to the number of attorneys in an office, and the overall R^2 is a healthy .55.[6] The most important influence on the size of the office is the number of business establishments in the office's jurisdiction. Its standardized coefficient (.64) is about four to five times larger than any of the other variable coefficients. Prosecutors located in large communities tend to have correspondingly large staffs. Other contextual factors associated with increased numbers of prosecuting attorneys are western location, high per capita income, and high rates of violent crime. Surprisingly, the violent crime rate has the weakest effect on number of attorneys. Its standardized coefficient is just over one-half the size of that of income per capita. Its statistical significance ($p = .0984$) is also marginal. Some factors tend to increase the size of the prosecutor's office; others tend to decrease it. Prosecutors located in communities with high rates of employment in manufacturing tend to have smaller offices. The percentage of the population with sixteen or more years of education also has a negative effect on the number of attorneys in the local prosecutor's office.

Taken together, these results show that the size of the local prosecutor's office is not solely a function of the size of either the local community or its crime problem. Other community characteristics—such as income, education, regional location, and type of economy—influence the size of the prosecutor's office and, hence, the availability of resources to fight corporate and other forms of crime.

Alternative Remedies. Although community context strongly influences the size of the local prosecutor's office, it does not appear to have a strong effect on prosecutors' attitudes toward the use of alternative remedies in corporate cases. Column 3 in Table 7.2 shows the results of our regression analysis of the alternative remedies scale. The R^2 is very small, only .03, and none of the community context variables has statistically significant effects on the scale. These results suggest that office culture is determined by factors other than community context, at least as we have conceptualized and measured it here.

We speculated that local prosecutors might be more willing to defer to state and federal regulatory action if they lacked organizational resources to pursue cases themselves. To investigate whether office culture was determined by office resources and structure, we regressed the alternative remedies index on the contextual variables with number of attorneys and special units included in the equation. Adding these measures made no difference, as neither had a statistically significant effect and the overall R^2 remained very small.

Special Units. The final office characteristic to be examined is the presence of a special unit. Since this variable is dichotomous, we use logistic regression to investigate the effects of community context. Table 7.3 shows the logit estimates. As in the model of number of attorneys, we see that the number of potential offenders is strongly related to the presence of a special unit. Prosecutors located in communities with large numbers of business establishments are more likely to establish a special unit than are their counterparts in communities with fewer business entities.

For theoretical purposes, the findings on violent crime and economic specialization are particularly important. The coefficients for both violent crime and economic specialization in manufacturing are negative (-0.001 and -0.010, respectively). Thus, as violent crime increases, the likelihood that a prosecutor will devote organizational resources to corporate crime appears to decrease. Similarly, the more a community's economic structure depends on manufacturing employment, the less likely it is to have a special unit devoted to corporate crime control. These findings provide support for the idea that the priority given to corporate crime control is influ-

Table 7.3 Logistic Regression Model of the Probability That the Prosecutor's Office Has a Special Unit

Variable	Logit Coefficient
Potential offenders	1.975***
Violent crime rate	−0.001*
Specialization in manufacturing	−0.010**
Percentage with 16 or more years of education	−0.017
Per capita income	0.000
Western region	0.776*

Note: −2 Log-Likelihood = 450.50; model chi-square = 166.46 with 6 degrees of freedom ($p < 0.001$); 418 observations.
*$p < .10$
**$p < .05$
***$p < .01$

enced by the stability and strength of the local community. Prosecutors located in communities that are beset with social and economic problems appear to be less willing and less able to devote resources to corporate crime control.

The final contextual factor that influences whether a prosecutor is likely to establish a special unit is regional location. Prosecutors located in the West are more likely to have a special unit than are their counterparts in other regions.

Prosecutorial Activity

When we examine prosecutorial activity against corporate crime (Table 7.4), we find that the characteristics of the prosecutor's office appear to have the most important influence. Indeed, number of attorneys and presence of special units are more powerful predictors of activity than our index of potential offenders. Office culture, as captured by the alternative remedies index, also has a statistically significant effect. In contrast, most of the contextual variables are either not significant or less important than in earlier models.[7] Overall, the model explains 40 percent of the variation in prosecutors' activity against corporate crime ($R^2 = .40$).

Both the organizational resources of the local prosecutor's office, as measured by the number of attorneys, and its organizational structure, as indicated by the presence of a special unit, influence activity against corporate crime. The availability of more attorneys permits more corporate crime

Table 7.4   OLS Regression Model of Prosecutorial Activity against
Corporate Crime

Independent Variables	Standardized Coefficient
Community context	
Potential offenders	.178**
Violent crime rate	−.028
Specialization in manufacturing	−.028
Percentage with 16 or more years of education	.075
Per capita income	−.042
Western region	.110**
Office characteristics	
Number of attorneys	.257***
Special unit	.222***
Alternative remedies	−.091**
Intercept	7.372
R^2	.40
F	25.411***

*p < .10
**p < .05
***p < .01

prosecutions, and if these attorneys are organized into a special unit, the level of activity increases even further. However, organizational resources and structure are not the only office characteristics that influence activity. Office culture is also important, as evidenced by the significant negative coefficient for the alternative remedies index. This index taps the extent to which the prosecutor's willingness to take a corporate case to court would be limited by federal or state regulatory action or by a private civil suit related to the case. Even though we do not yet know the sources of variation in office culture, we can say that it influences activity toward corporate crime. Local prosecutors who say they would be limited by actual or pending regulatory action tend to take on fewer cases than do those who pay less attention to the actions of regulatory agencies.

Among our contextual variables, only potential offenders and regional location have significant coefficients. Although still significant, the index of potential offenders is less important in the model of activity than it was in the models for number of attorneys and presence of special units. Similarly, location in the West is a less important determinant of prosecutorial activity than it was of office characteristics. The coefficients for specialization in manufacturing, percentage with college education, violent crime, and per capita income are not significant. These contextual variables do not have direct effects on activity.

Taken together, the analyses reported in Tables 7.2, 7.3, and 7.4 suggest that the impact of community context on prosecutorial activity is largely indirect. The strength and specialization of local economies, the violent crime rate, and the level of education in a community significantly influence the size of the local prosecutor's office. The violent crime rate and specialization in manufacturing are negatively related to the likelihood of an office having a special unit. These dimensions of community context determine the amount and organization of resources available for corporate cases. They influence the local prosecutor's capacity for control of corporate crime, which, in turn, directly affects the level of prosecutorial activity.

An ambiguous and difficult-to-interpret aspect of our analyses are the results on alternative remedies. Variation in attitudes toward alternative remedies influences activity in a predictable fashion. The effect is not large, but it is significant. However, the source of this variation is not clear at all. It does not appear to be a function of either community context or office characteristics. We suspect that attitudes toward alternative remedies may be a function of several unobserved influences. One such influence may be idiosyncratic: the background characteristics of prosecutors, such as their political orientations, which we could not assess in this study. Another influence may be unique historical factors involving the prosecutor's relationships and experiences with the state and federal regulatory agencies operating in their communities. In communities where local prosecutors have established good working relationships with regulatory agencies, they may be more willing to forego prosecution at the request of these agencies in order to maintain good relations. It is also likely that some regulatory enforcers are more strict in dealing with corporate offenders than are others. Prosecutors associated with these strict enforcers may feel that regulatory enforcement alone is an adequate deterrent.

Reconsidering Sutherland

The results of our multivariate analyses support the idea that community context shapes local reactions to corporate crime. This finding probably would not have surprised the man who first drew the attention of criminologists to the problem of corporate crime: Edwin Sutherland. Sutherland's contributions to the study of white-collar and corporate crime are both celebrated and disparaged. He is revered for his brilliantly original exposé of corporate wrongdoing and for inventing the concept of white-collar crime. The distinguished British criminologist Hermann Mannheim (1965, 470) suggested that, if there were a Nobel prize in criminology, Sutherland would have won it for his work on white-collar crime. But Sutherland also has had his detractors. From the outset, his definition of white-collar crime was criticized, and it continues to provoke controversy today (Tappan 1977; Hirschi and Gottfredson 1987; Shapiro 1990). Although the debate over the definition of white-collar crime is certainly important, it has had the unfortunate effect of overshadowing other aspects of Sutherland's thought on white-collar crime. His ideas about social reactions to white-collar and corporate crime, in particular, have not received sufficient attention. It is to these ideas that we turn now, as a starting point for considering the broader theoretical implications of the findings presented in this chapter.

An often overlooked dimension of Sutherland's theories about crime in general and corporate crime in particular is his argument that crime flourishes when communities are socially disorganized (1983, 255–57). Sutherland identified two types of social disorganization: *anomie* is a lack of standards for directing the behavior of members of a society in general or in specific areas of social action; *conflict of standards* refers to conflict between groups with reference to specified practices (1983, 255).

According to Sutherland, two factors contribute to social disorganization with respect to business practices. First, business "behavior is complex, technical and not readily observable by inexperienced citizens" (1983, 255). The complex and hidden nature of business activity makes the development of public standards of behavior difficult. Second, Sutherland argued that, for three to six decades following the end of the Civil War, business relations in America were undergoing rapid change. During this period of change, old standards were breaking down and new ones had not yet developed. In Sutherland's view, white-collar and corporate crime flourished because of both types of social disorganization. Because America was founded on the ideals of free competition and free enterprise, it had a long tradition of opposing government regulation of business. This tradition had considerable popular support. While the tradition had been largely abandoned in practice, Sutherland thought that it nevertheless retained much force as an ideology promoted by the businesses of his day. As a result, anomie with respect to business practices was common and widespread. The public, in Sutherland's view, was ambivalent about both business and government control of business activity. Lacking clear signals of concern from the public, law enforcers were not vigorous in their pursuit of business misconduct.

The second type of social disorganization, conflict of standards, also mitigated against control of business. According to Sutherland, the business community is tightly organized in favor of violations of business regulations. That is, within the business community, violations of business regulations are not discouraged or negatively defined. If anything, violations are defined favorably by business. But political society is not similarly organized against violations of business regulations. That is, no strong normative consensus exists against violations of law by business. Definitions favorable to violations of law exceeded definitions unfavorable to violations of law. From the perspective of Sutherland's differential association theory, then, high rates of business crime were to be expected.

Nearly fifty years have passed since Sutherland first presented his analysis of white-collar crime. Much has changed in American society in the intervening years, but much also has remained the same. And parts of Sutherland's analysis still ring true today. Business behavior is still complex, technical, and not readily observable. If anything, it is more complex, more technical, and more hidden than it was in Sutherland's day. Occasionally, a dramatic disaster—such as the terrible fire in a chicken-processing plant in North Carolina which killed twenty-five workers—will highlight the dangers of regulatory noncompliance and prompt public outrage against corporate offenders (Wright et al. 1995). But most corporate crime remains hidden, difficult to detect, and not obvious in its effects.

Certainly, government intervention in the economy has increased since Sutherland wrote, particularly during the 1960s and 1970s. But this increase has not gone unopposed. During the 1980s significant efforts to deregulate the economy were initiated by Republican administrations and have continued in the 1990s with the Republican takeover of the United States Congress. These efforts have been enthusiastically promoted by business organizations and just as enthusiastically resisted by consumer groups, labor unions, and environmental organizations. To say that, in present-day American society, there is a conflict in standards regarding business behavior and government regulation certainly would not be inaccurate.

Thus, the factors that Sutherland saw in his day as contributing to social disorganization with respect to corporate crime still operate today. And corporate crime still flourishes in the midst of this disorganization. We agree with the general thrust of Sutherland's argument, but we think that there are logical implications to his approach that have not been sufficiently appreciated. He argued that corporate crime flourishes because society is not socially organized to prevent it. But there is no reason to assume that the level of social organization against corporate crime is fixed. It may increase or decrease over time, and it may be greater in some geographic areas than in others. Just as communities may be more or less organized against street crime, they also may be more or less organized against corporate crime.

The results presented in this chapter show that community context strongly influences prosecutors' activity against corporate crime. From the perspective of Sutherland's disorganization theory, the findings suggest that the degree to which communities are socially organized against corporate crime depends at least in part on local economic, social, and crime conditions. Communities plagued by high rates of violent crime understandably focus their efforts against violent crime. But when violent crime appears to be under control, then the salience of other forms of crime may rise in the hierarchy of public priorities. Relatedly, communities with strong and diverse economies can afford greater control of corporate crime. Economically strong communities may not be willing to tolerate corporate misconduct for the sake of jobs. To their populations, the tradeoffs between economic growth and worker safety, pollution, and fraudulent business activities may appear less necessary and less palatable. These communities may, over time, develop local legal cultures that are less tolerant of corporate misconduct. That is, in Sutherland's terms, they may become socially organized against corporate crime. In response to this social organization, prosecutors may feel it necessary to devote more resources to investigating and prosecuting corporate crime.

A Note On Conflict Theory and White-Collar Crime Studies

Another theoretical tradition that can help illuminate the results of our analyses is the conflict perspective. It is the dominant perspective for organizing contemporary macro-level research on official reactions to crime (Liska 1992). The conflict perspective assumes that law is a source of domination. Those in power use the law and law enforcement agencies against behavior they deem threatening to their interests. Law making and law enforcement, according to the conflict perspective, reflect the interests of the advantaged (economic elites) over the interests of the disadvantaged (the poor, the unemployed, and minority groups). The perspective draws attention both to activities (crime rates) and people (the unemployed) as potential sources of threat and hence as important macro-level determinants of official reactions to crime (Liska 1992, 17–18).

Conflict theorists have paid particularly close attention to the relation between the economic order and the state's crime control apparatus. They contend that coercive control by the state is a function of perceived threats to social and economic stability (Hochstetler and Shover 1997; Box and Hale 1982; Jankovic 1977). In theory, social elites fear disadvantaged minority groups and the unemployed. Where these subject populations are large or growing, elites perceive them as threats to order. In response to these perceived threats, the panoply of control institutions—police, courts, and prisons—becomes more coercive. Empirical investigations have focused, with generally favorable results, on the relations between unemployment and imprisonment rates (Inverarity and McCarthy 1988; Inverarity 1992; Hochstetler and Shover 1997) and between minority group size and police per capita (Liska et al. 1981; Jackson and Carroll 1981). A fundamental proposition of the conflict perspective is that, as threats to social and economic stability increase, official reactions become stronger and more repressive (Liska 1992). The threat hypothesis has been used to explain variation in different forms of crime control, ranging from lynching to the expansion of the welfare system (Chamlin 1992; Tolnay and Beck 1992).

These and other studies have greatly advanced our understanding of large-scale variation in official reactions. Yet, they employ quite narrow conceptualizations of threat, which is conceived entirely as a bottom-up phenomenon. It flows from the bottom of the social structure toward the top, from the lower classes toward the middle and upper classes, from people of color toward white people. The sources of threat typically identified are limited to different groups of disadvantaged people (the poor, the unemployed, or minorities) and the threatening activities they engage in (ordinary street crimes). However, without denying the conservative, ethnocentric, crime-fearing nature of the middle and upper classes, it is reasonable to ask whether other sources of threat also influence community responses to crime. We suggest that they do.

The corporate crimes of legitimate businesses (e.g., manufacturers and retail outlets) may also act as sources of threat. Indeed, as documented in our opening chapter, there is substantial evidence that corporate crime is a matter of some concern to local communities and law enforcement. Since the mid-1970s, the salience of corporate crime as a social problem has risen, manifesting in growing public concern over it and more aggressive governmental policies against it (Cullen et al. 1987; Katz 1980).

White-collar and corporate crime theorists also posit an implicit relation between the economic order and the activities of control institutions. The relation, however, is the opposite of that proposed by conflict theorists: poor economic conditions reduce state control of business activity because of the state's interest in nurturing economic growth (Simpson 1986, 1987). For example, Box (1987, 55) contends that in economic recessions potential corporate offenders use their political and economic influence to lobby for reduced law-enforcement efforts in their industries.

What happens when economic conditions or other social conditions improve has rarely been explicitly considered by corporate crime or conflict theorists. Box (1987) does not directly address the impact of economic expansion on corporate crime control, but it follows from his analysis that corporate law enforcement increases during economic expansions. The empirical results presented in this chapter also suggest that economic health may be associated with more vigorous efforts to control corporate and business misconduct. Prosecutors located in communities with high per capita income levels tend to have large staffs and to conduct more corporate prosecutions than do their counterparts in less well-off communities. The violent crime rate is inversely related to the likelihood that a local prosecutor will make special organizational arrangements to respond to corporate crime. Traditional indicators of threat seem to be inversely related to activity against corporate crime.

We speculate that, according to the status of traditional sources of threat—such as the overall volume of crime or the state of the economy—local prosecutors focus more or less attention on corporate crime. Economically secure communities are less threatened by street crime and disadvantaged groups; therefore, they can pay more attention to other potential sources of threat—for example, that posed by corporate crime. They have greater freedom and more resources to focus on control of corporate crime than do communities that are less well-off financially. Similarly, communities with low levels of street crime may be more willing to allocate crime control resources to other forms of crime than are communities plagued by high crime rates. Increased local prosecution of corporate crime would be one form of reallocation. As social indicators such as the unemployment rate or the crime rate improve, prosecutors reallocate resources away from ordinary crime control and toward corporate crime control. These considerations lead us to suggest a revised threat hypothesis for corporate crime control: In contrast to ordinary crime control, local corporate crime control tends to increase as traditional types of social threat decline.

In addition to the data presented in this book, some historical evidence supports this line of reasoning. Friedman (1985b) argues that, since the turn of the century, a steady increase has occurred in controls placed on business activity. This increase has been caused in part by scientific and technological advances and in part by the gradual improvement in the American standard of living. As the middle class expanded and became more economically secure, it was less willing to accept business misconduct for the sake of economic prosperity. Advances in science and technology make life seem more predictable and more controllable. Environmental pollution, industrial accidents, poisonous food, and dangerous cars no longer are accepted as simply unavoidable parts of life. Rather, these and other business-induced harms are seen as preventable. This new view of harm has led to ever-greater social control of business activity (Friedman 1985b; Geis 1988) and to greater grass-roots-level activism against corporate misconduct (Cable and Benson 1993; see also Evans et al. 1993).

Notes

1. The literature in this area is large. For an excellent overview of prior research, see Allen Liska's *Social Threat and Social Control* (Liska 1992).

2. The alternative remedy scale has an alpha reliability of .81.

3. Information on the number of business establishments in a county is available in the *City-County Data Book*.

4. Because of the extremely skewed distribution and wide range of values for this index, its natural log is used in the analyses reported below.

5. Another reason for using a level of significance that is higher than customary involves our sample. Recall that we originally surveyed *all* prosecutors located in urban areas, and over two-thirds of them responded. When we compared the respondents to nonrespondents,

we found very few significant differences. Thus, the sample we are analyzing represents a substantial proportion of the population of urban prosecutors, and there are good reasons for thinking that it is highly representative of that population. Because we have surveyed such a substantial proportion of the population, our sample statistics can be considered closer to population parameters than is ordinarily the case. Using the traditional cutoff point of .05 for assessing statistical significance would make the likelihood of committing a type II error unnecessarily high. Arbitrarily sticking to the .05 level might lead us to overlook potentially important relationships and effects.

Statistically, the problem is that we are sampling from a finite population. Sampling from a finite population without replacement leads to overestimation of the standard error and, thus, to an increased likelihood of incorrectly accepting the null hypothesis (Hays and Winkler 1970).

6. Collinearity diagnostics indicate that multicollinearity is not a problem in this model. The largest variance inflation factor is 1.97, and the highest condition number is 25.79. Both of these values are below the suggested cutoffs for identifying problematic multicollinearity (Myers 1986).

7. Note, for example, that in the OLS model of number of attorneys, the standardized coefficient from potential offenders was .64, while in the model for activity it is only about one-fourth that size (B = .178).

PART III

The Culture of
Prosecution, Investigation,
and Networking

8

PROSECUTORIAL DECISION MAKING

Substantial consensus exists among prosecutors on a variety of issues related to corporate crime control. Prosecutors more or less agree on the factors that increase their willingness to undertake corporate cases and on the goals they pursue in prosecuting corporate crimes. When a corporate crime results in physical or substantial economic harm to victims, almost all prosecutors say they are more willing to prosecute. The goals pursued by most prosecutors in corporate cases tend to be general deterrence, boundary maintenance, and retribution. This consensus appears to be largely unaffected by social context, at least as context has been operationalized in this study. Regardless of the size of the jurisdiction served or its regional location, most prosecutors appear to share a common view regarding when and why corporate offenses warrant prosecution.

This consensus on what constitutes a serious corporate offense arises out of what we call a *common legal culture of prosecution*—that is, a set of norms and values about how corporate offenses are defined and the role that the criminal justice system should play in controlling this form of crime. While our survey data permitted us to identify this consensus among local prosecutors, they are not well suited to exploring the complex pattern of reasons that underlie it. This shortcoming is an unavoidable weakness of survey data. Hence, in the next three chapters, we set aside our survey results and turn to interviews we conducted during our field studies with prosecutors and other criminal justice and regulatory officials. Our goal is to delve more deeply into the reasoning that underlies prosecutorial decision making and to explicate the common culture of prosecution.

The interviews were open-ended but guided by a strong sense of significant areas to explore. When we were talking with prosecutors, we focused primarily on their priorities in corporate cases and on the legal and resource constraints that influence their decision making in corporate cases. We tried to get a sense of how prosecutors think about corporate offenders and why they decide to prosecute in one case but not in another. What are prosecutors trying to accomplish in corporate cases, and why are these goals, whatever they may be, important? One might say that we were looking for red flags, that is, for the characteristics of an offense or an offender that tend to trigger a criminal prosecution.

In what follows, we have focused on the general themes that arose in the interviews. To let the prosecutors, as much as possible, speak for themselves, a selection of actual responses is presented. For the most part, we have not attempted to analyze or explain differences in the views of the prosecutors across jurisdictions. Rather, we treat them as indicative of the range of opinions held by prosecutors nationwide.

Consumer Fraud and Environmental Crime

For the case studies, we chose to concentrate on two specific forms of corporate crime: consumer fraud and environmental crime.[1] We focused on consumer fraud because the national survey indicated that it is the corporate crime that prosecutors most often handle. Two recent surveys on fraud found victimization rates of over 50 percent (Titus et al. 1995; Van Wyk and Benson, 1997). When local prosecutors and state attorneys general first began showing an interest in economic crimes in the early 1970s, consumer fraud was a primary focus (Edelhertz and Rogovin 1982c). We chose environmental crime because it was an area that, at the time, appeared to be undergoing significant change. Although no hard data were available in 1988 on local environmental crime prosecutions, new survey data indicate that our suspicions were correct and that local environmental crime prosecutions are on the rise. The National Institute of Justice recently sponsored a survey of local prosecutors' offices representing jurisdictional populations over 250,000 (Rebovich and Nixon 1994). The survey found that local environmental crime prosecutions rose steadily from 1990 to 1992. Criminal prosecutions of environmental offenses rose from 381 to 756 between 1990 and 1991. They increased even more rapidly in the first six months of 1992, during which 882 environmental prosecutions were reported, eclipsing the total for all of 1991 (Rebovich and Nixon 1994). Environmental crime is one of the areas in which the limits of the law to control economic behavior are being redefined (Cullen et al. 1987, 312–19; Magnuson and Leviton 1987).

Consumer Fraud

Broadly construed, fraud refers to the "crime type comprising offenses sharing the elements of practice of deceit or intentional misrepresentation of fact with the intent of unlawfully depriving a person of his or her property or rights" (Rush 1986, 103). Fraud takes a variety of forms. Sometimes individuals defraud businesses, as in false insurance claims, or individuals may victimize governmental programs, as in welfare or medical benefit frauds. Consumer fraud occurs when a business deliberately defrauds an individual by misrepresenting the condition of a product or service so as to deliberately mislead the consumer.

Consumer fraud is an ancient offense. As early as the first century A.D., Pliny the Elder reported instances of manufacturers and retailers of honey and pharmaceuticals adulterating their products so as to increase their profits at the expense of consumers (Green 1990, 203). And T. Swann Harding (1935) has compiled hundreds of reported cases of consumer fraud throughout history.

Because fraud can occur whenever goods or services are sold, opportunities for fraud are virtually boundless. Fraud may be found in the high-culture business of international art trading and the blue-collar world of auto repair. The offenses may be relatively unthreatening, such as slightly over-weighting meat or produce by miscalibrating scales, or downright dangerous, as may occur when seriously ill individuals are led to rely on worthless quack medicine in place of traditional health care. The offenders range from individual, fly-by-night entrepreneurs to well-established, multinational corporations. Some consumer frauds are an incidental part of otherwise legitimate business activities, such as an auto repair shop that cheats a few of its customers. In other cases, fraud is the main purpose of the business enterprise. The types of consumer fraud most frequently mentioned in the field interviews were repair frauds and advance fee swindles. For example, auto repair and appliance repair frauds were often cited. The businesses involved were generally small to medium-sized companies and not major corporations.

Friedman (1993, 195–97) suggests that con games, rackets, and swindles blossomed in nineteenth-century America. During this century, conditions in American society made possible types of swindling that were impossible or at least difficult before. The development of the newspaper and the national postal system, for instance, made it possible for swindlers to reach more potential victims than ever before. Swindlers could advertise cheap or worthless products on a grand scale. Women, for example, were promised in newspaper ads "the best sewing machine" in the world for only three dollars. For their money, they received a large sewing needle (Friedman 1993, 196). The growing mobility and anonymity of American society also made it easier for con men to ply their trade. Con men could move easily and anonymously from one place to another, quickly victimizing the vulnerable and gullible before moving on to another town. Because the class structure of the new world was more open and the markers of class more ambiguous than in Europe, it was possible to pass oneself off as a doctor, a professor, or a member of the nobility. In short, for a variety of technological and social reasons, it became easier in the nineteenth century to fool people.

These conditions continue to the present day. In the late twentieth century, American society continues to be highly mobile. And technological advances—most notably television, the telephone, the computer, and direct-mail mass marketing—have provided more efficient ways for fraud artists to find good victims. Technological advances also have made the average citizen more dependent on experts to keep his or her automobiles and appliances running. Opportunities for consumer fraud abound in modern society.

Environmental Crime

Like consumer fraud, environmental crime comes in a variety of forms and sizes. Offenders may be homeowners who dump leftover paint into the city sewer system in violation of local ordinances, or they may be multinational corporations that manufacture, ship, and dispose of hazardous materials under conditions so ridiculously unsafe as to be criminally negligent and morally outrageous (Tallmer 1987; Stone 1987). Some offenses are complex, involving elaborate schemes by business executives to avoid detection. Others are blatant, almost mindlessly simple—so much so that the intent, indeed the basic intelligence, of the offender is open to serious question.

Because different types of environmental crimes are associated with different types of industries and businesses, the nature of environmental crime in a community tends to reflect local economic activity. Certain types of environmental problems, however, are widespread. A study of local law enforcement responses to environmental crime concluded that "illegal waste tire disposal, improper disposal of furniture stripping and electroplating waste, used motor oil disposal, and hazardous wastes dumped into streams and rivers are found in nearly all communities" (Epstein and Hammett 1995, 3). Along with these generic forms of environmental crime, some communities suffer unique problems as a result of their particular mix of local industries and businesses. For example, in the rural community of Yellow Creek, Kentucky, most if not all of the local environmental crime is committed by one particular business, a tannery (Cable and Benson 1993). Both Maine and New Jersey have problems with illegal disposal of hazardous waste, but the type of waste is specific to each state. In Maine, waste cases tend to involve the textile, wood, and fishing industries; in New Jersey, they involve the chemical-producing and petrochemical industries (Rebovich 1992, 33).

In a strictly legal sense, what counts as environmental crime varies a great deal across jurisdictions. Statutory inconsistencies and the lack of uniform codification in state environmental laws pose difficulties for prosecutors and investigators. At the same time, they create opportunities for environmental offenders, who can evade prosecution merely by moving their operations to jurisdictions that are legally more "user-friendly" from the offender's point of view (Hammett and Epstein 1993a). A full treatment of the state of the law with respect to the environment is beyond the scope of this book. We note, however, that environmental law at the state level is to a large extent patterned after federal statutes. Thus, a brief review of some of the major pieces of federal legislation may be useful, as many states have enacted parallel laws.

One of the most important pieces of federal legislation is the Resource

Conservation and Recovery Act of 1976 (RCRA). The RCRA established a framework to cover hazardous waste from generation to disposal. It empowers the United States Environmental Protection Agency (EPA) to regulate the labeling, containment, and transportation of hazardous waste, via record keeping and a complex permitting system. The RCRA authorizes the EPA to define hazardous waste and establishes criminal penalties for persons who knowingly violate EPA rules governing hazardous waste transportation, storage, or disposal. Under the RCRA, states may establish their own regulatory programs for hazardous waste, provided that they meet certain minimum standards. Most states have now been granted authority to implement at least partial hazardous-waste–control programs. Nevertheless, states vary considerably regarding the extent to which they use criminal as opposed to civil or administrative procedures to deal with violators (Hammett and Epstein 1993a, 3–4).

Although the passage of the RCRA in 1976 represented a big step forward in the control of hazardous waste, the need for further legislation was soon recognized, prompting the passage of the Hazardous and Solid Waste Amendment (HSWA) to the RCRA in 1984. The HSWA toughened the criminal penalties available under the RCRA and extended regulatory control to so-called small-quantity generators of hazardous wastes (SQGs), those that produce less than 1,000 kilograms (about 2,680 pounds) per month (Hammett and Epstein 1993a).

The HSWA increased the cost of legal disposal of hazardous waste and imposed these costs on smaller, less financially sound enterprises. Hammett and Epstein (1993a, 4) speculate that increased costs have prompted an increasing number of generating firms to seek out less costly illegal methods of disposal. Just as fraud offenders adapt creatively to new laws and new enforcement strategies, today's environmental criminals are also adapting to the new legal environment. They have negotiated a sharp learning curve and are using increasingly sophisticated methods to commit hazardous waste crimes. The new environmental criminals have adopted classic techniques, such as forgery and bribery, that have long been part of the corporate criminal's toolkit. Rather than simply dumping waste in some isolated area, the more sophisticated environmental criminal may forge a waste transportation manifest or bribe public officials to look the other way. Other techniques involve mixing hazardous waste with nonhazardous waste (known as *cocktailing*), mislabeling drums, or disposing of the waste on the generator's own property (Hammett and Epstein 1993a). *Midnight dumpers* have not disappeared, and they have been joined by more cunning and devious criminals.

Illegal disposal of hazardous waste may be becoming more like organized crime. It would not be correct, however, to say that traditional syndicate crime families of the type popularized in the *Godfather* movies are heavily involved in illegal hazardous waste disposal. Real syndicate involvement appears to be limited to New Jersey (Rebovich 1992). Nevertheless, it is clear that organized groups are common among illegal waste offenders. In some cases, the offender is a legitimate waste generator, and the offense is organized only in the most elemental sense that it involves a criminal conspiracy among company officials to enhance profits by cutting regulatory corners. Other cases involve more deliberately and formally organized criminal groups, such as enterprises established for the specific purpose of providing illegal hazardous waste disposal as a service (Rebovich 1992). In our interviews with investigators, no mention was made of traditional syndicate crime families in connection with environmental crime, but our interviewees often referred to legitimate businesses in connection with ongoing environmental criminal activity. Criminal organizations that service legitimate businesses also were frequently mentioned.

In addition to the RCRA and the HSWA, other components of the federal environmental and regulatory scheme include the Clean Air Act, the Clean Water Act, the Toxic Substances Control Act, the Federal Insecticide, Fungicide, and Rodenticide Act, and the Comprehensive Environmental Resource Compensation and Liability Act, more commonly known as the Superfund act. These statutory schemes criminalize certain acts and require that certain information be provided to the government. Falsifying and, in some situations, omitting information is also subject to criminal penalties.

The Clean Water Act (CWA) was designed to regulate the discharge of pollutants into streams, rivers, and lakes. In 1987, it was amended to create criminal provisions for "knowing endangerment," that is, for knowingly violating sections of the act and knowing that the violation places another in imminent danger of death or bodily injury. The maximum penalty for a person convicted of knowing endangerment is a fine of $250,000 and imprisonment of fifteen years. If the person is defined as an organization, the maximum fine is $1 million. For local prosecutors, the CWA is important, because states may be delegated authority by the EPA to implement their own CWA programs, provided that they establish minimum criminal penalties of $10,000 per violation for willful or negligent violations (Hammett and Epstein 1993a).

The Comprehensive Environmental Resource Compensation and Liability Act (CERCLA), or Superfund, was designed to complement the RCRA's regulatory coverage of hazardous waste. Whereas the RCRA addresses illegalities in the generation, transportation, storage, and disposal of hazardous waste as they occur, the focus of the CERCLA is on environmental damage wrought by past noncompliance. Under the CERCLA, contaminated sites that pose threats to the environment may be placed on the National Priority List (NPL). If a site is placed on the NPL, then all firms that contributed to its contamination are required to conduct or pay for its cleanup. The U.S. Attorney General has authority under the CERCLA to seek injunctive relief in situations where a release, or threatened release, poses an imminent danger to public health or the environment. The act also provides criminal penalties for failing to notify or intentionally misleading federal authorities about the release of a hazardous substance from a regulated facility. However, except for these provisions related to reporting, the CERCLA is generally not a source of criminal prosecutions (Hammett and Epstein 1993a).

Both the Toxic Substances Control Act (TSCA) and the Federal Insecticide, Fungicide, and Rodenticide Act (FIFRA) also provide for criminal penalties in their respective realms of activity. Because the TSCA is, for the most part, centrally administered by the EPA in Washington, local prosecutors rarely handle violations of its provisions. Some states have FIFRA programs that are designed to govern the misuse of pesticides. Acts that violate FIFRA regulations and result in physical injury or death are subject to criminal penalties. For individuals, the maximum penalties are imprisonment of one year and a $250,000 fine. If the defendant is a corporation, fines as high as $500,000 may be assessed.

Judges and Sentencing of White-Collar Offenders

The decision to prosecute is in many ways analogous to the sentencing decision made by judges. Both decisions are made by individuals who have substantial discretion; both decisions have dramatic impact on the offender's fate; and, both raise questions of equality, justice, and effectiveness in the treatment of offenders and offenses. In many ways, these decisions are guided by the same underlying principles.

In recent years, much research has focused on how federal judges sentence white-collar criminals (Mann et al. 1980; Hagan et al. 1980; Wheeler et al. 1982, 1988; Benson and Walker 1988). In an important book on this topic, Stanton Wheeler, Kenneth Mann, and Austin Sarat argue that, in sentencing white-collar criminals, federal judges are guided by three unwritten, yet core, legal norms (Wheeler et al. 1988). The first norm is that "offenses should be treated differently according to the *harm* they produce." The second principle holds that "offenders should be treated differently according to the *blameworthiness* of their actions." The third norm is that harmfulness and blameworthiness taken together constitute the basis for assessing the *seriousness* of a case, which, in turn, provides the foundation for sentencing decisions. These norms, Wheeler and colleagues argue, reflect deeply rooted cultural values. They underlie not only sentencing practices but also the development of legislative statutes designating what forms of behavior deserve punishment and how much punishment is deserved.

From the work of Wheeler et al. (1988), we clearly see that judges regard white-collar sentencing as an onerous and complex task (see also Pollack and Smith 1983). Judges see themselves as having to strike a delicate balance between the interests of society and those of individual defendants. However, as troublesome and difficult as sentencing is for judges, the decision to prosecute is in many ways even more complex. At sentencing, judges deal with individuals whose behavior has been formally declared illegal and criminal. By definition, some sort of criminal sanction is appropriate and required. Prosecutors, on the other hand, face a more ambiguous situation. They must make the initial decision as to whether behavior should be characterized as criminal. They determine whether a particular person deserves to be drawn into the criminal justice system. More so than judges, prosecutors function as gatekeepers to the legal system. They decide who will and who will not be pulled into the system as well as what will and what will not be officially recognized as criminal activity. In making this decision, prosecutors are guided by the same unwritten legal norms that direct judges in sentencing. These norms form what can be called a common culture of prosecution.

The Common Culture of Prosecution

Purposes

General Deterrence. To understand why prosecutors proceed against some instances of corporate illegality and not others, it is first necessary to understand the purposes prosecutors hope to serve in conducting prosecutions. The interview responses indicate that prosecutors decide to pursue corporate crime cases mainly, but not entirely, for the same reasons that judges decide to sentence white-collar offenders to prison. Like judges, prosecutors hope to achieve a general deterrent effect (Mann et al. 1980; Wheeler et al. 1988). But unlike judges, prosecutors also tend to be concerned with punishment and education. General deterrence stood out, however, as the purpose uppermost in the minds of prosecutors. As one prosecutor commented:

There's only one advantage to these prosecutions. One of these prosecutions is worth five hundred as far as deterrent value is concerned. I've prosecuted maybe fifty murderers, and I've never deterred the street murderer once. I've probably prosecuted one industrial murderer and I think we've deterred a whole lot of people, at least woke them up and some people are trying to do the right thing. So even with a lack of resources, one [of these] prosecutions is much more valuable than one streetwise, or what they call traditional, street crime prosecution.

This point was made just as strongly by a prosecutor in another district, who felt that achieving general deterrence was not only her goal but also her duty.

When I go to a Chamber of Commerce meeting or to some trade association meeting, and they say, "Well, we'd like to hear from the district attorney's office. Tell us what you do," I get up and I say just real simple, "My job is to put you in jail if you violate the laws [and] if you get caught." Now that may result in greater compliance or it may result in more sophisticated efforts at deception. It may result in an escalation of noncooperation with the regulators, but if the end result is less environmental noncompliance, then I'm set. And I just think that the criminal sanctions, and now more and more the criminal sanction with jail for individuals, and I'm not talking about the truck driver who drove the truck that dumped the drums off the side of the highway, I'm talking about the plant manager who told the truck driver to do it, or we will go as high up the corporate chain as we possibly can, then I think we have done what we are supposed to do.

As the preceding quotation illustrates, prosecutors recognize that achieving deterrence in a corporate setting may be difficult. One source of difficulty involves the connection between intention and act which prosecutors must establish to convict a person of a crime (Stone 1975). The organizational context of corporate crime complicates this connection. In organizations, the person responsible for deciding to break the law often may not be the person who actually carries out the criminal act. Prosecutors understand that this separation between intention and act can be used by corporate executives and employees to deny their own criminality. Indeed, this strategy is commonly used by defense attorneys in corporate cases (Mann 1985). Managers and executives claim that they do not actually do anything criminal; they just issue orders or establish policies. Workers claim that they do not knowingly or intentionally break the law; they just obey orders. Criminal prosecution, prosecutors believe, is one sure way to break through this haze of denial. As one prosecutor put it:

It's important if you're going to have deterrence to get a message to the corporate world that crime committed by corporations and their managers or supervisors will not be tolerated. And [it's important] for people [to realize] . . . that choosing to do a criminal act because you want to save your job, not just get treated in terms of raises or job assignments, but primarily it's a "if you don't do this, you're going to get fired" that they will have a criminal liability if their conduct violates the law. And it's not going to be a defense to say, "well . . . I was told that we had to do it, so I had to choose between my livelihood and damaging the environment." Maybe that's a hard choice but it's a choice that's going to, in some cases, bring liabilities.

The prosecutor went on to argue that, only by prosecuting individuals, could the structure of behavior in corporate organizations be changed.

You know, if corporate America realizes that (and it's not all corporate America that's the bad guys, but just the ones who are determined to break the law) it's the worker who has to do this, and if they know they can't threaten him and get him to violate the law just because it's a choice between working and not working, then they won't have anybody to do it. They're going to have to do it themselves, and if they do it themselves, that's even better because that means their liability is greater.

For criminal sanctions to have a general deterrent effect, they must be made personal. That is, they must be extended to individuals and not limited to just the corporate entity. As far as some prosecutors are concerned, it is the prospect of individual responsibility and criminal sanctioning that sends the strongest message. Two prosecutors, discussing a case in which both the corporation and individual executives were charged, described how this case in particular achieved a strong deterrent effect:

First prosecutor: I've always felt that that is the best deterrent you can get because you get a two-pronged attack. It's not just the guy sitting around at home on Sundays saying to his wife, "Well, my corporation isn't that dirty." He's saying to his wife, "I'm not that dirty." And he's got to defend himself personally and his corporation's reputation.

Second prosecutor: . . . [T]o a lot of these people, money doesn't mean anything. You can set, you know, whatever the amount of money you think [is appropriate] and it's no big deal. OSHA and EPA traditionally may levy the fine and then they back off and adjust accordingly, so it really doesn't matter. And to equate a person's life for worker safety isn't in them. To these people, it is nothing and they are not equitable. You can't just say "OK, $200,000." And it's not worth not having fresh air to breathe, not having the training they should have, because these are just people, because they are [an] expendable work force. They're not. And for those kinds of people the only thing that you're going to do is you're going to send them to jail.

First prosecutor: It's one thing that can't be passed on. You can fine a company a million dollars, and if they're a viable company the shareholders suffer, the consumer suffers in higher prices, what have you. But the culprits are not the people that are paying the price. So you give them twenty years in jail, and you try to pass that on to the consumer. And it really stops at that point and people start waking up. I mean as I talk around the country to these corporate people, there's no doubt in my mind that I think that they are prepared to pay the cost of fines . . . at the expense of life and limb in the workplace. But, boy, when Film Recovery came down and Penn Thermometer came down, and people are, like, going to jail, a businessman says "How do I pass that on?" And a criminal defense lawyer says "You don't. You do the time." And that's why people are paying attention now.

Like federal judges, then, prosecutors see general deterrence as the primary reason for undertaking corporate criminal prosecutions. As the preceding exchange illustrates, they imagine that the threat of criminal conviction elicits enormous worry, if not panic, among corporate executives and business owners. Based on the fear and anxiety they observe in indicted executives, local prosecutors generalize to the business community as a whole. In their view, the conviction of just one executive sends a loud and clear message to others, a message that they believe is getting through. Their evidence for the deterrent effect is mainly anecdotal; nevertheless, local prosecutors are convinced that corporate prosecutions have dramatic effects on local business practices. For example, in Chicago, where the famous Film Recovery case was prosecuted, an attorney involved in the case noted the following change in businesses:[2]

It's funny. It's really funny. I've got a friend who's a manufacturer's rep and part of his business is safety products, and his business is going up 40 percent a year since Film Recovery on safety products. And I turned to [another attorney] and I said "Well, do you think that these people's sense of consciousness has been changed at all?" He says, "Nope." I said, "What do you think?" He says, "They're scared. They're just plain scared. They're not doing this out of the goodness of their heart because it's a moral thing. They're just scared about jail."

Education and Boundary Maintenance. Although most prosecutors see general deterrence as the primary purpose for prosecuting corporate criminals, another closely related rationale is also considered. Corporate prosecution may serve to educate people in the business community. Hauling a corporate offender into criminal court makes explicit the boundary line between acceptable and unacceptable conduct in business. One prosecutor made the point this way: "We have to use the criminal tool aggressively if we are going to send a message that white-collar crime is not just a sort of regulatory function, analogous to the rule making proceedings of the FCC or whatever, but this is crime that we take seriously." The educational potential of criminal prosecution extends to the general community. Successful prosecution of a corporate crime sends a message to the general community that the system is fair. According to the same prosecutor, "We are serious about closing the perceived gap between street crime and white-collar crime as regards the sentencing and the sanctions. I think ten or more years ago we all as prosecutors were legitimately open to the criticism that we treated folks who dressed like us and looked like us and spoke as we did and went to our same college or the same school as a different class of wrongdoers." Commenting on the educational importance of criminal prosecutions, the prosecutor continued: "I believe we need to send the signal that crime in the suites is as important as crime in the streets, and that's one of the ways you do it."

A prosecutor in another district felt that education was particularly important in the area of environmental crime: "To treat environmental noncompliance in terms of civil sanctions just continues to feed the belief on the part of most of the businessmen that are involved in environmental noncompliance that these are just business decisions made for economic reasons. Treating them as crimes points out to them that what they are really engaged in is criminal conduct."

Punishment. As far as most local prosecutors are concerned, corporate criminals deserve to be punished. The offenses should be morally censured, and the offenders should suffer stigmatization and punishment. In this regard, prosecutors appear to differ from judges. According to Wheeler et al. (1988; see also Mann et al. 1980), punishment in the case of white-collar offenders is generally not a central concern for judges, who apparently feel that the process of adjudication is punishment enough for most white-collar offenders. Hence, when a judge sentences an offender to imprisonment, it is to deter others rather than to punish the individual. Prosecutors, on the other hand, seem to be motivated by a desire to make offenders pay for what they have done. They endorse principles of just desserts for corporate criminals and believe that punishment should reflect the seriousness of the offense (Schlegel 1990). Describing an environmental polluter, one respondent put it this way:

If he goes out and dumps PCBs on somebody else's land in the middle of the night and [some regulator] catches him, the first thing he's going to want to do is be real cooperative with you, so we won't get involved. So we want that guy. It's not enough just to take him and get him to clean it up. We want to prosecute this guy in court and ask for prison because he's endangered the lives of citizens in the water supply and everything else.

In many of our interviews, prosecutors expressed a real sense of moral outrage at some corporate offenders. Rather than defining them in morally neutral terms, our interviewees were more apt to call them contemptible, vile, and disgusting. They were incensed and insulted by what they perceived to be the offenders' arrogance and callous disregard for others. Offenders were described as a "blight on the public." This sense of outrage we uncovered in our interviews belies the notion that corporate crime receives short shrift at the local level. The prosecutors we interviewed certainly did not define these crimes as morally neutral. It is true that some of the passion displayed by prosecutors in our interviews may have occurred because we focused on environmental and workplace-related offenses. These are crimes that involve direct harm to others, and it is easy to see why prosecutors become irate. Yet, those who handle consumer fraud and other financial offenses also seemed to regard even these nonviolent offenses as very serious. Remember, though, that we were speaking with people in the units specifically devoted to corporate cases. They have a vested interest in taking these offenses seriously. Their views may not be representative of those of other attorneys in the office or even of the district attorney, who may view corporate crime as much less important than street crime. Nevertheless, the idea that local prosecutors do not care about corporate crime or do not take it seriously is clearly debatable. At least among the prosecutors we interviewed, a strong belief persists that corporate crime is an important form of criminality, comparable, if not exactly equal, to street crime in its threat to community wellbeing.

Selecting Cases to Prosecute

Although prosecutors are clear that deterrence is their major goal in corporate cases, they are less certain about how best to select or handle cases to achieve that goal. This uncertainty is understandable, given the complexity of the decision they face. It involves consideration not only of what to prosecute but also who and how. Prosecutors must determine whether an illegal act warrants prosecution, whether individuals or the corporation should be pursued, and whether civil or criminal charges are more appropriate.

We asked the prosecutors how they decide among cases. What determines whether a case is accepted for prosecution, referred to another agency, or simply ignored? How are the decisions reached to proceed with criminal as opposed to civil charges and to file charges against the corporate entities as opposed to individuals? We came away with a strong sense that, as one prosecutor put it, there are very few "hard and fast rules." The offices we studied generally did not have set policies or internal guidelines on corporate cases, especially in regard to environmental and work-related offenses. Our respondents often were reluctant to speak in generalities, saying that each case is unique and that the specific facts of a case determine how it is handled.

The apparent absence of general policies or internal guidelines may be explained by the fact that, although they are increasing, environmental and work-related prosecutions are still relatively new and infrequent. Internal guidelines may develop over time, as local prosecutors become more experienced in handling these cases and as they get a better sense of the variety of crimes that occur in their jurisdictions. But at present the selection of cases appears to be more a matter of personal judgment than one of policy. Discussing whether to proceed in a criminal or civil forum, one prosecutor put it this way: "There is a significant subjective factor there, and you have to ask yourself do you feel right about the decision you're making, and if you don't feel right about it, then you start asking questions about why is it wrong? What we find is that those are the cases that we generally will decline to prosecute." A prosecutor in another district made a similar point in discussing the difficulty of deciding how to handle environmental violations.

It's a fine line sometimes between what is a civil case and what is a criminal case, and it's a judgment call really that a particular defendant, whether corporate or individual, their state of mind, the egregiousness of the situation, there may even be mitigating and aggravating factors. You say, well, if it's a case of negligence or recklessness, the company that allows the condition to occur, whether it's asbestos being spewed into the air or something through their recklessness or negligence, is that a civil matter or is that a criminal matter? Is that criminal negligence? You know, what's the difference between an automobile accident and vehicular homicide? I mean, what's an accident and what's criminal negligence? It's a hard thing and as the prosecutor you're always trying to be as fair as you can and weigh out the laws and pros and cons. Looking at the aggravating and mitigating factors are the main things we have to do.

Despite the ambiguity surrounding the decision, criminal prosecutions do occur. The interviews suggest that the decision to file criminal charges depends on how prosecutors assess the nature of the offender and the nature of the offense. This assessment involves more than simply deciding whether an accused is legally culpable and whether the elements of the crime can be proved. It involves attention to what Wheeler et al. (1988) call the blameworthiness of the offender and the harmfulness of the offense.

Blameworthiness. Blameworthiness refers to the degree of personal moral culpability or fault that an offender has for the offense—that is, to the offender's state of mind. Before deciding upon a sentence, judges always assess the defendant's relative degree of fault or blame (Wheeler et al. 1988). Judges determine to their own satisfaction whether defendants knew that what they were doing was wrong and whether they intended to do what they did. The same appears to be true for prosecutors deciding whether to file criminal charges. They, too, must determine that the accused knew that what he or she was doing was wrong—and intended to do it anyway. In making this assessment, prosecutors, like judges, draw on deeply rooted principles of English common law (Wheeler et al. 1988, 81–82).

Thus, before proceeding with criminal charges, prosecutors must be convinced that the illegal actions in question were committed intentionally. Offenses that result from ignorance, sloppiness, or incompetence, even if technically they could be prosecuted, are less likely to lead to criminal charges than are those that result from a deliberate or callous disregard of the interests and safety of others. Prosecutors pay close attention to any evidence indicating that the accused corporation knew what it was doing. Where the facts suggest that the corporation or its agents deliberately intended to disregard the law, the likelihood of criminal prosecution increases. Intentionality, then, is an important part of blameworthiness.

How do prosecutors decide that a company or an individual executive intended to violate the law? The interviews suggest that the most important factor is evidence of a *pattern of conduct*—that is, any evidence that the offensive conduct has happened before, that the event is not a one-time violation. To establish a pattern of conduct, prosecutors pay close attention to input from regulatory agencies, which can provide historical data on the past conduct of an offender. Where the records indicate that an offender was repeatedly notified and warned of illegal conduct, prosecutors are much more likely to consider criminal charges than where the records show a history of compliance. Thus, depending on the pattern of conduct, similar illegal acts committed by different companies can provoke dramatically different responses from prosecutors. One prosecutor used the following hypothetical example to make this point: "Let's use AT&T. AT&T does

X and CMW [a fictitious name] does X, and AT&T can demonstrate for the last forty years they have appropriately done everything with regard to environmental issues. We know CMW, because we've been on CMW's case for thirty years. We're going to be much more inclined to go for the throat of CMW than we are for AT&T." Drawing a parallel between a street criminal's prior criminal record and a company's regulatory history, a prosecutor in another district made a similar point: "In a street crime case you can look at a defendant's prior criminal history. Here most of these people don't have a prior criminal history, but they have a track record as far as environmental conduct. You can look at that." Another exchange with two prosecutors on the subjects of environmental and workplace-related violations illustrated the reasons behind their focus on the offender's regulatory track record.

Interviewer: You mentioned a patterned course of conduct. Is that something that's really important to you when you're looking at a case? Maybe the situation turns out to be a one-time event and not a series of actions.

First prosecutor: It's clear that if you've got a corporation that has embarked upon a course of conduct which exposes employees to hazardous substances continually, and then takes those hazardous wastes and dumps them out on the general environment that exposes other people to it, and they would do it on the basis of a long-time continuum, [then] obviously agency requirements aren't doing the trick, a possible civil action is not doing the trick, and that would almost mandate that criminal action be brought against these people.

Interviewer: Suppose, though, that you found a fact situation like that, but then you had an organization that says, "We realize we made mistakes. We're going to mend our ways." Like we were talking about before, they'll say, "Oh, I won't do that anymore. Hit me with a fine. Do whatever you want."

First prosecutor: In a fact situation like that, no . . . we'd most likely have to address it criminally.

Second prosecutor: And the reason is that, by the time it would get to us, then that kind of situation is imperative, drastic. The agencies have been working with them for years. Both EPA and OSHA . . . have always been in a cooperative mode with it. They go in. They say, "Let me show you what your problems are, make you aware of them, and then help you change them." And . . . the agency is set up to give them thirty days, fifty days, ninety days, one hundred and twenty days, you know, six months down the road. And then they will come back and talk again. And so by the time it gets to us, they [the businesses] have had ample opportunities and extensions unlimited . . . And now they're going to come to us and say "We'll change our ways"?

From the prosecutor's point of view, at least for environmental offenses, the filing of criminal charges against a business is the last stage in a long process. The process begins with regulatory agencies and ends with the prosecutor only in cases where there is a history of repeated violations and where repeated warnings to the business to correct its behavior have been ignored. This history of violations and warnings is used by prosecutors to redefine the business's illegal actions from simple, but understandable, mistakes to calculated criminal acts. It is not clear exactly how many violations there must be before a business is redefined by regulators and prosecutors as criminal. Nevertheless, at some not-well-defined point, the shift in perspective is made.

A factor that contributes to the shift in perspective and also influences assessments of blameworthiness is what the offender does after the offense is exposed. Offenders who appear to be obstinate and to lack remorse provoke stronger reactions than do those who recognize and accept the wrong fulness of their actions. In response to a question about what factors would tip the balance toward criminal prosecution in a close case, one prosecutor responded in this way: "In my own mind, it's certainly the attitude of the defendant. Is he cooperative? Is he remorseful? What happened that made him have the accident? Did he try to cover up, found out he couldn't, and that's how it came to light? Or did he come up front, and was he initially up front about it? In my mind, a lot of it is the offender's conduct."

In essence, to decide whether criminal charges are warranted, prosecutors focus on the offender's character as manifested in his or her actions. They want to know what type of a person or company they are dealing with. They use information on historical patterns of conduct and behavior immediately following an offense to form a judgment about blameworthiness. Prosecutors appear to be much like the federal judges studied by Wheeler et al. (1988). In deciding how to treat an offender, both focus on broader aspects of the defendant's actions than mere legal culpability. Judges use blameworthiness to decide whether imprisonment is warranted; prosecutors use it to decide whether charges should be filed in the first place. Thus, blameworthiness plays a key role in determining whether offenders will be brought into the justice system and the treatment they receive once inside.

Harmfulness. The other key feature in the common culture of prosecution is the nature of the offense—most importantly, its harmfulness. In theory, offense and offender are analytically separable, but in actual practice a case is a combination of both for prosecutors. Indeed, the harmfulness of the crime may strongly influence the perceived blameworthiness of the offender. Although for purposes of explication we discuss the two concepts separately, we acknowledge a certain artificiality in this process.

Like blameworthiness, harmfulness is a matter of judgment. The precise criteria used to assess it vary by type of offense and by jurisdiction, as well. A prosecutor focusing on consumer fraud, for instance, has different criteria than one concentrating on environmental crimes. For the former, the number of victims may be the deciding factor; for the latter, the number of victims may be less important than the degree to which a victim experiences or is exposed to physical harm. The jurisdiction in which an offense occurs also influences how its harmfulness is assessed. An offense deemed egregious in one place may be thought routine elsewhere.

As one might expect, cases involving real or potential physical harm to individuals provoke the strongest response from prosecutors. In the interviews, prosecutors expressed moral outrage over business conduct that was or could be physically harmful. Activities that jeopardize the physical safety of others are likely to be defined as criminal. Consider this exchange with a veteran prosecutor:

Interviewer: Do you measure harm on a variety of dimensions? How many people—

Prosecutor [interrupting]: You know it's not so much or how many, like it would be OK if it was one person and not OK if it was two. When there are people involved, and we can immediately say it's people, our position is when you kill somebody and if you can't demonstrate to us that this was a freak thing where you took every possible precaution, you know, we're going to look real seriously at criminal charges.

Potential as well as actual harm also is evaluated carefully. One prosecutor elaborated on this issue for environmental violations:

I'm looking at the extent of environmental damage or the potential for environmental damage. What if someone has a large quantity of hazardous material sealed in drums, so it's not by one's intention released into the environment but it's disposed of off the side of the highway. As far as I'm concerned, that's an [illegal] disposal. The defense will say, but it's still in the sealed drums so where is the harm to the environment? The potential for the harm there is real significant. Small quantities . . . we had a case last week of a business that had small quantities of hazardous waste that they were just throwing into a common trash dumpster. We were asked to do a criminal prosecution. My view is let's make sure the business knows what the law is; ignorance is not a defense, but the quantities are so small and there was no effort at deception. I mean it was just open and blatant, and you say neither of these are very sophisticated criminals or these are very naive individuals. They just threw cans of hazardous paint, waste paint into a dumpster. It was a body shop, and I said we don't need a criminal case for that. We need to make sure it doesn't happen again.

As the two cases cited by the prosecutor illustrate, for environmental cases it is the combination of what was done and how it was done that determines whether criminal charges are warranted. A minor offense—that is, one involving small quantities of hazardous materials—committed blatantly and with no attempt at deception is handled with a warning; in contrast, a similar disposal-type offense involving larger quantities of chemicals, potentially more danger, and some deception is perceived as warranting criminal charges.

Unlike environmental and workplace-related offenses, risk of physical harm is less likely to be an issue in consumer fraud cases. Fraud involving health-related products or services clearly has the potential to result in physical harm to the victim. Yet, in the interviews, harmfulness in fraud cases tended to be assessed by different criteria. Obviously, the amount of money involved and the number of victims provide straightforward indicators of harm. Another factor considered in assessing harm is the vulnerability of the potential victims. Offenders who victimize the elderly tend to be viewed in an especially harsh light and to provoke criminal charges more quickly than are those who victimize the population at large. In one jurisdiction, criminal charges were considered for consumer-fraud–type offenses only when they caused an aggregate loss of $100,000. Smaller amounts generally were handled with other procedures. But an exception to the $100,000 standard was made for cases involving the elderly.

Constraints on Local Prosecutors

Despite their desire to achieve general deterrence, prosecutors often decide not to file criminal charges. As the preceding discussion implies, sometimes this decision is made because the principals in a case are not sufficiently blameworthy or their offense is not sufficiently harmful. Nevertheless, even in cases where blame and harm are evident, prosecutors may not proceed with criminal charges. How is this seeming inconsistency rationalized or justified?

The interviews suggest that several other factors shape the decision to file criminal charges. Two of these factors, legal and resource constraints, are interrelated. Legal constraints make corporate cases resource-intensive, but in turn resource constraints make it difficult to overcome legal constraints. A third factor is the potential negative impact that conviction may have on a community.

Legal Constraints

Legal constraints are statutes and procedural rules that make the use of the law more or less difficult for legal actors. For example, the probable cause requirement makes it more difficult for police officers to conduct legal searches and arrests than would be the case if only reasonable suspicion were required.

In discussing the impact of legal constraints on prosecutorial decision making, we must exercise some caution. The law never stands still; it continually evolves and changes. Legislatures can draft new statutes that ease the legal burdens prosecutors face. Courts can render decisions that clarify the meaning of ambiguous legal relationships. For example, in 1988, when we began this project, considerable confusion existed over whether federal OSHA regulations preempted state prosecution of unlawful conduct in the workplace. That issue has now been settled in favor of the states. Local prosecutors no longer have to worry that their cases involving workplace-related offenses will be thrown out of court because of lack of jurisdiction. Legal constraints also can vary dramatically from one jurisdiction to another. A constraint in New York may not be one in California. Thus, our description of the legal constraints faced by local prosecutors should not be taken as the last word or as an entirely accurate description of the current state of affairs nationwide. Our description and analysis reflect the situation at the end of the 1980s and beginning of the 1990s in four jurisdictions. Undoubtedly, in some jurisdictions things have changed since then, but we suspect that many prosecutors still confront the problems we describe here.

A major constraint on the decision to prosecute a corporate criminal case is the burden of proof required to win a conviction. This burden is especially hard to meet in the case of individual executives in large organizations. The fragmented and hidden character of decision making in large organizations makes it difficult to locate a responsible person. The person truly responsible is difficult to pin down without some form of documentation, which often is absent. As one prosecutor put it, "If you can show some document tying somebody high enough in the organization . . . I mean when you sue a company for selling sugared water as apple juice and you've got documents showing the heads of the company knew this was occurring and had to know, you got a criminal case. You don't have that and you [can only] show somebody below did it and there's no indication they knew of it, [then it's] very difficult."

The general view seemed to be that securing convictions was harder against individuals than against corporate entities. But in the case of corporate entities, convictions often were regarded as not worth the effort because no person would be exposed to a sentence of incarceration. Without the possibility of someone doing some time, the deterrence potential of a case was seen to decline, and hence the expenditure of resources became less justifiable.

In some cases, the difficulty of establishing *mens rea* arises out of poorly drafted statutes. Statutes can be poorly drafted in a variety of ways. They may require the prosecutor to prove something that is nearly impossible to prove. In New York, for example, a prosecutor complained about an unreasonable burden of proof in a case involving water pollution.

We're working on a case now that [it's obvious] this statute was never drafted by someone that had proved a case in court. Seventy-one dash nineteen dash thirty-three is a water pollution statute, and it subscribes a [class] C felony, a highest felony, to one who knowingly pollutes, or puts a pollutant into a sewer, which subsequently causes a serious physical injury, i.e., down the stream to the sewage treatment plant. [Now] how are you going to prove that causal relationship up here and down here without intermingling forces, other reactions [affecting] the integrity of this stuff? How do you know it's the same stuff? How do you know somebody else didn't double-quantity down the pipe? It's ludicrous.

The problem is that, to obtain a criminal conviction, the prosecutor must show a direct connection between the illegal emission and a specific injury. It is nearly impossible to demonstrate this connection given the physical distance between the polluter and the potential victims.

Statutes can be poorly drafted in other ways besides posing an unreasonable burden of proof. They may be ambiguous as to exactly what is being declared illegal. Ambiguity creates problems for prosecutors with respect to *prior notice*. An example of this situation also comes from New York. Two prosecutors complained that the environmental law had evolved in disorganized fashion. The result is "a hodge-podge or patchwork quilt," which made it extremely difficult for prosecutors and potential violators to know exactly what is illegal. As the two prosecutors put it:

First prosecutor: They [the state legislature] criminalized the regulatory scheme.

Second prosecutor: Right, so now we have a statute that says anybody having any degree of culpable mental conduct, whether it's negligance, recklessness, knowingly, intentional, any degree whatsoever, any of those culpable mental states, who violates any of your regulations found in blah, blah, blah, blah is guilty of a misdemeanor. You now have a statute that says it. Now that presents a lot of problems for a prosecutor, because you have to give the defendant notice of what he's being charged with. Is he being charged with being reckless? Negligent? Intentional? And here you have a statute that doesn't even differentiate. Any of those mental states is fine. Or it violates any of these regulations, and then you have a set of regulations that's this thick . . .

First prosecutor: That's not an exaggeration. The regulations are impenetrable, a great disservice.

Second prosecutor: By scientists, by anybody. They're impossible no matter how well-intentioned you are, really. When you say any violation of that complex set of regulations with any state of mind, there's a crime.

According to these prosecutors, some of these problems can be ameliorated by drafting what are called *endangering statutes*. Such a statute makes it a crime to release a toxic substance in such a manner as to endanger public health, safety, and the environment. It does not require the prosecutor to show that the release resulted in a specific injury or harm; it does not even require the prosecutor to show that release involved medical waste, since the definition of waste is debatable. Instead, the prosecutor must show only that a toxic substance was released in such a manner as to endanger public health.

Simple as they may be, endangering statutes can still have problems if they are not carefully constructed. Endangering statutes may be drafted by environmental law specialists instead of criminal law specialists. Specialists in environmental law may draft laws that are difficult to use, because they lack experience with proving criminal cases in court. As the prosecutors quoted above see it:

They [environmental law specialists] really don't understand the due process requirement, and the problems of proof, and the problems of notice to the defendant of what he's being charged with . . . You have to charge them under the specific section of the crime that puts them on notice of what . . . the proscribed conduct is. And when you have a section, a single section of a statute, that, let's say, has several different mental states, you have a problem there.

As we noted above, legal constraints may change over time as the law evolves. Sometimes courts make it easier for law enforcement officials to apprehend and convict offenders; at other times they make it harder. What we have described here regarding legal constraints may well have changed and, indeed, probably has changed in the interim. A more constant, less changeable obstacle confronted by prosecutors stems not from the legal system but, rather, from the organizational system in which they work.

Resource Constraints

Like most organizations, the prosecutor's office must pursue multiple objectives with limited technical, budgetary, and personnel resources. These resources can be severely taxed by the difficult and time-consuming process of investigating, preparing, and prosecuting a case against a corporation (Bequai 1978). The evidence in these cases may be little more than an elusive paper trail of memoranda and files. Organizations and individuals often go to great lengths to control the prosecutor's access to this crucial information (Mann 1985). For example, documents may be destroyed or deliberately hidden from investigators, or the corporation may hire skilled defense attorneys to restrict the government's access to information. The difficulty of gathering evidence buried in corporate files severely limits the ability of prosecutors to investigate corporate crimes and to convict corporate criminals (Cullen et al. 1987; Rakoff 1985; Schudson et al. 1984; Vaughan 1983).

According to many of our respondents, the difficulties of investigating and convicting corporate offenders make prosecutors reluctant to invest scarce resources in these cases. Resources tend to be invested in criminal investigations mainly where evidence can be easily gathered, especially evidence that incriminates a specific individual who can be sentenced to prison. If it appears unlikely that an individual can be convicted, civil proceedings are favored. According to one prosecutor, "If there's a feeling that you can get the evidence fairly easily, and if the case is easy to explain to a jury, and if the person is likely to get a good sentence, I think they'd go criminally." The importance of convicting an individual stems from the prosecutor's desire to deter and belief that incarceration is the only real deterrent.

Precisely how inadequate resources are at the local level became obvious during the case study visits. Prosecutors and investigators in these relatively large and well-to-do offices have to make do without the most basic equipment. For example, prosecutors in Cook County, Illinois, lamented that they did not even have dictaphones. Memoranda, briefs, and other documents had to be written in longhand before office secretaries could type them. An investigator pointed out that simply having a car phone and an answering machine would greatly improve her efficiency and productivity. It would enable her to make and return calls as she traveled around the city working her cases. Without the phone, her time in the car was, as she put it, "mostly wasted." The interviewees noted that these simple items are standard equipment in all but the smallest private law firms.

On a more substantial level, prosecutors in one district commented that their ability to develop and properly to dispose of environmental cases was seriously diminished by lack of access to adequate laboratory facilities. A long delay in having a substance identified can limit the prosecutor's options in responding to cases of illegal disposal or handling of toxic wastes. As one prosecutor explained, to "find out what's in a substance six months later is too late in an environmental case you're dealing with. How can you walk in [to a court] and [ask] for injunctive relief and say there's an immediate need to close this [business] down when you've waited six months? . . . how can you really do anything criminally and talk about how bad this is if we let it go six months at a time?"

When undertaking corporate cases, prosecutors must consider not only their own resource constraints but also those faced by judges and the correctional system. What the corporate crime prosecutor views as a serious case may not appear so to others in the justice system who see a different mix of cases. Almost without exception, the prosecutors we interviewed noted that their corporate crime cases receive lower priority than do drug or gang cases. In every jurisdiction we visited, prosecutors noted that the war on drugs, for all its intrinsic merit, was devouring resources at a tremendous pace and severely undermining law enforcement in all other areas.

Indeed, according to some of the prosecutors we interviewed, drugs and violence have become such high priorities in large cities that environmental crimes actually receive more attention in rural areas than in urban areas. In urban jurisdictions, the press of violent and drug-related offenses is so great that prosecutors with environmental cases have difficulty getting judges to take their cases seriously. A New York prosecutor described the situation in this way:

Within the state we have rural counties upstate that are much more attuned to environmental problems. Because, let's say, they're a rural county and if there's a landfill or a factory that's polluting, it becomes a major political issue. That'll be front page news. New York City has such a terrible crime problem in terms of regular street crime, and violent crime, and drugs, murders [that] when you go to court in a New York City criminal court with a polluter, unless it is a major, major case, the courts are so overwhelmed by the drug problems, they are so understaffed, so crowded . . . [and] the judges are so hardened by what they are seeing, because they deal with such a huge quantity and overwhelming amount of violent crime that . . . it's hard for them to take this [the polluter] seriously. And although they may be a committed environmentalist, they're not going to waste a lot of court time or what they deem is a waste of court time, because they don't even do it in the serious felonies. [Even] the serious violent felonies go assembly-like justice, because it's the only way the system can manage. And if you come in with a complex environmental case, which nobody in the court system is familiar with, no judge has any idea what you're talking about. They don't know anything about any of the statutes or regulations . . .

Thus, prosecutors recognize that judges always assess the seriousness of a case relative to other cases. From the prosecutor's perspective, it makes little sense to pursue environmental offenses aggressively if judges do not treat them seriously.

The justice system has been described as a loosely linked system (Hagan et al. 1979). This characteristic means that lack of resources is best viewed as a constraint that affects priorities in the entire justice system, not just in the prosecutor's office. Beginning with the police and continuing through each stage of the justice process, caseload priorities set at one stage are, at least in part, determined by the priorities and capabilities of the following stage. For example, before the police decide to crack down on a particular form of crime, they must have some reasonable assurance that their cases will be accepted and pursued by the prosecutor. Prosecutors, in turn, would be unwise to bring cases that judges are not interested in hearing. Finally, sentencing judges must keep in mind the capacity of the prison system to absorb convicted offenders. This is not to suggest that prosecutors have absolute veto power over decisions made by police or that judges can override prosecutors with impunity. A certain amount of give and take between stages in the justice process always exists; prosecutors cannot simply ignore the police, and neither can judges simply ignore cases brought by prosecutors. Nevertheless, actors at one stage can make it more or less difficult for actors at another stage to do their job.

As we have argued throughout, the role of the prosecutor cannot be considered in isolation. The prosecutor may well occupy the most powerful position in local criminal justice but is, nevertheless, situated within contexts which constrain his or her ability to act. The prosecutor must attend not only to community context but also to the context of the rest of the justice system.

Indeed, it may make most sense to conceive of the prosecutor as situated within a set of nested contexts. The prosecutor's most immediate context consists of other actors in the justice system—police, regulatory officials, and judges. These actors influence prosecutors through their ability to affect the prosecutor's workflow. They either bring cases to prosecutors (as do police and regulators) or take cases from them (as do judges). The context of the justice system, itself, is then situated within the larger community context, which, in turn, influences not only the prosecutor but all other stages of the system as well. This point was particularly well illustrated by two prosecutors in the New York state attorney general's office. They explained how environmental cases are treated differently in New York City than in upstate jurisdictions:

I could tell you that it's very difficult to bring any white-collar criminal cases into the court system in New York City because of the drugs and the street violence. They just don't want to deal with that. They just feel that it's not . . . I mean unless it's a real celebrated type of case, they're just not going to really put that much attention to it. Upstate since we do handle cases outside of the New York City area all over the state you can see the difference. It's black and white. An environmental case in an upstate county that has very few violent crimes and not a terrible drug problem, all of a sudden that case is much more important, and that case becomes front page news.

Later the prosecutors referred to a specific case in which a judge in an upstate county apparently had not been sympathetic to the prosecution's recommendation that an executive convicted of an environmental violation receive jail time. The judge's statements generated enormous local interest and publicity.

Now it seems the fact that the judge himself expressed a lot of hostility towards the case and towards the prosecution in that case . . , it was a front page story every day throughout the trial, before the trial, at the sentencing. That's the kind of treatment it gets in those areas as opposed to New York City, where, I mean unless it's a major action involving city landfill or something, if we were to bring a criminal case against a company in criminal court it's not going to make the New York Times. I mean, if it does, it's going to be a tiny little word or filler material and that's it. These cases are not going to generate publicity down here.

The preceding example illustrates, once again, the importance of community context for prosecutors. Knowledgeable, as they are, of local crime conditions and local concerns, prosecutors can assess, or at least have a rough idea, how any given case is likely to be received in the community and by the court system. An offense that provokes outrage and headlines in one community may receive little more than passing notice in another. Thus, the importance of an offense is determined in part by its characteristics and in part by where it fits in the mix of cases that make up the daily workload of the local justice system.

Political Contraints and Community Impacts
Two important and controversial issues regarding prosecutorial decision making involve the politics of law enforcement and the impact of pros-

ecution on the community. As elected officials, most local prosecutors are members of the local political establishment. They know and interact with local political leaders, some of whom also may be leading figures in the local business establishment. To conduct election campaigns, local prosecutors, like all elected officials, must raise money, some of which comes from corporations or their executives and leaders. It is reasonable to wonder whether the prosecutor's links to the political and business establishment influence how the law is enforced against other members of the establishment.

Corporations often make valuable contributions to community well-being in the form of employment and taxes. Some communities are dependent on particular corporations or businesses for their economic livelihood. This dependence provides a source of power for those who own or manage these organizations—power which, it has been argued, enables them to break the law with impunity.

The complaints that justice is not blind and that the well-to-do and powerful fare better than others in the justice system are old and hotly debated matters. White-collar crime scholars, from Sutherland's time to today's conflict theorists, have argued that economic and political elites receive special consideration in the justice system (Reiman 1995; Barnett 1981; Snider 1982). Naturally, this issue is sensitive for prosecutors, one they do not discuss enthusiastically. Nevertheless, on several occasions the prosecutors we interviewed openly addressed the influence of political and economic constraints on their decision making.

As noted earlier, in the 1980s the war on drugs had top priority for many law enforcement agencies. At the same time that the national war on drugs was consuming the lion's share of criminal justice resources, other developments on the national political scene reduced local prosecutors' effectiveness against corporate crime. The election of Ronald Reagan as president ushered in an era of pro-business and anti-regulation politics. In this new era, local prosecutors found that they could no longer automatically count on federal agencies for support of their enforcement efforts. According to some local prosecutors, federal agencies such as the Environmental Protection Agency (EPA) and the Federal Trade Commission (FTC) became much less aggressive, and in some cases actually hostile, toward law enforcement against business. One discouraged local prosecutor described the situation for us:

Without getting excessively political about this, there was a clear sea change in the 1980s as a result of the Reagan administration's policies . . . the attorneys general through the National Association of Attorneys General and the district attorneys have been very critical of the federal administration in the last nine years for failing to prosecute consumer and antitrust and environmental cases. EPA and FTC and the Anti-Trust Division of the Justice Department have done much less than they did historically to aggressively pursue these areas. Now partly it's a philosophical difference, and I understand that when you win the White House you have the right to bring in a new prosecutorial philosophy. But without waxing at great length on a subject that's of great sensitivity to us here in the state and local prosecution business, I'll say that many of us of all political stripes have been very disappointed by the retrenchment of these federal enforcement agencies.

This prosecutor went on to describe how the state attorneys general and local district attorneys have been forced to step in and take over responsibilities once assumed by federal agencies. In some cases, local prosecutors have even found themselves fighting against the federal government in court. Needless to say, these developments had detrimental effects on relationships between local and federal agencies. The prosecutor continued:

I could name a dozen areas including environmental prosecution where AGs and the large DAs have gotten involved in what I consider filling the vacuum of the void left by the federal agencies. In fact, for a while there, and I do see this changing, for a while there some of the federal agencies were actually entering on the sides of the defendants. The U.S. Anti-Trust Division would file *amicus* briefs repeatedly on the side of defendants to ease the antitrust laws. I understand that there's a philosophical difference there and such, but you must know—in your study you might want to reflect in a footnote someplace—how enormously demoralizing it is for state and local officials to have the feds do a complete about-face and change their prosecutorial standards dramatically, cease prosecuting certain kinds of things, and actually file *amicus* briefs for defendants. I mean that's just horrible for our relationship with those agencies.

How widespread these views are among local prosecutors is difficult to ascertain exactly. The prosecutor quoted above was particularly forceful and articulate on the change in federal policies during the Reagan years.

Other prosecutors paid little or no attention to these issues. Some evidence from the national survey suggests that this prosecutor's views are commonly held. Recall that in chapter 4 we found that most local prosecutors conduct joint investigations with federal agencies only rarely, if ever. And federal agencies are generally regarded as much less helpful to local prosecutors than are state and local agencies.

Conclusions

In assessing our interviews with prosecutors, we are struck by the apparent consistency in how they view corporate crimes and how federal judges evaluate white-collar offenders. For both groups, a common legal culture rooted in concepts of harm and blameworthiness appears to guide reactions to white-collar and corporate crime. We suspect that prosecutors may differ from judges in precisely how they define these concepts in practice. Prosecutors may have more expansive definitions of harm and blameworthiness than do judges. They may be more likely than judges to regard any given instance of corporate criminality as deserving of harsh sanctions. At least in their remarks, they appeared to believe that judges often are too lenient in corporate cases.

We speculate that prosecutors' more punitive attitude toward offenders may stem from their greater awareness of all the facts involved in a case. To prepare a case, prosecutors necessarily try to gather as much information as they can about the offender and the offense. But defense attorneys, of course, go to great lengths to make inadmissible in court as much of this information as possible. Because of the rules of evidence, judges may only be exposed to a small part of the offenders' conduct during the trial. They see, in effect, a sanitized version of the crime. This is especially true in cases where the defendant pleads guilty and does not go to trial. However, regardless of how much more seriously prosecutors may view corporate cases than judges do, the difference is a matter of degree only. It concerns where the members of both groups place people and events on their private scales of blameworthiness and harm. Although placements may vary systematically between prosecutors and judges, both groups are using the same scales. Another area of consistency between judges and prosecutors involves their general goals. Both groups see general deterrence as their primary goal in carrying out their respective official responsibilities.

Where local prosecutors may differ from federal judges is in the context in which their decisions are made. Local prosecutors are more constrained by organizational realities than are federal judges. Prosecutors work with quite limited resources, so the potential of a case to consume resources becomes an important factor as they decide how to respond. To pursue general deterrence through use of the criminal law is a noble but often unrealistic goal for prosecutors. Federal judges, on the other hand, do not have to consider resource constraints quite as seriously when they make sentencing decisions in white-collar criminal trials. It may take a long time for a case to be tried in court, but the decision to sentence an offender to some form of incarceration does not directly affect the judge's organizational resources. The decision to prosecute, in contrast, always directly affects the prosecutor's organizational resources.

Notes

1. In Los Angeles and Chicago, we also investigated prosecutions of workplace-related offenses (that is, occupational safety and health violations), because these two offices have conducted landmark prosecutions in this area.

2. *People vs. Film Recovery Systems, Inc.*, is a famous case that originated in Chicago. Stefan Golab, an employee of a company called Film Recovery Systems, died from inhaling poisonous fumes while working in the company's plant. What makes the case unusual is that individual executives and the company, itself, were convicted of murder. The case is now on appeal to the U.S. Supreme Court.

9

INVESTIGATING CORPORATE CRIME

Prosecutors are not the only soldiers in the fight against corporate crime. They have allies in other law enforcement and regulatory agencies as well. Cases often are referred to local prosecutors by the local police and by state regulatory investigators. In many communities, prosecutors work with the police and with regulators on a continuing basis. In this chapter, we turn our attention to the investigators and regulatory officials with whom prosecutors interact in handling corporate offenses.

Our goal is to describe how the police and regulatory officials view the problem of corporate crime. Do they share the views of prosecutors with respect to the purposes of corporate crime prosecutions? We argue that, by and large, they do. The influence of the norms of harm and blameworthiness is not confined only to the courtrooms inhabited by judges and prosecutors. These norms are as important to police and regulators as they are to prosecutors. Their influence extends in varied form throughout the criminal justice and regulatory control systems.

We focus first on consumer fraud offenses, which are handled primarily by the police. Then, we turn to the more complex arena of environmental crime, which often involves the police, health officials, fire departments, and many other governmental agencies.

Investigating Fraud

The interest of local prosecutors in fraud is not new. Since the early 1970s, consumer fraud has been a priority concern for both state attorneys general and local prosecutors (Skoler 1982; Edelhertz and Rogovin 1982c). The survey results reported in chapter 3 showed that it is the corporate crime most frequently handled by local prosecutors. Indeed, about 70 percent of local prosecutors process at least one consumer fraud case in a typical year.

Fraud cases are investigated by a variety of different agencies. Local police departments in large cities such as Chicago and Los Angeles usually have a special unit devoted to financial crimes or fraud and forgery-type offenses. Because of the volume of cases, prosecutors in some local offices have hired their own in-house investigators to support assistant prosecutors who specialize in financial offenses. In Nassau County, New York, prosecutors work with the Insurance Frauds Bureau of the State Insurance Department. They also receive cases from the Insurance Crime Prevention Institute, a private organization funded by the insurance industry. In Duval County, Florida, cases involving fraud by professionals are developed and investigated by the State Department of Professional Regulation. The Better Business Bureau also refers complaints to the local prosecutor.

The types of crimes investigated by these different agencies vary enormously. They range from deceptive advertisements by well-known and supposedly reputable retail stores to the outright scams of fly-by-night, telemarketing, boiler-room operations. Dishonest auto mechanics, crooked appliance repair technicians, unlicensed doctors, and deceitful home repair services are but a few of the schemers with whom fraud investigators tangle.

Fraud comes in a variety of shapes and forms. It can be perpetrated by "legitimate" businesspeople against individual consumers. For example, a generic form of fraud is the advance fee swindle, in which someone promises to provide a service for a fee and then, after being paid, never fulfills his or her end of the bargain. The service that is promised can be anything from finding a job or an apartment to locating a scholarship program for a student who cannot afford college without help. In other forms, fraud is perpetrated against large institutions rather than individuals. For example, fraud against medicare programs and the health insurance industry by doctors and other health professionals is common (Sparrow 1995; Green 1990, 193–94). Although fraud comes in an almost countless variety of forms, all frauds share two characteristics. To be successful, those who would perpetrate a fraud must appear to be legitimate or engaged in a legitimate undertaking, and they must secure the trust and cooperation of the victim, if only for a short period of time. These characteristics—the appearance of legitimacy and the cooperation of the victim—influence the detection, investigation, and prosecution of fraud.

Because fraud perpetrators assume a guise of legitimacy to carry out their schemes, detecting skillful frauds can be difficult. Victims may be taken in by the scheme and fail to realize that they have been victimized. A truly successful fraud is one in which the victim never realizes that an offense has occurred. For example, many people really do not know much about their cars. Their ignorance and their unavoidable need to trust the automotive experts make them easy prey for unscrupulous mechanics who diagnosis and repair problems that do not exist. Similarly, victims of bait-and-switch schemes by retail stores may not realize what has happened to them.[1] Thus, the traditional means by which cases are brought to the attention of law enforcers—that is, a victim who complains—may not operate as effectively for fraud as for other types of offenses.

Once detected, though, frauds may be easier to investigate than ordinary street crimes. The main reason is that, with a few notable exceptions, the perpetrator is generally easy to identify and locate. The exceptions are fly-by-night operations, such as home repair frauds run by migrant gangs. In these operations, the offenders plan all along to leave the area as quickly as possible after making a few scores. The idea is to get out of town before victims have time to realize that they have been defrauded and identify the perpetrators to the police. Excluding the fly-by-night operator, the person who hopes to make a living by running a fraudulent business must, like any other businessperson, stay in one place and try to attract customers. Staying in one place is risky, though, because it makes it easier for investigators to locate the offender.

The fraud offender's need to appear legitimate helps investigators in other ways. To appear legitimate, one must have the trappings of legitimacy. In the case of business, the trappings often take the form of paper documents such as newspaper advertisements, printed flyers, prospectuses, order forms, invoices, and checks. These documents create a paper trail that investigators follow in order to link the offender to the victim and, hence, to the crime. Indeed, for fraud investigators the key element to establish in many investigations is that what is on paper does not match what actually happened. Thus, investigators must show that the claimed repair was not actually made, that the diagnosis of the problem (for example, a broken part in a machine) was egregiously incorrect, that the victim's money was never actually invested as promised, or that the employment company never really had any lines on jobs. One investigator described how the paper trail left by an offender is used to show criminal intent:

If it's a business credit fraud, how do you show that the guy intended to rip everybody off versus he's a bad businessman? Is he competent? Is he a little short on capital, or does he really have a fraud going in the beginning? And that's what we have to show, the misrepresentation and the phony credit reference. They're all phony, the phony financial statements that they provide to their victim, the phony reports that they feed to Dunn and Bradstreet showing the company history. We show that the information that is provided them is all phony, thereby showing the intent to defraud.

The fraud offender's reliance on the cooperation of the victim creates opportunities for investigators. It permits investigators to employ proactive strategies against fraudulent businesses. Investigators who become aware of a potentially fraudulent enterprise can pose as customers or have others pose for them. In effect, like undercover vice investigators, the fraud investigator can participate in the crime itself and gain an insider's view of how the fraud is perpetrated. This tactic, known as a sting operation, has been used successfully against fraud in a number of industries, such as auto repair, appliance repair, home improvement, insurance, and the health care professions. Ironically, perpetrators of fraud often are caught by the very duplicitous means that they use to commit their offenses.

For fraud investigators, the major purpose of criminal prosecution is punishment, and their major goal is "to put the bad guys behind bars." As they see it, their job is to get a conviction on a serious charge and, if possible, a heavy sentence for the offender. In their view, taking this approach is the only sensible way to allocate their scarce resources. Since the number of cases to be investigated always exceeds the resources available for investigation, it makes sense to concentrate on the cases most likely to be solved and to result in criminal conviction. To expend resources on other cases would waste time and money. Three fraud investigators in Los Angeles made this point in particularly clear fashion:

We have sort of a philosophy here at this place that if we can't take that case through prosecution and get as heavy a sentence as possible for that case, then we're not going to work that case. What's the point? I mean . . . if I can't reach a successful conclusion, and I define that as conviction for a stated crime that we bring to the DA, then we might as well be working another case that we can get a conviction on. Because we have a responsibility to the citizens of the Los Angeles area, taxpayers, to spend their money wisely. Why spend money on a case that's going nowhere? It doesn't make much sense to me. Spend money, resources and like that, on taking a case through prosecution and conviction. That's the bottom line.

The types of cases that are selected for investigation and prosecution influence the investigator's attitude toward offenders. Investigators tend to focus on cases involving multiple victims and large amounts of money. Like prosecutors, they look for patterns of events. A single complaint against an auto repair shop, for example, is unlikely to generate an investigation or sting operation. But repeated complaints against the same establishment eventually will draw the attention of investigators. Even though each individual victim may have lost only a relatively small amount of money, the aggregate impact of the offense is large. From the perspective of investigators, this aggregate impact makes the perpetrator especially blameworthy and deserving of harsh punishment. For example, a police investigator in Chicago related the details of an advance fee scheme involving an employment referral service. According to the investigator, over 850 people paid ninety-five dollars each to a company that promised to find them jobs but never did. In this type of situation, the investigator felt that the local prosecutor's office (in Chicago, the Cook County state's attorney) would probably pursue some sort of injunctive relief for the victims. While recognizing the constraints on the local prosecutor, the investigator noted that this sort of case was "an area that grates at people, including law enforcement." Because so many victims were involved and because the victims were mainly low-income, minority group members, the investigator was adamant that the perpetrators of this scheme deserved to be incarcerated: "Would it be sufficient to say that the organizers of this scheme should do sixty days in the county jail? To me that would be ludicrous. These people should be sent to the penitentiary, because the aggregate impact they have is certainly of a felony nature."

Investigators are aware, of course, that other considerations may be relevant to the handling of particular cases. In many cases of fraud, for example, restitution may be a prominent concern, especially for the victims. Although investigators are cognizant of the importance of restitution, it is often treated as secondary to the primary goal of punishment. As the investigators from Los Angeles see it, typically they can do little to help victims recover their money.

What it really boils down to is that we're looking for convictions. Convict that person of the crime that we filed, not a lesser crime, but the crime that we bring for filing. Secondary to that is if we can get the person's, the victim's money back or property back or whatever, good. We'll try to do that, but it's secondary. 'Cause in these cases we find that that's almost a pipe dream, getting the victim's money back. 'Cause these people, they spend this money as fast as they make it, fast as they make it. You know, if you live high on the hog, you buy consumable items, cars, jewelry, who knows, whatever, you know by the time we hook them up, yeah, they may have defrauded the half-a-million dollars [but they] don't have a pot to pee in.

Whether money is available for restitution depends, in part, on the nature of the fraud. Frauds that are an ancillary part of ongoing legitimate business operations hold greater potential for restitution than do frauds in which the business is purely a front. For example, perpetrators of advance fee swindles or investment frauds have the potential to reap a great deal of money relatively quickly. They may spend it just as quickly, because these sorts of schemes inevitably must collapse and offenders know it. Those who pay the advance fee eventually realize that they are not getting their money's worth, and investors figure out that the returns they were promised are not going to materialize. In effect, the perpetrator is taking the victim's money and giving nothing in return. To continue for a long period of time in this sort of "business" is not likely. The personality characteristics that cause offenders to be attracted to these sorts of schemes—impulsivity and a preference for immediate, as opposed to delayed, gratification—reduce the likelihood that offenders will save rather than spend their ill-gotten gains. Hence, there is often little left for restitution to victims by the time the offender is arrested and convicted.

Other frauds are based in more enduring enterprises, in which the object of the fraud is to improve profit margins over the long run rather than trying to make a bundle quickly. For example, in businesses such as auto repair and home appliance repair, fraudulent and legitimate activities are combined. Some repairs are made, some services are provided, although they may not be exactly what victims want or need. Offenders hope to stay in business over the long term and, therefore, attempt to accumulate capital to solidify their businesses. Hence, when these schemes are exposed, assets may be available out of which victims can be paid back.

In addition to punishment and restitution, other goals are pursued by fraud investigators. Investigators in all of the four field sites we visited noted the importance of trying to reassure the public that con artists are not allowed to operate with impunity. Yet, investigators also noted that they are fighting an uphill battle; like other forms of crime, fraud will never be completely eliminated. An investigator from Los Angeles had this to say about how cases are selected:

We try to pick the ones that will get some publicity and give the citizens the impression that we're on top of everything, but the truth of the matter is that we just, that we and other law enforcement agencies in the county, just don't have enough people to investigate more than perhaps 25 percent of the crimes that are committed. The rest of them, they end up having to get some remedy through civil action and that's the reality.

The possibility of garnering public goodwill through publicity is one reason why sting operations are popular with fraud investigators. Because investigators can control the timing of events in sting operations, they are able to alert the media in advance of arrests and thereby ensure publicity for their efforts. Publicity increases the general deterrent effects of the investigation on other offenders and has the added side effect of increasing public confidence in the effectiveness of law enforcement. For example, in Nassau County, New York, an investigator noted that, "the auto repair sting is an interesting area that we've done over a number of years, and we've been very successful at it. I think the public has a good feeling about it because they feel it may deter the next repair place from ripping them off." Even when stings do not result in arrest and conviction for a criminal charge, they can still serve as a means of sanctioning repair shops that rip off their customers, while generating good publicity for investigators. For example, in the following exchange, an investigator speculates on the two-fold effects of a recent investigation:

Investigator: We had a home improvement repair [sting] recently that worked out very well. We rented a house and had a washing machine set up with a minor malfunction and we had the area covered by videotape. Repairmen would come in and, of course, the person representing the homeowner would leave the area, so he would feel he was all alone there while we would be videotaping the whole episode. And that resulted in eight out of ten repairmen being cited in some way or another for doing poor work, unnecessary repairs.

Interviewer: Do you make a great effort to publicize these types of operations once they are concluded?

Investigator: Yes, we do because we feel it's helpful. The public wants us to do that, and they feel better about it and then we get good results as far as putting the home improvement guy on notice that he's being watched, and he should give the public a fair break, I think. The same with auto repair.

Although the publicity generated by sting operations can have many positive effects, it can also have unintended and unwanted side effects. The publicity that accompanies the prosecution of a high-profile case may alert potential offenders to the tactics and strategies in use by law enforcers. Offenders may then modify their behavior so as to make detection and successful prosecution more difficult. Investigators must then figure out new ways to ferret out fraudulent schemes. An evolutionary spiral of response and counter-response between control agents and fraud offenders is the inevitable result.

In effect, as Malcolm Sparrow has argued with respect to fraud in the health care industry, fraud control is a dynamic game. Investigators and prosecutors play against opponents who "think creatively and adapt continuously" to new control efforts (Sparrow 1996). The opponents, in this case potential fraud offenders, watch the strategies used by police, prosecutors, and other control agents and then adapt accordingly. Thus, the effectiveness of any given set of fraud control strategies is usually temporary. Strategies that work well today may be of little use tomorrow, "once the game has progressed a little."

While complex, multimillion-dollar frauds are common in the health care industry, it would be inaccurate to conclude that these are the kinds of offenses typically handled by local prosecutors and investigators. The schemes that come to the attention of local officials tend to be smaller and less complex. Auto repair frauds and advance fee swindles rarely, if ever, involve millions or even hundreds of thousands of dollars. Nevertheless, the basic dynamics of the fraud control game remain the same regardless of the type or size of the offense. The skill level of the players may vary considerably, with the less skillful players being more likely to come to the attention of local authorities. Yet, it is probably safe to assume that even the relatively unskilled fraud offenders found at the local level adapt to whatever strategies are used by local enforcers. An example of this dynamic was given by an investigator in Duval County, Florida, discussing charity benefit frauds:

> *Interviewer:* Is it your impression that the business offender . . . is becoming more educated in response to your activity?
> *Investigator:* Oh, yeah. I think they are. Anytime you go through an ordeal like we go through to prosecute somebody, they've got to get an education out of it. They see where they made their mistakes and they go back and they try to fine-tune those and they polish them up. Might get somebody else to run the organization. See what I'm saying? Anytime you make a case against any of these bandits, you educate them and you just polish them up to fine-tune them to come at you again, make it three times as hard to get to. They're walking a fine line. You gotta wait till they fall off on the wrong side and then be there to catch them and put them where they belong. A lot of the time they'll be able to walk that fine line a long time and it's hard to get them on the other side.

Investigating Environmental Crime

The involvement of local prosecutors in environmental crime is a relatively new development. In 1978, in response to a raft of hazardous-waste–dumping incidents, officials in New Jersey established a statewide Toxic Waste Investigation/Prosecution Unit, which was the first unit of its kind in the nation. Since then, a handful of local prosecutors have devoted extensive resources to environmental crime (Hammett and Epstein 1993a, 14). Our survey data suggest that many other local prosecutors are now prosecuting environmental offenses. Recall from chapter 3 that nearly three-quarters of our survey respondents said that they had jurisdiction over environmental crimes (72.9 percent); more than one-half (54.9 percent) said that they had prosecuted an environmental offense at some time; and almost one-third (30.6 percent) reported prosecuting an environmental offense in our reference year of 1988.

Styles of Enforcement

Because of their complexity and scope, environmental crime cases often involve both regulatory and criminal justice agencies in the investigative and prosecutorial process. Interagency interaction and, in the best of all worlds, teamwork have long been recognized as virtually required to resolve criminal environmental problems. But the agencies involved in investigating and prosecuting crimes against the environment historically have been based on contrasting philosophies of how the law should be enforced: conciliation and compromise versus compulsion and coercion. A conciliatory approach views law enforcement as a method of "social repair and maintenance," with the goal of securing compliance and thereby preventing harm (Hawkins 1984, 3–4). Harm is prevented when violators are induced to act in conformity with regulations. Regulatory agencies typically are thought to employ an enforcement style that is predominantly conciliatory (Braithwaite 1985a; Hawkins 1984, 3; Shover et al. 1986).

In contrast, criminal justice agencies, such as the police and local prosecutors' offices, typically take a penal approach toward law enforcement. Its defining characteristic is the use of sanctions to impose punishment on offenders. Rather than emphasizing harm reduction, the focus of criminal justice agencies is on punishing offenders for their wrongful actions. If a law has been broken and if the lawbreaker can be identified, then the breach of law deserves punishment (Hawkins 1984, 3–4). To the extent that harm prevention is a concern for criminal justice agencies, they assume that punishment deters and that deterrence is the best form of harm prevention.

It is tempting to think that criminal justice and regulatory agencies manifest completely different approaches to law enforcement. However, like other researchers, we found that the reality of their enforcement activities is more complex. Regulatory agencies sometimes take a coercive, penal approach to enforcement, and criminal justice agencies sometimes respond in a conciliatory, problem-solving manner (Hawkins 1984; Shover et al. 1986). It would be a mistake to characterize regulatory investigators as exclusively preoccupied with issues of problem solving. Indeed, among our interviewees, a great deal of similarity appeared in the perspectives that criminal justice and regulatory officials hold regarding environmental offenders and offenses.

The similarity in perspective that we observed between criminal justice and regulatory actors should not be overemphasized, because it may have been influenced by our research design. In the field sites, we used snowball sampling to identify potential interview subjects. At each site, we began with the local prosecutor or the prosecutor's designated representative. We relied on prosecutors to identify individuals in other agencies whom they felt it would be important for us to interview. This approach naturally led us to people with whom prosecutors have good working relationships and with whom they work on a more or less regular basis. With respect to environmental crimes, we were usually referred first to either the prosecutor's own in-house investigative staff or the directors of the local police department's HAZMAT or environmental crime unit.[2] Next, we were referred to people in regulatory agencies, such as the Illinois Environmental Protection Agency or the Los Angeles County Public Health Department.

Time and resource constraints prevented us from conducting in-depth investigations of the operations of the regulatory agencies. Our contacts were generally limited to the agents or investigators who tended to work on criminal environmental cases or to their supervisors. Our interviews with regulatory agency personnel thus were limited to a select group of regulatory officials. This group may have more experience with the penal approach to environmental regulation than is, perhaps, typical of most agency personnel. Our perspective on the regulatory view of environmental offenders, then, is not based on a broad cross section of regulatory personnel. Rather, it relies primarily on investigators and agents who may in a sense be de facto law enforcement operatives.[3] Given that they work together on similar problems, it is not surprising that the views of the regulatory agents we interviewed bear a strong similarity to those of prosecutors and police investigators.

Many of the investigators we interviewed clearly believed that those who violate environmental laws deserve to be punished with criminal sanctions. Like prosecutors, they saw general deterrence and retribution as the primary goals of the criminal enforcement process. The imagery and language used by investigators to describe the impact of criminal prosecutions were virtually identical to those of prosecutors. For example, in Chicago an investigator who works for the federal EPA expressed the view that the regulated community traditionally has thought that the costs of being caught violating environmental laws simply could be passed on to customers. But when criminal sanctions are imposed, violating the law becomes "a personal issue":

Now, criminally, both on the state and federal level, what we can do is we make the environmental violation a personal issue, so that whoever signs that form that says we are within compliance . . . and those people that make a mental decision that they are going to direct the foreman and they're going to direct their people to dispose of waste illegally, now we make it a personal issue. And it's much more difficult once we prosecute people criminally for them to pass on a jail sentence to the public. You can't do that. . . . The criminal enforcement of environmental laws puts teeth in the regulatory process.

A similar viewpoint was expressed by an investigator for the Illinois Environmental Protection Agency. In his view, the chief advantage of criminal enforcement is that

it sends a message to other individuals in the regulated community who might be tempted to save a few bucks and do it the wrong way or who may already be doing it the wrong way and running afoul of the law. When they read in the paper that somebody went to jail for an environmental crime, whether it's a one-man company . . . or a multinational corporation, and a vice-president ended up going to jail and had a felony conviction on his record, they sit up and take notice.

The penal approach taken by investigators is linked to their image of who the environmental offender is. In their view, the offender is first and foremost an opportunist, one who takes advantage of the opportunities for illegal profit created by the introduction of environmental regulations into the marketplace. Environmental regulations create profitable criminal opportunities in two ways. First, regulations on the disposal of toxic chemicals and other forms of hazardous waste create conditions under which a black market in illegal disposal services is likely to arise. Whenever laws or regulations prohibit or tightly control a commodity or service that is in demand, a black market is likely to arise to satisfy the demand. To dispose of hazardous waste in accordance with regulations is expensive. This expense motivates waste generators to seek alternative, less costly means of disposal; fly-by-night waste haulers and midnight dumpers move in as a criminal class to provide this service.

In a second, and more general way, regulations create criminal opportunities by providing a means for unscrupulous, "legitimate" businesspeople to undercut their competitors. Because regulations raise the costs of doing business, they provide such businesspeople with an incentive to avoid meeting them. As one investigator put it:

As I suggested, depending on what the material is, I guess it costs anywhere from about one hundred and fifty dollars to one thousand dollars a barrel to dispose of hazardous waste legally. And so a businessman in a cost-conscious economy says, "Boy, if I don't have to pay to get rid of that stuff, I can undercut Jones down the street with the cost of my product."

As far as investigators are concerned, some portion of the business community always will "ignore the law for the benefit, in this case, of holding down costs."

Because both the fly-by-night waste hauler and the cost-conscious businessperson set out deliberately to evade the law, the only morally appropriate response, say investigators, is to punish them with criminal sanctions. As an investigator put it, these persons deserve punishment "because of the intent factor that we talked about earlier. This isn't an accident. This is deliberate." Particularly in the case of illegal waste haulers, the deviance in question has a categorical, unproblematic quality that triggers a penal response (Hawkins 1984, 6). Dumping a truckload of cyanide plating waste in a field represents a discrete activity, a specific incident, which neatly corresponds to the traditional legal categories of *actus reus* and *mens rea*.

Regulatory agencies often are accused of having been captured by the very industries they are supposed to regulate. A captured agency is one that has been co-opted by those it seeks to regulate, so that the concerns of the regulated are incorporated into the agency's decision making. The process involves a subtle shift, in which the agency comes to define its own interests in stability and self-preservation as being best served by adopting the regulated community's point of view, by going along with the industry rather than vigorously representing the public interest (Bernstein 1955). An assessment of the empirical adequacy of capture theory is beyond the scope of this book. However, in the interviews with regulatory investigators, we found little evidence of an understanding or sympathetic viewpoint toward the regulated community. To the contrary, investigators openly expressed the view that criminality is an ongoing feature of some sectors of the business community.

Selecting Cases

Not all cases of known environmental crime end up in the criminal justice system. Indeed, many violations that could be handled in a criminal forum instead receive treatment via administrative or civil proceedings. A number of interrelated factors influence how law enforcement and regulatory investigators decide which approach is most appropriate. These factors include whether the case is solvable, the intent of the violator, the violator's past record of behavior, and the nature of the threat the offense poses.

Similar to other forms of deviance, the facts of an environmental crime must be interpreted by enforcement agents. Interpretive judgments made by enforcement agents define the meaning of events and the actions of specific individuals. As a result of this interpretive process, some events are classified as criminal while other ostensibly similar events and actions are not.

Not all environmentally harmful or threatening events that are legally definable as crimes result in criminal prosecution, illustrating Becker's point that "an infraction of a rule does not mean that others will respond as though this had happened" (1963, 12). For an event to become a crime, it must be defined and assessed by enforcement agents in reference to its setting and context. Judgments about the offending actor's inner character and motivation must be made, and the act in question must be placed in the context of the offender's overall history and pattern of behavior. The crimes that result from this interpretive process justify the imposition of criminal sanctions on those who violate environmental laws (Hawkins 1984, 72).

Solvability. Like fraud, a primary consideration in the selection of environmental offenses for criminal prosecution is the criterion of solvability. The assessment to determine whether a case is solvable begins early in the investigative process, often the moment information about a potential offense comes to light. Solvability involves not only the issue of detection— that is, whether a perpetrator can be identified; it is also a matter of whether the event, itself, can be viewed as a crime. As Katz (1977) has noted in regard to federal prosecutors, in white-collar crime cases investigators often have to bring the prosecutor into the case early in the investigative process. The same is true at the local level for environmental crimes. An investigator noted that "more than once, we've gotten the prosecutor out of bed at eleven o'clock at night and taken him off to some site where some buffoon has dumped some barrels." Investigators will apprise the local prosecutor of the situation and try to obtain a reading from the prosecutor on whether the fact situation points toward a criminal prosecution before they invest much time in the investigation. This scenario is especially common for environmental investigators, who are housed in police agencies, prosecutors' offices, or special units within regulatory agencies devoted to environmental crime.

Solvability refers, of course, to the potential the case has of being solved in the classic and traditional police sense of identifying a specific, culpable offender and linking that person or organization to the offending behavior. For most white-collar crime investigations, it is generally easy to identify the perpetrator but difficult to prove the crime. But some environmental investigations are like ordinary street crime investigations. The criminality of the behavior may be obvious, but the offender's identity is hidden. This investigative problem arises often in cases of the illegal dumping of hazardous waste in barrels. Various federal and state regulatory codes require such barrels to be identified with serial numbers and other identifying information. Knowledgeable midnight dumpers grind off or otherwise obscure this identifying information before disposing of the barrels. In these cases, unless there is some other fairly obvious way to identify the offender, investigators are likely to write the case off and turn their attention to other matters. According to one investigator, "if it's absolutely not solvable then why expend our limited resources when there's a lot of other things we could be doing just as well? Don't beat a dead horse, I guess is what we're saying."

In other cases, solvability, in the sense of identifying a culprit, is not a problem. For example, in situations where a manufacturer is storing hazardous waste material in an illegal manner on the premises, the identity of the offender is not problematic. Likewise, if a regulatory compliance officer measures how much pollution a local plant is releasing into a river and finds the amount to be in excess of regulations, the offender is immediately at hand. In these cases, the important investigative and interpretive issue is the intent of the offender.

Intent. For enforcement agents who handle white-collar or corporate crimes, interpreting the actor's intent is always a key element in the investigation and adjudication of cases (Benson 1985; Mann 1985). There often is little dispute between prosecution and defense over what happened. Both sides can agree that a person said or did certain things, such as signing a shipping manifest or dumping a load of barrels. But at the same time, they can disagree completely over the intent behind those actions. Did the person knowingly sign an incorrect manifest, or was it simply an oversight? Did the person mean to dispose of barrels containing regulated hazardous chemicals in the town dump, or was he or she confused about the legal status of the contents? Answers to these questions determine the moral reputability of the actor's actions and shape the enforcement actions that follow. Mistakes, errors, omissions, and oversights deserve to be noted and corrected in the future. Deceptions, evasions, and deliberate falsifications, however, warrant a much stronger response.

When an offender takes evasive action to avoid detection, the investigator's job becomes more difficult, but this is a double-edged sword. Evidence that the offender took evasive action and tried to avoid detection can be used as proof of criminal intent. For investigators, it is an important factor, one that calls for the redefinition of the event from an administrative or civil matter to a criminal offense. Like prosecutors, investigators pay close attention to evidence of criminal intent, because it establishes blameworthiness. Blameworthy behavior requires that a different moral framework be applied to the individual. The individual is moved from the category of businessperson to that of environmental criminal. At the same time, evidence of intent is a source of motivation to investigators to work hard on the case. Thus, events that, from an objective standpoint, are similar, if not identical, may be treated dramatically differently. For example, two individuals who illegally dispose of hazardous waste in barrels will provoke drastically different law enforcement reactions if one attempts to hide the offense while the other does not. Consider this exchange with a veteran investigator for a state police environmental crime unit:

Interviewer: So, it's possible that you could have two offenses equally serious, but in one case you've got a perpetrator who's gone to some lengths to cover his tracks, like grinding off his serial numbers or taking his barrels somewhere else and pitching them—

Investigator [Interrupting]: But, yet, we might spend more effort in working on that individual because you have a state of mind there that's unreal. In other words, this person has deliberately sought about to . . . it's not a technical violation.

It's not an accident. It's not a situation where he got caught without enough money to dispose of it. This is a clear-cut indication that he's out to circumvent the environmental control system. So, I guess I took you all the way around the horn and brought you back again, but that factor does enter into it. Maybe if we got a company that . . . let's say a shipping plant. A shipping plant worker, for example, was told to get rid of some barrels and misinterpreted that these two particular barrels that had paint thinner in them were to go. In other words, he thought the boss wanted to get rid of those and he put those on the load. Now that's a violation. That's a criminal violation. But what's more likely to happen with something like that when it's that clear-cut that it was one man acting not out of malice or anything else, just an honest error in effect, is that we're going to look at that real quick and we're probably going to slide that one across for a civil administrative hearing. Whereas you get the same scenario where once a month the guy is shipping barrels out and in the barrels of nonhazardous waste he is grinding off the numbers, the labels, and so forth, and every month he's putting in two barrels of highly flammable paint waste, we'll spend a lot of time on that guy. Because there's a guy who is . . . who has the intent to violate the environmental protection statutes.

"Grinding off . . . labels, and so forth" adds the component of moral disreputability to the actor's behavior. The person not only violates the law. More important, he or she does so knowingly and with the *intent to violate the law.* Criminal intent and moral disreputability also may be established in other ways.

Prior Record. Regulatory compliance agents generally do not start with a penal approach. Securing compliance from as broad a cross section of the regulated community as possible is the preferred goal, and a conciliatory style of enforcement is the method of first choice. But when a business enterprise repeatedly fails to comply, investigators begin to reassess and consider more punitive responses. At some not-well-defined point, a record of noncompliance becomes evidence that the offender has a criminal mind and is, therefore, someone who cannot be deterred easily by fines or warnings. Exactly when this shift in the investigator's perspective should be made is a matter of judgment. An investigator in a state public health department outlined the process:

A lot of times with the world of people that we inspect here, we run into small mom-and-pop operations. People who don't have the staffing, the environmental staff that the bigger companies have to advise them. A lot of times, we have ignorance coming into play. And, you know, we have our inspectional staff and in those types of situations where there's no gross violations, perhaps there may be a can of paint or something in the trash, we may not pursue that criminally. We would pursue that through our regulatory avenues, which is notice of violation, and then we reinspect for compliance and things like that. What we have is an escalating compliance mode that we would enter into if, upon subsequent reinspections, we find no compliance . . . We have a transition from the typical regulatory role of going out and inspecting, issuing a notice, coming back at a later time. If there's no compliance, we may go to hearings, administrative hearings, and we may go through that whole process. At some point in time if there's still no compliance, we may escalate it to a criminal situation.

The idea of an "escalating compliance mode" suggests that the interpretive process applied in environmental cases takes place over time. Environmental offenders, in effect, sometimes have to work at the role before regulatory enforcement agents are convinced that administrative sanctions alone will not secure compliance. In the case of ongoing business concerns, it is only after routine administrative sanctions fail to produce the desired compliance that regulatory agents begin to consider using the criminal law against violators or referring the case to the criminal justice system. The point at which a case is transferred from the regulatory control system to the criminal justice system often is a matter of some controversy, which we address in the next chapter, on networking.

Threat. The potential impact of an environmental violation on the health and safety of other individuals figures prominently in investigative decision making. Like prosecutors, investigators pay close attention to the harmfulness of the offender's behavior in deciding whether to pursue a case for criminal prosecution or to refer it for administrative or civil action. Although investigators often use the term *environmental impact* when discussing how they assess harmfulness, they are clearly more concerned with impact on individuals than that on the general environment. According to one investigator:

If a guy is out dumping cyanide plating waste in maybe an abandoned gravel pit or something. There's no residences around anywhere for some miles and the water table—that's not endangered. OK, that doesn't have the huge environmental impact. It's gotta be dealt with. The stuff's gotta be cleaned up so it doesn't seep, and what have you. But by the same token, if he's dumping it right near the head point of a well across a street from a playground of a school in a residential area, well, now you have a whole different scenario of environmental impact.

From the perspective of investigators, the point of environmental enforcement is not to protect the environment in an abstract sense. Rather, it is to protect individuals. The state of the environment is seen as directly and causally linked with individual health and wellbeing. Violations of environmental laws which pose direct threats to public health thus can be equated with ordinary street crimes, in the sense that the violator engages in criminally negligent behavior. The causal connection between the offender's actions and harm may take longer to manifest itself in the case of environmental crimes than in the case of street crimes. Nevertheless, the connection is present and establishes the criminality of the offender's behavior. An investigator for the Los Angeles Police Department's Hazardous Materials Unit noted, with respect to environmental crime, that

you've got something that's very insidious. You got something that is out there and the only difference between a major violator in the environmental area and the current murderer, or rapist, or robber is the impact of what they do. In order to commit a homicide in the state of California a person has to die within a year from the results of the injury or [precipitating] event. In environmental crime, a person may well die, but it's probably not going to be within that one year from an exposure from a contamination from a working environment, which is really a criminally negligent occurrence. Something that somebody deliberately made the decision to continue, a particular practice which is illegal because it's been found to be detrimental to people's health as well as to the environment, as well as to everything around.

The moral characterization of the victims of environmental crime also influences the imputation of blameworthiness to the offender. Innocent victims, those who in no way facilitate or precipitate their victimization, engender especially protective responses in law enforcement officials and especially harsh views of offenders. The victims of environmental crime are seen as innocent, and therefore the offender's conduct is deemed as especially reprehensible and warranting punishment. One investigator commented,

When you go down to the water fountain down here and turn it on and drink it, you have the legitimate right to expect that the water is going to be a reasonably safe product for you to drink, and I don't think that the misdirected businessman has the right in his quest for finances to change that. I guess what I'm saying is one of the reasons I think we need to use the criminal laws is I can think of no other area of law enforcement where there are more potential innocent victims than in chemical crime.

That investigators in environmental units emphasize the potential for physical harm from environmental offenses is understandable. Doing so speaks to important and traditional moral justifications for the state's monopoly on law enforcement. It taps into a cherished dimension of the police officer's self-image—that of guardian. To protect the physical security of community members, to not permit the strong to victimize the weak, to prevent those with evil intent from harming the innocent and vulnerable—these are among the strongest moral justifications for the police. They represent symbolic and heroic ideals of public service, which the officer on the street aspires to fulfill. Thus, it is understandable that investigators in environmental units portray their work as serving these goals and want its importance recognized. Those who work in environmental units most certainly are not unique in attempting to make their work appear vitally important. Like other complex organizations, criminal justice organizations pursue multiple objectives with limited budgetary, personnel, and technical resources. Since they cannot meet all of the numerous, conflicting, and shifting demands made on them, criminal justice administrators must make strategic decisions on the priority of objectives. Competition for resources among organizational subunits is inevitable, and it makes sense to assume that the priorities are established and resources allocated roughly on the basis of the perceived importance of a subunit's work.

Paradoxically, although the science underlying environmental regulation and pollution control is sophisticated, it can be difficult for environmental units to document the importance of their work in hard quantitative terms. In laboratories the identity of toxic chemicals can be scientifically determined with great accuracy. Regulatory agencies routinely measure the discharge of contaminants into the air and water in exceedingly small amounts, such as parts per million or billion. But this technical precision in quantifying the precise nature or extent of an environmental offense does not extend to its long-term consequences. Even though there is a widespread belief that toxic chemicals and hazardous wastes are extremely dangerous, it is rare that illegal disposal of such substances actually results in immediate physical harm to anyone.

Since it is difficult to connect particular environmental offenses to specific harms to individuals, it is hard for environmental units to establish a baseline against which to measure their effectiveness. The indicators of harm in environmental cases often are ambiguous, and so the indicators of harm prevented are correspondingly ambiguous. This ambiguity makes it difficult for environmental units to compete with other specialized units for resources. Environmental unit leaders must justify their requests based on theory and intuition, as opposed to concrete facts. While they think their efforts will save lives, they can't say how many, when, or where. As one investigator observed:

I think if the facts could ever be quantified, the number of lives that we're trying to save, the number of dollars in property damage that we can bring to an absolute minimum, is tremendous. You contaminate an aquifer and it's contaminated. You prevent it and it's a permanent resource. You prevent certain materials from being dumped in the areas where children play. And I don't know what the health effects are going to be, but I can hazard a guess that we're going to save a lot of lives, or at least a lot of premature deaths or lingering illnesses. [But] you just can't quantify it. It's hard for me to go to an administrator and say, "Look, here's what I'm going to do for you. I'm going to save you six whole lives, and I'm going to prevent this many illnesses, and I'm going to be able to ensure that the air is better, the water is better, the soil is more productive." I can't quantify it, but intuitively I know it's got that possibility, and if we have more people working in concert, we could be much more effective to realize those results.

Conclusions

In chapter 8, we described how local prosecutors think about corporate crime cases. We argued that prosecutors' reactions to corporate crimes and to corporate offenders are guided by the concepts of harm and blameworthiness. These concepts are the twin pillars of a legal culture that provides a moral framework for the interpretation of acts and actors, a culture broadly endorsed by judges and prosecutors. In this chapter, we have tried to show that this legal culture also shapes how investigators react to instances of corporate wrongdoing.

Like judges and prosecutors, investigators consider more than just the law in making decisions about cases. For investigators, deciding which cases to pursue, how hard to work on them, and how to channel them in the system is not just a matter of matching the facts to the law. Investigators also assess the facts in relation to a moral framework. The law sets the parameters of the investigator's authority. It empowers them to make observations, ask questions, and collect evidence when certain types of events or factual situations appear to have occurred. But it is where an event fits within the moral framework of harm and blameworthiness that determines the amount of time and energy investigators are likely to invest in it.

Investigation may be viewed as the first stage in the moral interpretation of a case. It starts what Garfinkel (1956) called a "status degradation ceremony," in which the offender's actions are reinterpreted to show the essential evilness of the offender. Investigators provide the preliminary screening and ordering of the facts, which are then passed on to the prosecutor. The prosecutor, in turn, further shapes the facts for presentation in court. At each stage of this process, the person whose duty it is to make a decision about the case—be it investigator, prosecutor, or judge— is guided, we believe, by the same legal culture. Individual investigators, prosecutors, and judges may, of course, differ from one another in how they assess particular cases, and collectively investigators may differ from prosecutors and judges in how they tend to assess cases in general. But the differences are matters of degree, not kind. The justice system may be, as some have argued, a set of only loosely linked institutions, but the institutions are, nevertheless, linked (Hagan et al. 1979). One important form of linkage is a common legal culture.

The investigation of environmental crimes may be a more complex undertaking than is the investigation of fraud. More and different types of agencies tend to be involved in the former than in the latter. Environmental investigators often must either know a good deal about manufacturing processes, basic chemistry, and hydrology or rely on those who do. Nevertheless, the complexity of environmental crime as opposed to that of fraud should not obscure an essential similarity in their investigation. In both types of cases, investigators are engaged in an interpretive process aimed at determining the moral character of the defendant and his actions.

A final note: We focused on two specific types of corporate crime.

There are many other types. We speculate, however, that an investigation of how other types of corporate crime are investigated and prosecuted would uncover much that is similar to what we report here. Some of the police investigators we interviewed had worked on other types of crime before being assigned to fraud or environmental crime investigations. While acknowledging that some types of crime are more complex and difficult to solve than others, they also left us with the strong impression that the basic focus of investigation is always the same: You look for evidence of intent, for a guilty mind (Benson 1985). Except for the most massive offenses, it is evidence of moral disreputability—intended or repeated violations—that makes a corporate crime serious.

Notes

1. A "bait and switch" occurs when a retail store entices customers into the store by advertising or in some way publicizing a product at an extremely low price. Once the customers are in the store, they may be told that the advertised product is temporarily unavailable and steered toward buying a higher-priced product.

2. HAZMAT is short for hazardous materials. Many local and state law enforcement agencies now have either permanent HAZMAT units or teams of specially trained individuals who can be assembled on short notice to respond to emergency situations.

3. Even though regulatory inspectors usually are not referred to as police, they are, nevertheless, "special police forces for industry" (Wells 1993, 4).

10

NETWORKING AND INTERAGENCY
RELATIONS

Investigating and prosecuting corporate cases often requires interaction between people located in different agencies, jurisdictions, and levels of government. This interaction—or networking, as it is sometimes called—is widely touted as absolutely necessary for effective local control of corporate crime. Although networking long has been recognized and promoted as an important control strategy, little is known about how it works in local corporate crime prosecutions. How do prosecutors interact with other agencies in corporate cases? What forms does networking take? How are the interests and perspectives of different agencies coordinated, so as to avoid jurisdictional disputes and conflicts? This chapter attempts to address these and other questions related to networking and interagency cooperation by continuing our analysis of the field study interviews.

Our discussion focuses primarily on the generic dimensions of networking—that is, on the processes and problems common to local networks generally. We begin by focusing on the different forms and types of networking manifested in the four field sites. Next, we discuss how formal and informal networks are related and examine the problem of conflict in networks. Because regulatory agencies are particularly important to the control of environmental crime, we devote a section to the special features of networks involving regulatory agencies. We also address the difficult area of relations between local prosecutors and federal agencies.

Types of Networks

Networks can take many different shapes and forms. For analytical purposes, they can be roughly divided into two major types: formal and informal. Formal networks are constituted by explicit agreements reached between different governmental agencies to cooperate on particular types of cases. Formal networks go by a variety of names. They may be called task forces, strike forces, or working groups, or they may go by some sort of acronym, such as CHEMHIT. They vary in size from as few as two or three agencies to as many as twenty or more. In theory, representatives from the various network agencies meet on a regular basis to discuss cases, share information, coordinate investigations, and develop new initiatives.

Sometimes formal networks arise in response to a particularly important or egregious offense or series of related offenses. For example, an egregious toxic waste spill may cause regulatory and criminal justice agencies to come together in an effort to formulate a comprehensive response. Or, the manufacture of an unsafe product, such as the Dalkon Shield, that harms many consumers may lead to coordinated action by a variety of different regulatory and criminal justice agencies. In these cases, the network is temporary and is disbanded after the particular case is resolved.[1] At other times, formal networks are organized to attack a particular type of offense, such as consumer fraud or environmental crime, on a permanent basis. The distinction between temporary and permanent formal networks is useful for analytical purposes, but in the real world the two forms may overlap. Permanent networks sometimes evolve out of temporary ones, if the networking arrangement is viewed by the participants as having been a success and worth continuing.

Informal networks develop over time out of the casual, day-to-day, cooperative, case-related interactions that occur between particular individuals in different agencies. Formal networks are like bureaucracies in that role positions are permanent but role occupants may change without affecting the status of the network. An agency may be a permanent member of a formal network, even though the specific individual designated as its representative on the network may change from one meeting to the next. In contrast, informal networks are necessarily personalistic; their existence depends on the specific individuals involved and the strength of their working relationships. Informal networks arise spontaneously as investigators, regulators, police officers, and prosecutors interact during the course of their day-to-day duties. As we argue below, formal and informal networks are related in complex ways.

Networks and networking also can be conceptualized according to the level or levels of government represented by agencies participating in the network. Vertical networks involve agencies at different levels of government. For example, a task force on environmental crime may involve local, state, and federal officials. In a horizontal network, the agencies involved all represent the same level of government—either local, state, or federal.

Networking in the Four Field Sites

Networking is a fluid, evolving, and ever-changing phenomenon. What works in one jurisdiction may not work in another, and what is needed in a jurisdiction at one time may not be needed at another. Task forces, working groups, and strike forces come and go over time. Not surprisingly, the extent of formal network arrangements varied dramatically across our four field sites. Thus, in describing networking in the field sites, we do not attempt a complete enumeration of the formal networks in each of the field sites. Rather, we concentrate on describing the major players who work most with local prosecutors in the field sites, paying particular attention to networks that handle environmental and consumer fraud types of cases. We take this approach partly because, in the time since the field studies were conducted, things have probably changed considerably in the jurisdictions we visited. In addition, as we argue below, formal networks—that is, those that have formal names and are instituted via the exchange of official memoranda of understanding between agencies—are less important and less prominent than are informal networks.

Los Angeles County, California. In Los Angeles, the prosecutors we interviewed mentioned several different task forces and strike forces focusing on a diverse set of problems. For example, there were task forces on foreclosure and bankruptcy fraud, telemarketing, and environmental crime, all within Los Angeles County or the southern California area generally. In addition, the California District Attorneys' Association has established a

Consumer and Environmental Protection Council (CEPC), which involves district attorneys throughout the state. At meetings of the CEPC, prosecutors hold roundtable discussions on their current cases.

One of the most important formal networks is the environmental crime strike force organized by the Los Angeles County district attorney's office in the early 1980s. This complex network involves prosecutorial, law enforcement, and regulatory agencies from Los Angeles County. The cities of Los Angeles, Long Beach, Pomona, Santa Monica, and Signal Hill, the region, and the state of California also are represented on the strike force. Figure 10.1 shows the membership on the strike force as it stood in the early 1990s (Hammett and Epstein 1993b).

Cook County, Illinois. In Cook County, Illinois, an organization known as CHEMHIT involves the state's attorney's office, the attorney general's

Figure 10.1   Los Angeles County Environmental Crimes Strike Force

County of Los Angeles
Los Angeles County District Attorney's Office, Environmental Crimes/OSHA Division
Hazardous Materials Control Program of the Los Angeles County Fire Department
Los Angeles County Department of Public Works

City of Los Angeles
City Attorney's Office, Environmental Protection Section
City Fire Department, Underground Tank Unit
Port of Los Angeles Police
Los Angeles Police Department
City Sanitation Enforcement Division, Industrial Waste Operations

City of Long Beach
Department of Health and Human Services, Hazardous Materials Division
Long Beach Police Department
City Prosecutor

City of Pomona
Fire Department, Fire Prevention Bureau

City of Santa Monica
Industrial Waste Section

City of Signal Hill
Police Department Hazardous Materials Unit

Regional Agencies
Los Angeles County Sanitation Districts
South Coast Air Quality Management District, Enforcement Division

State of California
California Highway Patrol, Environmental Crimes Unit
California State Department of Fish and Game, Wildlife Protection
California State Department of Health Services, Toxic Substances Control Division and Toxic Substances Control Program

office, Illinois State Police, and the Illinois Environmental Protection Agency. CHEMHIT was originally organized for the purpose of providing training to law enforcement officers, and it has held several training sessions. CHEMHIT also provides a phone number for citizens to call to report environmental problems and violations. With the exception of CHEMHIT, there appeared to be no other formal networks in Cook County focused on corporate crime. For fraud crimes, the local prosecutor works primarily with local police departments and United States Postal Service inspectors.

Duval County, Florida. Unlike Los Angeles and Cook Counties, no formally named networks exist in Duval County, Florida. But the local prosecutor's office has been instrumental in organizing regular meetings among several agencies with interests in environmental crime, including the state Department of Environmental Regulations, the Fish and Game Department, the highway patrol, the marine patrol, a regional water management district, the sheriff's office, and the city of Jacksonville's fire department, public services department, and water division. This group meets every other month to discuss potential cases and is used by the local prosecutor's environmental prosecutions division as a forum for soliciting agencies to bring cases.

Nassau County, New York. At the time of our study in fall 1989, the local prosecutor's office in Nassau County was in the process of organizing a formal system for handling environmental emergencies and crimes. A formal protocol had been developed which outlined the responsibilities and duties of a number of agencies in the event of environmental emergencies. This network is designed primarily to respond to blatant environmental problems, such as hazardous waste spills. It is not organized to respond to ongoing or longstanding problems, such as a manufacturer who continually violates environmental regulations.

Positive and Negative Aspects of Formal Networks

There are many reasons why the development of formal networks can improve local responses to corporate crime. For example, because regulatory agencies often have regular contact with corporate enterprises, they can serve as important sources of discovery and referral of cases for prosecutors. Some corporate offenses involve complex, technical evidence. To develop and properly present these types of corporate cases, local prosecutors may need to call on the expertise of regulatory personnel. Sometimes corporate offenses cross jurisdictional lines. For example, telemarketers may set up shop in one jurisdiction but work their fraudulent schemes on victims located in other jurisdictions. To respond effectively to these types of cases, local prosecutors must interact with their counterparts in other jurisdictions or at other levels of government. Like prosecutors, investigators also regularly find that they must work with counterparts in other agencies to discover and develop good corporate cases.

Besides improving the process by which cases are discovered, investigated, and prosecuted, formal networks offer other advantages as well. Members of the network can learn about one another's priorities and problems. By sharing information on cases, agencies can avoid duplicating efforts or unintentionally jeopardizing ongoing investigations. Formal networks are particularly important for effective response to the emergency types of situations that can arise involving environmental violations. By providing a set of guidelines for responding to emergencies, formal networks can dramatically improve the coordination of efforts among different agencies. Better cooperation makes for a more efficient response. For example, in Nassau County a formal protocol was developed by the local prosecutor and adopted by local law enforcement and regulatory agencies. The protocol established clear lines of authority and an explicit division of labor for responding to emergency situations. Comparing how environmental emergencies were handled in his jurisdiction before the protocol was adopted, the prosecutor noted:

If we'd go out three or four years ago to something, there'd be somebody from all the different agencies. And everybody would be trying to gather evidence, and [to be] the first one to get to the lab and to have a press conference. So, it doesn't work. It isn't efficient. It's a waste of what are limited resources . . . So, it makes much more sense to pool those resources.

Another important potential benefit of formal networks besides pooling personnel resources is the opportunity to pool intellectual resources. In newly emerging areas of the law, such as environmental and workplace-safety–related prosecutions, it is easy for prosecutors to make mistakes. Knowing precisely when to bring charges or how to respond to defense motions is not simple for local prosecutors the first time around. By communicating with their peers and sharing information and knowledge, local prosecutors can avoid making mistakes. Avoiding mistakes is particularly important in areas where the law is not yet settled, because there is the potential that an ill-advised prosecution will result in a bad appellate decision that could affect prosecutors in other jurisdictions. In effect, through the open discussion of cases, prosecutors as a group can provide checks and balances over the exercise of prosecutorial discretion by individual prosecutors.

This sort of intellectual resource sharing seemed to be one of the major functions of the Consumer and Environmental Protection Council in California. All local prosecutors in California have an interest in making sure that cases are not brought which might result in unfavorable appellate decisions. To avoid this, prosecutors in California talk with one another about what cases to pursue and how to pursue them. Even though the group has no formal authority over its members, it nevertheless exerts influence over individual decision making through collegial discussion of cases. According to one member of the group:

We know that one case brought in San Francisco that produces a bad appellate decision will very much affect the workers down in Los Angeles and vice versa. We have developed over the last fifteen years a tradition of very close liaison in criminal prosecutions. By that I mean . . . we have roundtable discussions of consumer and environmental matters. Each office makes a presentation as to the cases they're working, the decisions they're making as to prosecuting criminally versus civilly. They ask questions of their colleagues as to what are the sanctions you recommend, how many, how much? Right down to the nitty-gritty, what do you think this case is worth in terms of civil penalties? What's a fair plea in this case? And there's a lot of collegial peer discussion, if you will, that results in surprising consensus.

The consensus, of course, is not uniform. There are mavericks who pursue cases that the group as a whole may think are ill-advised and that may jeopardize the law in particular areas. But, overall, consensus and agreement are more common than conflict and disagreement. Agencies can learn from one another about new problems or potential problems before they get out of hand.

Formal networks also can provide opportunities for cross-training personnel. Regulatory agents from environmental agencies, for example, can teach their law enforcement counterparts about the rudiments of hazardous waste identification. At the same time, police agencies can teach regulatory personnel about due process requirements in criminal investigations. To the extent that they provide opportunities for personnel from different agencies to learn about one another's work, formal networks improve the ability of agencies to cooperate on solving problems.

For all their advantages, however, formal networks have disadvantages, too. Working with people in other agencies takes energy and patience. To establish, maintain, and manage a formal network takes time, which must be taken away from other important tasks. The benefits to be gained from having a formal network through which to share information on cases must be balanced against the costs of having to allocate someone to coordinate the flow of information. For example, when asked whether a formal procedure to share information on cases would be valuable, a prosecutor responded:

I don't think that because of the scope and size of the offices and the ability to communicate between them that is necessary at this stage in time . . . Certainly, there is a constant, almost daily [contact] between some agency and another. "Hey, we got complaints against this guy. Do you have anything? Do you have any investigations going? Do you have anything administratively going? What do you have that you can tell us on that?" And we do that on a fairly regular basis. So, we get the information that way.

The prosecutor acknowledged that instituting a formal procedure might be more efficient, but he worried about the "manpower time involved . . . and also the cost." From this prosecutor's point of view, the trade-off was not worth it. He continued:

Being like everyone else, we're greedy. We'd rather have two environmental investigators than someone coordinating that kind of information. I think we can serve our own local needs in terms of coordinating information by the networking and phone calls that we have. I don't see how it would be harmful, but I don't know if it would necessarily justify it in terms of expenditure of resources to gather all that unless it could be done more cheaply or easily than I would conceive sitting here right now.

The difficulties of sustaining a formal network over time are multiplied if the participants do not see a direct benefit from their participation. From the perspective of network members, attending network meetings takes time and energy, resources that are always in short supply and that could be spent on other matters. What is needed to hold a network together is a steady flow of important and solvable cases. Such cases serve to focus attention and to provide a set of common problems on which the network can concentrate its energies. Unless there are concrete cases to work on, the benefits of participating in a network decline rapidly, and other priorities begin to take precedence. The opportunity to get together informally just to talk and share information is not enough to sustain a network. For example, in Duval County, Florida, a working group organized to fight consumer white-collar crimes was experiencing difficulty resulting from a lack of focus at its meetings. One prosecutor explained:

There has been, up until just a few months ago, a monthly meeting, a roundtable type meeting with federal, state, and local agencies on consumer white-collar crime. We went through two or three meetings where we had poor turnout, just two or three for one reason or another. . . . I think what we're going to be doing after the first of the year is revamping that, getting some sort of input as to what people are looking for, and making sure . . . we've got everybody's goals in mind to make it worth meeting. . . . I think it probably got a little too informal. It was just basically discussions around the table, and we were trying to make it informal enough, a sort of brown bag lunch thing. Kind of make it informal enough so that we could communicate about ongoing things, and it got so informal that it wasn't being of benefit for some of the agencies. So, I think we need to take a hard look at it and revamp it.

Formal networks also require prosecutors to share credit and control over investigations and prosecutions. For ambitious and busy people, as prosecutors tend to be, these are important disincentives to networking. Sometimes the benefits of cracking a big case are worth the trouble of coordinating with others and sharing credit. But much of the time the motivation to put up with the difficulties of networking comes only from the individual prosecutor's sense of professional duty.

Formal and Informal Networks

The field studies suggest that networking involves a delicate balance between formal and informal arrangements. Formal networking arrangements, such as task forces with regularly scheduled meetings between large groups of agencies, were rare in the sites we visited. Where present, they seemed to be viewed with some skepticism. One investigator in a district attorney's office recounted how his district attorney had initiated such a task force on environmental crimes. After a while, however, the attorneys and investigators concluded that the meetings were not producing significant information sharing. Representatives from each agency tended to try to get information from the other attendees rather than share information with the group in general. As a result, the attorneys handling these cases decided to meet informally with smaller groups of agencies on a case-by-case basis.

While the formal task force may not have been as useful for information sharing as anticipated, it had important side effects that operated on an informal level. By establishing the task force, the district attorney and his administrative counterparts in other agencies created an environment in which their subordinates (investigators, regulatory officials, and assistant district attorneys) felt free to develop informal working relationships with one another. These informal relationships established between these street-level operatives constituted the real network in this jurisdiction.

This pattern was repeated in the other jurisdictions we visited and has important lessons to offer. Networking appeared to work through informal and personal relationships established between street-level operatives and their immediate superiors. It appeared most effective where operatives felt that they could work with their counterparts in other agencies without fear of being sanctioned by higher-level administrators. Whether in the prosecutor's office or in other agencies, administrators may promote networking by letting it be known that interagency cooperation will be rewarded rather than punished.

Administrators also can impede the informal networking process. Regulatory investigators in one agency reported that, although they had good contacts with their counterparts in other agencies, their superiors were opposed to cooperation with those agencies. The investigators clearly felt that too much initiative on their part would result in punishment rather than reward. Thus, networking and all of its attendant benefits may be inhibited as much by an atmosphere that discourages cooperation among street-level operatives as by a lack of formal interagency arrangements.

Almost without exception the prosecutors, investigators, and regulatory agents we interviewed were more favorably disposed toward informal than formal networking. They spoke in very positive terms about their ability to get in touch with "so-and-so" in another agency and get something done quickly and smoothly. Several reasons may explain the popularity of informal networks. One is that the members of informal networks are self-selected and include only people who get along well with one another most, if not all, of the time. Investigators and prosecutors tend to call and work with people in other agencies with whom they have had success in the past. If someone is difficult to work with or unwilling to share credit on a case, then that person is unlikely to be called by others when a potential case comes to light. Hence, informal networks inevitably include only individuals with compatible personalities who have developed bonds of trust and friendship with one another.

Another reason why informal networks are popular is that they are virtually always oriented toward handling specific cases, and solving cases is what investigators and prosecutors like to do. An informal network is activated when a potential case comes to light, and the prosecutor or investigator realizes that someone in another agency may be needed to help solve it. If the case is handled successfully, the experience provides positive reinforcement to all those involved with it. Having a series of successful cases can quickly cement the personal bonds needed to establish an informal network. Conversely, if working with someone in another agency does not lead to success often enough, then the informal connection between the individuals will be activated less and less often until it ceases, because it will be viewed as pointless. Thus, informal networks inevitably tend to be successful, because if they are not successful they cease to exist.

Formal networks lack some of the inherent advantages of informal networks. Formal networks may bring together individuals who do not have compatible personalities and whose interaction is unpleasant for both parties. In addition, formal networks are less likely to be as case-oriented as informal networks. Formal networks often must spend time on other matters, such as training and interagency relations, instead of confining themselves to solving particular cases. Although prosecutors and investigators may recognize the importance of these issues in the grand scheme of responses to corporate crime, they are, nevertheless, inherently less appealing than working a good case.

Turf Battles: Conflict Versus Cooperation

The criminal justice system sometimes is portrayed as a collection of warring fiefdoms, a hodgepodge of uncommunicative agencies independently pursuing their own goals and agendas and often working at cross-purposes to one another. *Turf battle* is the colloquial term used to describe this conflict between law enforcement agencies over the investigation and disposition of cases. These jurisdictional disputes long have been regarded as a persistent and particularly troublesome feature of local criminal justice and regulatory control systems (President's Commission 1967b, 68). When agencies compete for cases or refuse to cooperate with one another, the public interest suffers (Jacobs 1990). Separate, rather than cooperative, investigations inevitably result in duplicated efforts; precious time, money, and personnel resources are squandered. Cases fall through the cracks or are not handled as efficiently as possible. While lack of communication and interagency conflict certainly are not rare, the reality of working relationships within the criminal justice and regulatory control systems is complex and perhaps not as dismal as it is sometimes presented.

Local prosecutors, law enforcement officials, and regulatory agents are acutely aware of the negative consequences of turf battles. They understand that jurisdictional disputes over cases reduce productivity and waste resources. Furthermore, they know that, when a dispute becomes public, it can reflect poorly on the agencies involved, often becoming a focal point of negative publicity and criticism from the media. Agencies can appear in an unflattering light as more concerned with protecting their bureaucratic self-interest than with pursuing the public interest. Hence, agencies have many reasons to promote cooperation and to avoid or reduce conflict over cases.

Nevertheless, despite the drawbacks and costs, jurisdictional disputes and conflicts still occur all too often. The reasons for their persistence involve both organizational and individual interests. From the perspective of criminal justice organizations, cases are an important, if not the ultimate, measure of organizational effectiveness and significance. Solving cases demonstrates that the organization is working and that there is continued need for its services. Both regulatory and criminal justice agencies have a natural tendency to define situations such that they fall under agency jurisdiction. This tendency is exacerbated for many corporate crimes, because different agencies may have legitimate claims to jurisdiction. This ambiguity can lead to conflict. For example, an investigator in the Los Angeles County district attorney's office described how a hazardous waste crime could lead to conflict between agencies:

An example, the highway patrol is charged with enforcing transportation crimes in the state, and transportation of hazardous wastes is one of those. The health department also enforces those laws. They enforce the hazardous waste control law, so they may have some different ideas about who is responsible for a particular case, who should take the lead in investigating a certain case. [However,] an argument can be made for any site disposal of hazardous waste that involves transportation, so the highway patrol may decide to claim that case as theirs. It would seem simple to say "We'll work it together," but other interests enter into it. Like some unit might say, "My unit needs to have so many felony cases in a year if I am to get another man" or "I need to file this many cases in a year if I am going to stay in existence" or "We need to prove that we are cost effective." There is also funds, money that is available that I think may enter into some of this turf protection.

In the competition between governmental agencies for increasingly limited tax dollars, a heavy caseload can be used to justify requests for more financial and personnel resources. Thus, criminal justice organizations have an incentive to take credit for as many cases as they can and a disincentive to cooperate or share credit on cases with other agencies.

Cases also are important on the individual level. For individuals, cases are a source of status and prestige within the agency. Successfully handling a case gets one noticed and improves one's chances for advancement. For investigators, solving cases is the point of their job and the measure of their success; getting convictions is the measure of success and raison d'être of prosecutors. Understandably investigators and prosecutors often have strong proprietary interest in their cases.

Prosecutors and law enforcement investigators also tend to view incidents of suspected wrongdoing from the perspective of the criminal law. If the facts of an incident indicate that the elements of harm and blameworthiness are present, then the incident can be treated as a criminal case, and prosecutors and investigators are inclined to do so. They have strong organizational and personal reasons for applying the criminal law, regardless of the availability of other civil or administrative sanctions. Thus, at times prosecutors will pursue a case regardless of what other agencies are doing. In Chicago, we asked a prosecutor what effect the pending actions of other agencies might have on the decision to prosecute. He responded:

I think you just throw it into the hopper, and you just juxtapose your efforts and resource allocations with what the possible outcome of these other reactions are going to be. If it's so gross that only criminal action is appropriate, then as far as I'm concerned the other agency action is irrelevant, a la Film Recovery. OSHA's action in Film Recovery has had no impact on our decision whatsoever. If there is a $100,000 cost to the state for a cleanup and the agencies are moving quickly on getting that back, and we look at it, and we don't see a course of criminal conduct there, and we see how our resources are going to be drained off away from other cases, we might, say, accomplish our goal with the agency people. But generally speaking, if there is a good, viable, criminal charge, other agencies are irrelevant.

The chance to get "a good, viable" criminal case is a welcome prospect for prosecutors and criminal justice investigators. Getting a good case is as important for those who handle fraud cases as it is for those who concentrate on environmental crimes. A supervising fraud investigator with the Chicago police department noted that he keeps track of how often his detectives refer cases to other agencies:

Everybody covets good cases in law enforcement, and I don't care what agency you're in. If you're in law enforcement, you covet good cases. If I find that one of our detectives is giving away cases to another agency, because any referral has to come through a supervisor, but you know if I detect that every time he gets a case he's willing to refer this to another agency, I say, wait a minute. These people came to us and they wanted some service. . . . We don't want to give them the bum rush. . . . I don't want to see our guys saying, "Well let's send this over to the IRS, let's send this to the FBI, let's send this to the postal inspector, let's send this to the attorney general, let's send this to the state police." We have jurisdiction. We have responsibility for follow-up in these areas. Can we pursue it successfully? You can't say that at the front end, but if there's a reasonable expectation of success with this thing, let's have some impact if we can. Let's go for it.

Thus, when a good case comes along, it is not uncommon for agencies to initiate efforts to establish a stake in it. Generally, establishing a stake requires investing time and resources in the case. A prosecutorial or investigative agency may spend time checking out witnesses and developing information about a case before making its existence known to other agencies. This does not mean that prosecutors or investigators always try to keep good cases to themselves or that they never bring cases to the attention of other agencies that may have a legitimate interest in them. Communication and exchange of information about good cases goes on regularly, but cases discovered by one agency are not just handed over freely to another agency or jurisdiction if it can be avoided. Rather, the discovering agency tries to establish a stake in the case and thereby ensure that they get at least some, if not most, of the credit for its eventual disposition. For example, under New York's environmental conservation laws, local prosecutors and the Environmental Protection Bureau (EPB) of the state attorney general's office share criminal jurisdiction over certain types of environmental cases. Environmental cases may be initiated by either the local prosecutor or attorneys in the EPB, and it is not uncommon for them to work together on cases. In an interview with two attorneys for the EPB, we asked about competition and cooperation with the local prosecutor's office over environmental cases.

First Prosecutor: I think both [meaning there is both competition and cooperation]. My own experience and from what I've heard, I guess, is that sometimes there's more of a perception of competition than probably exists in reality, I think. But my limited experience has been I've gotten pretty good cooperation with district attorneys, but it's usually in everybody's interest to share. This office particularly, I think, takes the attitude that we're not looking to curry headlines for ourselves, or to take publicity away from a local official or something like that. We are perfectly willing to share credit in cases that we prosecute jointly. But you [referring to second prosecutor] may have different . . .

Second Prosecutor: Very circumstantial. I agree with most of what _____ has said that cooperation is pretty much the rule. Lack of cooperation is the exception. There is a sense of competition, you know, for premier status in these prosecutions, but that is not . . . the same as lack of cooperation. You know what I mean. Competition is very different.

First Prosecutor: I agree. I think that may come up for example in an investigation before there's an actual crime charged. Let's say we have our own set of investigators. Sometimes we may get a referral from investigators from another agency, such as DEC [Department of Environmental Conservation] or local or New York City has DEP [Department of Environmental Protection]. We may get a call from them. They may come across something and call us. But our own investigators may get a tip on something and start investigating it. [For example] a steel company. They heard there's a stack of drums in the backyard that they're dumping into the ground or down the sewer. In that case, usually we will work on it ourselves and think, "Well, this is a good case that we're going to generate for this office." The first thing that would happen wouldn't be to call up the DA's office and say, "Hey, we got a case in New York County; we're going to investigate it." We'd probably keep it in-house initially. I suppose you could say there's some competitive aspect to that, *but we got our tip. We're working on it. It's our case.* That doesn't mean to imply that, if the DA found out about it, or if at some point we would tell the DA about it, that we're going to fight over whose case it is. Chances are that if there is a prosecution to be had, it may very well be prosecuted by either us or them jointly. And I don't think there'd be a real conflict about who's going to do it.

As this long response illustrates, there is a degree of tension between the desire to be, or at least to appear to be, cooperative and the desire to get credit for solving a good case. A subtle distinction is drawn between "a sense of competition" and a "lack of cooperation." The former is acceptable, while the latter is not. Thus, communication about a case from a discovering agency to other interested agencies is neither immediate nor automatic. Rather, it is considered carefully and timed so as not to jeopardize the initial agency's stake in the case.

The reasons why information about a good case may be held in confidence during the initial stages of the investigation are understandable. Investigators and prosecutors sometimes do not trust their counterparts in other agencies. They worry that, if the facts of a case become public, other enforcement agencies may initiate their own investigations and prosecutions. The discovering agency would then lose control of the case and perhaps the credit for handling it. Losing control over the case means that one risks losing control over one's investment of time and energy. Quite naturally, many investigators and prosecutors are reluctant to take this risk for reasons which, to them, appear both reasonable and natural. As a prosecutor from New York put it, suspicion of others and a desire to get credit for one's work are part of human nature and an unavoidable part of the reality of the criminal justice system. The prosecutor continued:

There still exists, and I don't know a way around it, there still exists a degree of jealousy between various prosecutorial agencies, and it's hard for me to believe that cards are not held close to the vest when one is in the middle of an investigation of any import. . . . If there was a case of import being investigated, it's unlikely that a call would be made between that investigating agency, prosecutorial agency, to another prosecutorial agency for help, because there would be the old-fashioned theory: well, if you tell them about it, then maybe they're going to go into a grand jury and indict before you get a chance to indict. Now that's reality. That's the human nature thing. . . . I'm not talking about hostilities. I'm not talking about anger. I'm just talking about people saying, "Well, I did all this work, and if they indict, then what was the value of my working for all of those months?" That does exist.

Despite this clear-eyed and unflattering view of the *realpolitik* of the criminal justice system, the strength of the forces promoting competition and lack of cooperation among agencies should not be overestimated. Countervailing forces also operate, and interagency cooperation is not uncommon. Indeed, the prosecutor quoted above also noted that, "at the same time, there are cross-designations, and there is work that is done. It's an area that's evolving all the time." Balancing the sense of competition between agencies and the proprietary interest that enforcement agents have in "their" cases, factors which tend to reduce cooperation and communication, are values held in common by agencies and enforcement personnel. One such common value is the desire to punish those who cause harm to others.

The desire to punish harm doers or, as one investigator put it, "to put the bad guys in jail" is shared throughout the criminal justice system. It is part of the common legal culture of criminal justice and serves to bind agencies together. It promotes a sense of solidarity against a common enemy. Everyone agrees that preventing the continuation of harm and bringing the culpable to justice should be the primary goals of investigation and prosecution. The commitment of enforcement personnel to these shared goals can moderate their natural self-interest in keeping control of their cases. The shared legal norms of harm and blameworthiness promote rationality and consistency in the assessment of cases throughout the justice system. The common objective of making sure that the guilty are caught and punished promotes cooperation among agencies. Ironically, good cases serve as both a source of cohesion and a source of dissension among agencies.

When there are no cases to provide a common focus, interagency relations become more difficult to manage. In Los Angeles, for example, the local prosecutor's office has organized a relatively successful strike force on environmental crime. The strike force involves a large number of law enforcement and regulatory agencies. Even though this strike force has had a number of significant successes, the prosecutor currently in charge of managing it acknowledged the difficulty of maintaining good relations absent specific cases to work on:

There are times when I feel like I'm a parent dealing with a whole bunch of children in terms of some of the rivalries of strike force agencies, but then it gets down to working on specific cases. And we sit down in a room together and we say this is the target—and that's the word we use—and this is what has to be done, and this is what your agency needs to do, and that's what your agency needs to do, and that's by default and also by the fact that this office created the strike force concept. We lead it and we get them to work together. In between those types of meetings there are times when I can't tell them apart from my children in terms of the sibling rivalry. My predecessor, _____, he told me, he said, "You're going to find that you're going to spend a lot of time mediating between the various agencies." And that's true.

The common focus provided by a specific case can align the interests of disparate agencies. If a common focus is missing, rivalries between agencies and personal animosities between individuals are likely to surface, threatening the stability and cohesiveness of the network. Indeed, occasionally it may be counterproductive for the members of a formal network to meet if a specific case does not require the attention of the full network. For example, the prosecutor in charge of the Los Angeles County environmental strike force found that weekly meetings of the entire strike force were not productive. He reduced the frequency of strike force meetings from weekly to monthly. Instead of having the entire strike force meet to discuss cases, he would convene what he referred to as "mini–strike force meetings" involving only three or four agencies working on a specific case. He explained:

It became very clear to me that what was going on is that the major strike force meetings became a weekly coffee klatch where information was exchanged but not much. . . . I also realized quite honestly that I had individuals that don't like one another, who don't trust one another. . . . After the strike force meeting people would come and sit down with me privately and tell me things. I'd say, "Why didn't you say that at the strike force meeting?" [They would respond] "Well, there were people there that I didn't feel comfortable talking in front of." They're human beings and there's paranoia. There's suspicion. There are personal agendas. There are personal animosities.

Another factor that can bring agencies together is the recognition that plenty of cases are available to keep everybody working. Because resources are always limited and usually exceeded by the number of cases, cooperation is seen by some prosecutors and investigators as the only rational response. Failure to cooperate on cases and to communicate about ongoing investigations inevitably results in duplication and waste. The press of cases, then, can make fighting over jurisdiction in any particular case seem irrational. In Chicago, for example, an attorney from the attorney general's office argued that cooperation is the only rational way to extend limited resources:

I think that the only answer is to cooperate to the extent so that everybody's manpower isn't doing the same thing. They can get together and talk about an individual case and decide . . . how it is best sent through the available manpower, so that the crime's being prosecuted but not everybody is investigating the same crime. It's just a waste of time. . . . We should never fight over a particular case in terms of jurisdiction. There's too many cases. Anybody who'd fight over one case isn't doing their job because there's a hundred other cases just like it to go and find. So, make sure that things are being looked at and divide it up. Do it that way.

Despite this prosecutor's view, to say that there are hundreds of cases to divide up is not always accurate. When an investigative or prosecutorial agency begins to look into a new type of crime, good cases may be few and far between. In this situation, the agency cannot take a reactive approach and simply wait for cases to appear. Rather, a more proactive approach to case development must be taken. Taking a proactive approach is particularly necessary in the case of environmental crime, especially if environmental crime is a new area of interest for the local prosecutor. Thus, unlike the investigators and prosecutors who handle consumer fraud types of crimes and who are inundated with cases, those who work in the environmental area tend to engage in more outreach activities. They make special efforts to contact other agencies, particularly regulatory agencies, and to let other agencies know that they are interested in these sorts of cases. As a local prosecutor in Jacksonville, Florida, put it:

Normally in prosecuting cases, even in consumer fraud which you've been looking at, normally we don't have to go out there and drum up cases or drum up victims or complainants. We have more than we know how to handle in most cases. With all the armed robbery cases and drug cases—they're bringing in drugs everyday— it's all we can do to keep up with what they're bringing in. It's that way with every single [type of] crime that I've been associated with . . . except for two areas: environmental crime and public corruption. Those are the two areas where you don't [have a lot of cases]. Even in public corruption you get a lot of people complaining about it. But in environmental crime you just don't get it. And you sit here and you wait for those cases to come in and don't do anything proactive, you'll never get any cases. So we've sort of gone out and we've begged, screamed, whined, moaned, everything you can imagine, to get these people to bring us these cases.

Cooperation Between Regulatory and Criminal Justice Agencies

Cooperation between regulatory and criminal justice agencies raises special problems and considerations. As we noted in chapter 8, criminal justice and regulatory agencies traditionally have been guided by different philosophies on how the law should be enforced. Whereas criminal justice agencies take a penal approach toward law enforcement, regulatory agencies are more prone to adopt a conciliatory stance. The former focuses on punishing wrongdoing; for the latter, improving compliance is the main goal of law enforcement. Networks that involve both criminal justice and regulatory agencies must find ways to bring these different philosophies into alignment.

Besides differences in philosophy, other more practical problems are involved in linking criminal justice and regulatory agencies. One such problem concerns the legal status of police and regulatory agents to conduct searches and to gather evidence of wrongdoing. Regulatory enforcement agents typically have greater latitude than do the police to enter and inspect private property. As part of their normal duties, regulatory enforcement agents usually have the authority to enter a private business for the purpose of conducting routine regulatory inspections. In contrast, the police typically cannot enter a privately owned establishment unless they have a search warrant, probable cause to believe a crime is being committed, or the permission of the owner. But the greater ease with which regulatory agents are able to gather information from private entities comes at a cost. Information that is gathered as part of routine regulatory inspections generally is not admissible in court as evidence of criminal wrongdoing. It would not be acceptable, for example, for a regulatory agent to enter a private business under the pretense of conducting a routine inspection of production processes when his or her real objective was to gather evidence for a criminal prosecution of unsafe working conditions. The point at which an administrative investigation becomes a criminal one must be negotiated carefully.

Another practical problem that arises in networks involving regulatory and criminal justice agencies is evidence handling. The rules governing the handling and processing of evidence that is to be used in a criminal prosecution are elaborate and strict. When the police gather evidence concerning a crime, they must maintain a secure chain of custody. They must be able to document that the evidence in question was handled properly and under police control at all times. Failure to maintain the chain of custody properly may result in charges from defense counsel that the evidence has been tainted and is, therefore, not admissible in court. For most police officers, proper evidence handling procedures are a routine matter. The correct techniques are covered extensively in training and by departmental policies.

Personnel in regulatory agencies, on the other hand, often may not be familiar with the legal concept of chain of custody. An agency's lab technicians may be highly skilled chemical analysts and able to identify the chemical makeup of an unknown substance with great precision. However, if their technical skill is not exercised in accordance with the rules of evidence, it is of little value to the local prosecutor interested in prosecuting someone for illegally disposing of hazardous waste. For example, lab technicians may not realize how carefully they must handle samples after they have been turned in by investigators. It is not enough just to identify the unknown substance. The lab must be able to document that the substance in question did indeed come from the alleged crime site and that no one had an opportunity to tamper with the sample after it was collected. For regulatory agencies to work well in the context of the criminal justice system, they must learn to operate more like traditional police agencies.

It is essential for successful networking for regulatory enforcement personnel to understand the legal constraints under which police and prosecutors work. As regulators become more involved in situations defined as crimes, their role in the investigative process may become ambiguous and a source of conflict with the police. To the consternation of police, regulatory agents may begin to think of themselves as law enforcement agents or as quasi-police. For example, in Los Angeles County, the Public Health Department plays a very active role in the local prosecutor's strike force on environmental crime. A special unit has been created within the department to handle environmental crime situations. The investigators assigned to this unit are encouraged to get involved with all aspects of a potential case and to follow it through to conclusion. In doing so, they occasionally come into conflict with the police over who should be doing what in the investigation. While not considering themselves to be police officers, neither do the agents in the special unit think of themselves as merely regulatory inspectors. As one investigator described it, "We're sort of a hybrid animal in between the two, at least in my department here, and that has brought some problems. Police agencies come saying, 'Hey, you don't do interviews, and you don't do surveillance.' And our response is, 'Yes, we do and we have for a long time.' We just can't get any continuity in our cases if we don't get involved in some of these things."

From the perspective of some police investigators, though, the involvement of regulatory agents in certain aspects of criminal investigations is troubling. It blurs the line between administrative and criminal proceedings. A detective described a situation in which, after cleaning up a hazardous waste spill, inspectors from the health department continued to investigate the case:

They can't talk to the suspect and ask him, "Well, when did you start doing this? When did you start dumping this stuff?" Because then, you know, then you're walking a fine line . . . especially in the state of California. Very, very tough on that situation. And the health department is on a quest to be the all-round toxic cop, and believe me, that's what they want to be. The want to handle it all. They want to be able [to go] from the inspections to the prosecutions. You know, we have some problems with that. Because for one thing, they're not trained to be police officers, and there's a lot of things here in the state of California you have to be a police officer to do. You know, like the search warrant, and things like that, the arrest, you know, the surveillance, things like that. They're getting so much more involved in this situation. And they've crossed that line.

Later in the interview, the officer returned to this issue: "The problem is holding back the other agencies sometimes. Now the health department wants to be in there. They want to be stride by stride with you. And you can't do it. You got to somewhere down the line say, 'You got to do your job. We gotta do ours.' You gotta kind of hold them back somehow."

For local prosecutors, one of the most important potential advantages of strong links with regulatory agencies involves the discovery of cases. In theory, regulatory agencies can be an important source of environmental crime cases for local prosecutors. Regulatory enforcement personnel are in regular contact with potential violators, and they have the expertise to recognize environmental crimes in the making. For regulators to refer criminal environmental cases to local prosecutors would seem to be a simple matter. For a variety of reasons, the transfer of cases from the regulatory to the criminal justice control system is a weak point in the control of environmental crime.

One area of conflict between criminal justice and regulatory officials concerns the timing for transferring cases from the regulatory system to the criminal justice system. From the perspective of local prosecutors and the investigators who work for them, regulatory agencies often are too slow to hand over cases for prosecution. According to those who work in the criminal justice system, regulatory officials are not accustomed to viewing environmental violators as criminals. Their perspective is based on the notion that fixing problems is more important than punishing wrongdoers. Thus, regulatory agents are more inclined to work with environmental violators to solve the underlying problem that led to the violation than they are to pursue criminal sanctions against the violator (Hawkins 1984).

Besides having a regulatory mindset, regulatory agents have another reason to be reluctant to refer cases for prosecution. If criminal proceedings are instituted against a suspected environmental violator, the regulatory agent is likely to be called to provide evidence regarding the case. The proceedings may require the agent to make multiple appearances in court or to sit through lengthy depositions with defense attorneys. Fulfilling these time-consuming legal formalities distracts the regulatory agent from his or her normal professional duties. If criminal proceedings are instituted, the case is likely to drag on for an extended period. A prosecutor in Florida, discussing his relations with local regulatory agencies and the difficulty of getting them to refer cases, noted all of these problems:

We've sort of gone out and we've begged, screamed, whined, moaned, everything you can imagine to get these people to bring us these cases. And the biggest problem with it is not that they want to cover up environmental crimes, that's not true. The problem is that the people that work in these areas are regulators, and they're administratively minded people. Their whole mindset, their whole training and their goals and everything else is just to get the environmental polluter. They don't look at him like a criminal, though. The person who creates the environmental problem, if you get him in and get him to pay fines and to clean up, that's all they care about. They never think about prosecution. As a matter of fact, a lot of them think, "Well, if the prosecutors get involved it may draw out my case longer. I may have to go to court and give depositions and get tied up, and it'll maybe hurt my effectiveness." That's the way they look at it. They don't want to bring up the case.

The problem of timing is not unique, of course, to Florida, though the reasons for the delay in referring cases may be different. In California, for example, regulatory agencies appeared more inclined to undertake criminal proceedings against environmental violators than were their counterparts in Florida. This did not mean, though, that they were quick to refer cases to the local prosecutor's office. Instead, precisely because regulators were interested in criminal cases, they tended to attempt to handle the investigation of potential criminal cases in-house. According to an investigator in the Los Angeles County local prosecutor's office, the result was slowdown and delays in processing that jeopardized the case.

They [regulatory agencies] try to hold on to as many [potential criminal cases] as they can, and every once in a while they'll throw out some bad ones out there, you know, just to relieve themselves of the load. But they're trying to hold on to the good ones. But they're not designed to examine them. They just don't have the manpower to handle even one or two large cases. So they hold on to fifteen or twenty of them, hoping one of them will pan out and be real easy. And they're letting all these others go by the wayside. That's what killing us with some of these other agencies.

The investigator continued, explaining that regulatory agencies tend to be too slow and bureaucratic in their handling of cases. Within the local prosecutor's office, investigations move quickly. Once it is decided that a case warrants prosecution, speed is a priority. But in regulatory agencies, the decision as to whether to go with civil or criminal proceedings is handled more slowly, and the whole process of investigation takes longer. As a result, by the time the case eventually gets to the local prosecutor, too much time has gone by. The investigator went on to say:

The problem with these other people, let's say _____, you start with the inspec-tors, and the supervisor of inspectors, and you get the legal side, and you still don't know if it's going to be criminal. And finally they'll say, "Oh, let's go criminal." Well, then they go to the criminal side. You go to the criminal side's attorney. They look at it and then they pass it on to the investigators. The investigators look at it and start doing some work on it, and they pass it back to the attorney. They look at it again and say, "Ok, now it's lined up." By then nine months have gone by. So by the time we get it, you know, we're on our last legs. We've got to move fast, and in some cases you can't take it. There's no time to permit it.

Yet, from the regulatory point of view, the story has another side. To move fast requires certainty. It requires quick decisions about whether a criminal violation has or has not occurred. From the perspective of regula-tory agents, though, the police sometimes make decisions too quickly. They tend to see the world in absolute terms; either a crime has occurred or it has not. In contrast, regulatory agents are accustomed to recognizing and appreciating degrees of culpability and degrees of harm. They are ac-customed to making more finely grained distinctions between serious and technical violations than do the police. Because they have more training in environmental science and more experience with a broad range of environ-mental violations than do the police, they are better equipped to place indi-vidual instances of violations in perspective and to take a more flexible approach toward handling them. For regulatory agents, environmental en-forcement requires flexibility. To take a dogmatic, crime-busting attitude toward offenders would be neither appropriate nor effective. Police and prosecutors want regulatory agents to be more attuned to potential crimi-nal violations, but regulatory agents want police and prosecutors to be more sensitive to the complexities involved in protecting the environment. A regulator from Los Angeles described the type of person that, from his point of view, is needed in environmental enforcement:

If you have a cop, for instance, or even a health person, or anybody else, who is, you know, twenty years in the marines and sees things only his way, and nobody else's way is right, that person isn't gonna work, because in the environmental field it has to be a personality there that is open to change from what he is traditionally used to. That person and that agency as a whole is going to have to make a lot of adjustments. One of the problems is, for instance, in this whole area of what you're concerned with [is that] as a regulatory agency and sort of a mixed hybrid cop type of person, we can often see the relative degrees of seriousness of the crime, whereas a cop cannot. A cop sees something, a violation, [and] that's all he sees. In his mind, that's [something you take] straight to court, or write a ticket or whatever else he's been doing. And he doesn't see that one guy [dumping] waste oil is not that serious like we see. We have that perspective. We had a case two weeks ago where some sheriff's deputies saw somebody dump a couple of one-gallon cans of some residue that turned out to be latex [paint], and they arrested him. They said, "Call the disposal unit! Get out here right now!" And it's not their fault or anything like that. They just don't have the sense that we do on the degree of seriousness of the crime that occurs.

Thus, a general problem in networks involving regulatory and criminal justice agencies is that of integrating different perspectives. This problem is particularly pronounced in the case of environmental violations committed by ongoing legitimate business concerns in the course of otherwise legitimate business activities. Differences in perspective are less likely to be a problem in the case of a midnight dumper whose business consists of nothing more than providing an illegal dumping service. Consensus on the appropriateness of criminal sanctions for these purely criminal operators is widespread among both regulators and criminal justice officials. But the legitimate businesses that make up the bulk of the regulator's workload are a different matter. In the case of legitimate businesses, local prosecutors tend to view the "regulatory mind-set" as an obstacle to intensified prosecution of environmental crime. They can become frustrated with the willingness of regulators to work with offending businesses and with the cautious, graduated approach taken by regulators toward environmental enforcement. From their perspective, the tendency of regulators to turn to prosecution only as a last resort means that businesses are getting away with crimes that ought to be punished (Hammett and Epstein 1993a, 38–39).

To suggest, though, that the difficulties of network integration arise solely from the unwillingness of regulators to take a tougher stance toward environmental offenders would be a mistake. From the perspective of regulators, their approach works. Most businesses comply with most regulations most of the time. When violations do occur, they usually are minor and easily corrected. Regulators can point to many instances in which they have successfully negotiated and gently coaxed companies into compliance. These successes are the cases that prosecutors never hear about. And therein lies the problem. Success in regulation tends to be less visible than failure (Diver 1980, 274). Prosecutors tend to see only the cases where regulation has failed, and, hence, it is not surprising that they draw the conclusion that regulation is therefore ineffective. When prosecutors learn, after an egregious chemical spill, for example, that the offending business has a history of violations, they quite naturally wonder why the offender was not brought to their attention earlier. Having the advantage of viewing the case in hindsight, they may think it obvious that the graduated regulatory approach was not working and that the offense could have been prevented had strong criminal sanctions been applied earlier. Whether prosecutors are correct in this assessment, of course, would be difficult, if not impossible, to determine. It is easy to identify the repeat offender or career criminal in the middle or latter stages of his career. It is much more difficult to identify early on those who will become repeat offenders, regardless of whether they are street criminals or legitimate businesses.

Those who must make the decision to refer a case from the regulatory to the criminal justice system confront a dilemma familiar to many criminal justice decision makers—especially judges. The dilemma involves predicting the offender's future conduct from past behavior. For example, consider a judge who must decide to sentence an offender either to prison or to probation. If the offender will be deterred from future offending by probation alone, then a prison sentence would be an unnecessary waste of money and prison space, not to mention an unnecessary deprivation of the offender's freedom. On the other hand, if the offender will continue to commit crimes unless he or she is locked up, then a sentence of probation unfairly exposes the community to more harm. Regulators who oversee ongoing legitimate business concerns confront a similar quandary in deciding whether to refer a case for prosecution. Will more lenient administrative sanctions be sufficient to bring an offender into compliance, or will the offender continue to flout the law until confronted with the prospect of criminal sanctions?

Local Prosecutors and Federal Agencies

Both the survey and the case studies strongly suggest that networking is particularly difficult to coordinate between local prosecutors and federal officials. Whether measured by referrals or joint investigations, cooperation between local prosecutors and federal agencies is rare. Analysis of the field study data suggests that local prosecutors are disenchanted with federal agencies. Our questions about how their offices worked with federal agencies often were met with only polite smiles and disclaimers about not wanting to say anything negative. To the extent that we received answers, they suggested that local prosecutors and investigators see federal agencies as uninterested in local problems and intent on pursuing private agendas.

Outright conflict between local and federal agencies is rare and so is strong supportive cooperation. The relationship between local prosecutors and federal agencies is perhaps best characterized as mutually benign neglect. The main reasons for this neglect appear to be scarce resources and different agendas. In Los Angeles, for example, an assistant to the local prosecutor described the relationship between his office and the U.S. Attorney's office as basically cordial but infrequent:

I would characterize the relationship between our office and most of our DAs offices and those agencies as cordial. We have good lines of communication. We pick up the phone and call those agencies. In fact, in some of the agency's cases, and I'm thinking now of the Justice Department Anti-Trust Division with its San Francisco office, which is responsible for California and the Federal Trade Commission, which has L.A. and San Francisco offices responsible for the state, we have . . . a very good working relationship with. We're cordial, pick up the phone, call, exchange case ideas, refer cases back and forth. . . . But there is a very real problem, notwithstanding the basic cordiality and pretty good level of communication. There really are some breakdowns in the way in which the U.S. Attorney's office and our office and offices like ours work together. I think they are not a function of bad will or unwillingness to work collegially. It's a function of very short resources and somewhat differing agendas. The U.S. Attorney's office here in Los Angeles, for example . . . is greatly overburdened. It has enormous responsibilities for drug prosecutions and immigration problems, as the southern district here in California, San Diego, really does as well. They have too few U.S. attorneys.

Because of the shortage of resources, federal agencies, such as the FBI and the U.S. Attorney's offices, tend to have high thresholds for the cases they will accept. The prosecutor quoted above, for example, noted that the U.S. Attorney's office in his area generally required at least a million-dollar loss before it would take on a fraud case. The U.S. Attorney was usually unwilling to investigate or prosecute cases that fell below this threshold and, hence, did not accept referrals from local prosecutors on such cases. What happens to cases that are not accepted for referral by the U.S. Attorney's office depends, of course, largely on the resources and priorities of the local prosecutor. In some situations, the local prosecutor may take on a case refused by the U.S. Attorney, but in others, neither local nor federal prosecutors may be in a position to respond effectively.

Most of the local prosecutors and investigators we interviewed described their relationships with federal agencies in neutral terms, indicating that they had little contact with federal personnel. Yet it was clear that some of our interviewees had a much more negative view of federal agencies. They were particularly skeptical of the willingness of federal agencies to refer cases to local prosecutors. One prosecutor noted:

You don't get a lot of referrals from the U.S. Attorney's office. During my lifetime as a prosecutor, one of the things Justice did to try and stop this black hole is that, if a federal agency investigated a case and there was a determination by the U.S. Attorney that there was no federal jurisdiction, they changed the rules to mandate them to bring it to the attention of the local prosecutor to determine if he wanted it or not. Now I don't know if anybody checks on it to see if it's adhered to or what, but I can count on my hands the number of times that I've had federal investigative agencies say, "The U.S. Attorney doesn't want to do this; do you?"

Another prosecutor made the same point more succinctly:

I don't think you'll find a state court prosecutor anywhere who'll ever tell you that the federal government is doing anything for local prosecution. Most of them will say it's a one-way operation. Information comes up but doesn't come down. Sharing comes up but not down. That's not a criticism of this U.S. Attorney, the U.S. Attorney for the state of Illinois. That's just how the procedure works.

Although we did not find extensive interaction between local prosecutors and federal agencies in the four field sites, cooperation between local prosecutors and federal agencies is not completely lacking. In some instances, local prosecutors do cooperate with federal agencies on joint investigations and prosecutions. The likelihood of cooperation is increased if the crime has multijurisdictional elements. Thus, in Duval County, Florida, for example, a local prosecutor indicated that his office has worked harmoniously with various federal agencies, such as the Postal Inspector's Office, the FBI, and the Secret Service, on multijurisdictional fraud cases. Yet, as this prosecutor noted, positive working relationships with federal agencies may be more the exception than the rule for local prosecutors:

We have a real good rapport with people we work with in the fraud arena at the federal level. It's pretty much open book. If they want our file, they're welcome to it. They give us within the constraints they have what they can give us. That doesn't necessarily permeate the system in terms of the interrelationship, but I've found it to be pretty positive in our area.

Because we found such little networking between federal and local agencies, it is difficult to say much about why it works in one place but not in another. One factor that is helpful to networking success, though, is the presence of someone in the local prosecutor's office who has credibility with federal agencies. In Duval County, for example, the local prosecutor had on staff two retired FBI accountants as fraud investigators. These individuals knew the local federal agents and were, as the prosecutor put it, "a real benefit in terms of keeping the door open and getting and giving assistance." As with networking, in general, the long-term success of local-federal networking probably depends primarily on the development of strong personal ties of trust and respect between individuals in different agencies.

Conclusions

The prosecutors and investigators whom we interviewed routinely remarked on the virtual necessity of interagency cooperation but also noted that it is difficult to initiate and maintain. Because we chose the field study sites in part because they had relatively high levels of cooperation between agencies, it is probably safe to assume that networking problems are even more pronounced in other jurisdictions. Yet, despite all of its difficulties, cooperation between agencies at the local level is common. Most of this cooperation is informal and based on personal relationships between individual investigators, regulatory agents, and assistant prosecutors. Formal networks involving the chief local prosecutor and agency heads are rare.

The interviews suggest to us that formal and informal networks can best serve different purposes. Informal networks are particularly important when it comes to responding to specific cases. Precisely because they are informal, these networks can respond rapidly and flexibly to the many and unpredictable forms of corporate criminal activity. Information about suspected criminal activity can be passed quickly through the network by means of a few quick phone calls. There is no need to take time to convene formal meetings or to prepare official memoranda. Because they have relationships based on trust and compatible working styles, the members of an informal network can work together smoothly. They have fewer reasons to worry about protecting their agency's turf or not getting credit for their work on a case.

Despite the advantages of informal networking, it would be a mistake to rely on this form of interagency cooperation alone. Informal networks have disadvantages, too. One problem is that informal networks may not include all of the agencies that could potentially have an impact on corporate crime. This problem is especially likely to occur with respect to environmental offenses, because so many different types of agencies are, or could be, involved in responding to them. Recall, for example, Los Angeles County's environmental strike force, which involves nearly twenty agencies. That an individual in one of those agencies would have occasion to develop informal contacts in all of the other agencies seems highly unlikely. Thus, informal networks may miss opportunities for interagency cooperation, because all of the relevant agencies may not be connected to the network.

A second problem with informal networking is that it is a reactive rather than proactive strategy toward corporate crime control. Informal networks tend to be case-driven. They are activated when suspected criminal activity somehow comes to light, and they concentrate on solving specific cases. Hence, informal networking provides little in the way of opportunities or incentives for long-range planning or for the identification of new problems.

Formal networks can overcome some of the shortcomings of informal networks. They can legitimize and provide a means for expanding informal networking among agencies that may not have had reason to cooperate with one another in the past. Formal networks can provide opportunities for personnel to meet, interact with, and learn from their counterparts in other agencies. In addition, formal networks can provide a forum for long-range planning and for developing proactive strategies toward corporate crime control. In short, formal and informal networking should be viewed as complementary strategies of corporate crime control.

Note

1. This form of networking is also commonly used against street crimes. Most famous are the task forces that have formed in response to serial killers such as the Green River murderer and that Atlanta child killer.

PART IV

Conclusions
and Policy
Considerations

11

A REVIEW OF MAJOR THEMES AND SUGGESTIONS FOR THE FUTURE

Over the past two decades, corporate crime has emerged as a salient public issue. As part of a broad social movement against white-collar crime (Katz 1980), growing numbers of citizens, lawmakers, and law enforcers have recognized that the illegal conduct of business corporations exacts a heavy toll from its individual, business, and governmental victims (Cullen et al. 1987). Historically, the federal government has assumed primary responsibility for controlling corporate crime, but in recent years state attorneys general and local prosecutors have grown increasingly concerned with this social problem (Edelhertz and Rogovin 1982c). While federal efforts against corporate crime have been the subject of extensive research, we know relatively little about local reactions.

Consequently, we undertook this project to gather national data on what local prosecutors are thinking and doing about corporate crime. We hope that these data will further understanding of the corporate crime problem and help policy makers to assess its seriousness and extent in local jurisdictions. Our results illuminate the obstacles that local prosecutors face in responding to corporate crime and thereby provide a firmer empirical base on which to debate and to establish public policy. In this concluding chapter, we review our major themes and findings, discuss their implications, and make several recommendations for improving the effectiveness of local reactions to corporate crime.

Context and Activity Against Corporate Crime

Criminal justice organizations do not exist in a vacuum. Rather, they operate in a community context. This context influences the number and types of cases they must deal with and the community expectations regarding how cases should be handled (Wilson 1968; Myers and Talarico 1987). The norms, concerns, and activities of local communities shape how local criminal justice organizations operate and the styles of enforcement they employ. Local prosecutors are no exception to this rule. Indeed, because local prosecutors are elected officials, they may be especially sensitive to the concerns and priorities of local constituencies (Cole 1988).

How prosecutors view the direction and seriousness of the corporate crime problem depends a great deal on the size and location of the jurisdictions they serve. Prosecutors located in small or in rural districts tend not to regard corporate crime as a serious problem. They report that, during their tenure in office, the number of prosecutions has remained about the same, and most do not anticipate handling more such cases in the future. But prosecutors located in large districts take a significantly different view. In large districts, three out of four respondents see the corporate crime problem as at least somewhat serious, and one in eight sees it as very serious. A majority of this group also has observed an increase in the number of corporate criminal prosecutions during their tenure in office and anticipates that this trend will continue in the future. These views were particularly prevalent among prosecutors located in large districts in western states.

The influence of population size on how prosecutors perceive the corporate crime problem is predictable. As we showed in chapter 7, population size correlates strongly with the number of business establishments in an area and, hence, with the number of potential corporate offenders. Although we cannot say for certain, we believe that the number of potential offenders is strongly tied to the number of actual offenses committed in any given jurisdiction. It follows that, the greater the number of corporate offenders and offenses, the more likely prosecutors are to view them as a serious problem.

Regional variation in perceptions is not as easy to explain. Prosecutors in the West, regardless of the size of the jurisdiction they serve and presumably the level of corporate crime they encounter, view corporate crime as a more serious problem than do prosecutors in other regions. This difference in perceptions of the corporate crime problem becomes important in light of the data on levels of prosecutorial activity. Western prosecutors are more active against most forms of corporate crime than are other prosecutors. Furthermore, western prosecutors are more likely to have implemented special control procedures. Their attitudes toward the corporate crime problem appear to correlate with higher levels of activity and use of innovative strategies against it. We suggest that, to enhance the capabilities of prosecutors nationwide to respond to corporate crime, policy makers should closely examine the experiences of western prosecutors and try to communicate those experiences to prosecutors in other regions of the country.

However, population size and regional location are not the only factors that influence how active local prosecutors are against corporate crime. Other dimensions of the community context also are important, especially the condition of the local economy and the violent crime rate. Both influence the size and specialization of the prosecutor's office and the resultant level of activity against corporate crime. Prosecutors located in communities that have strong and diversified economies tend to have larger staffs and to have established a special unit for economic crimes. Having a special unit is particularly important, because it leads directly to higher levels of activity against corporate crime. High rates of violent crime, on the other hand, tend to be associated with reduced levels of activity against corporate crime.

To explain the empirical associations between economic conditions, violent crime, and prosecutorial activity against corporate crime, we suggested two related causes: threat and social disorganization. Like other forms of crime, corporate crime can pose a perceived threat to the stability and wellbeing of local communities. A solid and growing body of survey data indicates that many corporate crimes are viewed as very serious and threatening events by the general public (Schrager and Short 1980; Frank et al. 1989; Evans et al. 1993). It is especially likely that offenses against the environment provoke strong public reactions, which are no doubt driven by the potential threats that environmental violations pose to public health. For over two decades, survey research has found that public support for environmental protection is extremely high and widely spread throughout the population (Dunlap 1991; Jones and Dunlap 1992). Furthermore, over the past two decades, there has been a growing awareness that environmental problems pose threats to human health (Dunlap et al. 1993). Because they are elected officials, local prosecutors have been attuned to these developments and responsive to shifts in the concerns and fears of their local constituencies. As the local populace becomes more concerned about corporate crime, so does the local prosecutor. Thus, just as increased levels of threat from street crime can lead to more vigorous efforts to control it, increased levels of threat from corporate crime can lead to stronger governmental reactions.

However, communities are not equal in their ability to respond to the threats posed by crime, regardless of whether it is street crime or corporate crime. Some are more disorganized than others. The link between social disorganization and street crime has been extensively explored and well established (Shaw and McKay 1942; Sampson and Groves 1989). As Sampson and Groves (1989) have shown, economic conditions influence social disorganization, which in turn affects rates of street crime and victimization. We suspect that economic conditions and social disorganization also are related to rates of corporate crime and to the ability of communities to respond to this problem. Residents of communities that are economically disadvantaged and that suffer from high rates of violent street crime may not perceive corporate crime as posing much of a threat, simply because poverty and street crime are more immediate and pressing matters of public concern.[1] In these communities, local prosecutors are less likely to feel pressured by public opinion to do something about corporate crime. Hence, they are not as active against corporate crime as are their counterparts in more well-off, less-troubled, and better-organized communities.

As for the types of corporate crime that local prosecutors are pursuing, the survey revealed some surprising findings. As expected, local prosecutors appear to be most active against economic crimes such as consumer fraud, but a sizable percentage also report handling nonfinancial crimes. In 1988, nearly one out of three local prosecutors in urban areas prosecuted a corporate environmental crime. One out of ten prosecuted a workplace-related offense. These findings confirm the observation made over a decade ago by Edelhertz and Rogovin (1982c) that local prosecutors are moving beyond simple economic crimes to take on more complex and potentially more harmful corporate offenses.

These survey results suggest that programs to enhance the capabilities of local prosecutors to deal with environmental and workplace-related offenses would find a receptive audience. Our interviews in the field also support this idea. The prosecutors, investigators, and regulators we interviewed felt that these offenses were important and that local law enforcement could play a more active role in their containment. With respect to environmental crimes, the interviewees noted, in particular, a need for better access to laboratory resources to identify toxic materials quickly. Quick identification was seen as important not only for the obvious reason of protecting public health and safety but also to help build prosecutable cases in a timely manner. Prosecutors complained that, when they have to wait months for laboratory results, cases grow cold and become more difficult to prosecute successfully.

Goals, Constraints, and Legal Culture

Although local prosecutors strongly believe in the general deterrent effects of corporate criminal prosecutions, not all cases that come to light are brought before a grand jury or judge. In many instances, prosecutors elect not to file charges or, after charges are filed, not to bring cases to trial. These decisions are made on a case-by-case basis and in light of more or less unique sets of facts. Nevertheless, both the survey and the field studies permit some generalizations about the exercise of prosecutorial discretion in corporate cases.

According to the survey respondents, the decision not to prosecute is shaped primarily by legal and resource constraints. Lack of cooperation from victims, the availability of alternative regulatory remedies, insufficient investigatory personnel, and the difficulty of establishing *mens rea* in a corporate criminal context all were cited by large majorities of the respondents as factors that would limit their willingness to prosecute a corporate criminal offense. Conspicuous by their relative insignificance were the community context factors often thought to militate against prosecution of corporate wrongdoing. Very few respondents reported that insufficient public support or a potential negative impact on the local economy would limit their willingness to proceed against a corporate criminal offender.

A similar picture was revealed by the field interviews. Prosecutors and investigators often spoke at length about the difficulty of successfully prosecuting corporate cases without sufficient technical and personnel resources. Clearly, they desired to do more, but the reality of limited resources prevented them from doing so. In brief, local prosecutions of corporate crimes are relatively rare not because local officials regard these offenses as harmless violations of technical regulations or as someone else's problem but, rather, because the offenses at times are simply too complex and difficult to handle.

Besides legal and resource constraints, decision making in corporate cases also is shaped by what we called a common legal culture of prosecution. This culture is based on three core norms. First, offenses should be treated according to the *harm* they produce. Second, offenders should be treated according to the *blameworthiness* of their actions. And third, taken together, harm and blameworthiness constitute the *seriousness* of a case. Stanton Wheeler and colleagues argue that these unwritten norms guide federal judges in sentencing white-collar offenders (Wheeler et al. 1988). We suggest that they also guide how investigators and prosecutors evaluate corporate crime cases. Indeed, we suggest that these norms permeate the entire criminal justice system and, to a lesser degree, the regulatory system as well.

This common legal culture serves two important functions. One function is to provide a common vantage point from which actors in different agencies and positions in the criminal justice and regulatory systems evaluate corporate crime cases. Hence, it is a source of consistency in the treatment of offenses and offenders. This consistency is not universal in the sense that corporate cases are everywhere treated the same. What counts as a serious case in one community may be regarded as much less serious in another. Even so, within jurisdictions there is informal consensus on how cases should be treated and on the types of cases that deserve to be prosecuted. The consensus is strongest among criminal justice agencies. Regulatory agencies are more inclined to view prosecution as a last resort, and the proportion of cases they would consider for prosecution is smaller than would be found among criminal justice agencies. Yet, there are cases on which everyone agrees.

The common legal culture also motivates agencies to cooperate with one another. It provides a sense of collective purpose to the disparate agencies that make up the criminal justice and regulatory systems. For many reasons, though, it is not in the interest of agencies to cooperate with one another, and the power of organizational self-interest should never be dismissed lightly. But neither should it be regarded as an insurmountable obstacle to interagency cooperation. In all of the field sites we visited, we found considerable informal networking and cooperation among local prosecutors' offices, law enforcement organizations, and regulatory agencies. The survey data also indicated that many local prosecutors work with state and local regulatory agencies on a regular basis. We suggest that one reason why agencies can and do work together despite their often competing interests is that they share a common perspective on corporate offenses. Because they have similar perspectives on how cases should be evaluated, personnel from different agencies can agree about the cases which deserve to be investigated and prosecuted. If it is agreed that a case is serious and that something needs to be done about it, then it becomes more difficult for agencies to put self-interest ahead of serving the public good. As the prosecutor in charge of Los Angeles County's environmental strike force noted, once a target is identified and agreed upon, rivalries are set aside and interagency cooperation begins.

Networking

Successful prosecution of corporate crime cases often requires the coordinated efforts of multiple agencies. Because corporate crimes often are hidden behind ordinary business routines, the prosecutor's traditional source of information about crime—reports from victims—is less reliable for corporate crime than for traditional street crime. Indeed, without the efforts of regulatory agencies, some corporate crimes would never be discovered. Once discovered, corporate crimes can be difficult to investigate because of the complexity of the evidence involved and the ability of business entities to hire lawyers to legally obstruct the investigative process. In addition, corporate crimes sometimes cross jurisdictional lines, as when telemarketers set up shop in one state but make calls to other states or when toxic waste generated in one county is illegally disposed of in another. For all of these reasons, local prosecutors are ill-equipped to undertake a concerted effort against corporate crime by themselves. Accordingly, the importance of networking in the fight against corporate crime has long been recognized and promoted.

Both the survey and the field study data indicate that, to some extent, local prosecutors have heard and responded to the call for greater use of networking. Informal networking appears to be quite common, although formal networking arrangements are still more the exception than the rule. The survey revealed that less than 8 percent of prosecutors located in urban districts belong to an interagency task force or strike force devoted to economic or white-collar types of crimes.[2] Although formal networks are rare, evidence indicates that on an informal basis there is substantial interagency contact at the local level. Nearly 65 percent of the survey respondents said that they work with state regulatory agencies on joint investigations of corporate crimes; 56 percent work with prosecutors from other jurisdictions; and 61 percent work with the state attorney general's office.

In the field study sites, prosecutors also told us that they routinely call upon personnel from a variety of different state and local agencies to help them with corporate offenses. From the field studies, we learned about the importance of winning cases in keeping networks alive. Formal networks that do not have a steady supply of important and winable cases are difficult to maintain. Participants in formal networks must believe that their contribution matters and that, for their contribution, they get something in return. Successfully closing a case is the most sought-after reward.

Informal networking is common among local and state agencies, but networking of any sort with federal agencies is rare. The survey revealed that relatively few local prosecutors receive referrals from federal agencies and few work with federal agencies on joint investigations. Our interviews in the field study sites painted the same picture. Local prosecutors simply do not interact much with federal regulatory agencies, the FBI, or the U.S. Attorney's office. Taken together, the survey and the field study results suggest that federal agencies are perceived by local prosecutors and investigators as unhelpful and as largely uninterested in local problems. For some local prosecutors, the apparent reluctance of federal agencies to get involved with local corporate crime problems is understandable. Federal agencies, they believe, have scarce resources and different priorities. Other local prosecutors take a less charitable view. They think that federal agencies are simply more interested in protecting their turf than they are in helping to solve local corporate crime problems. Regardless which of these views is more accurate, the relative paucity of local-federal networking is troubling. Despite the growing recognition of the seriousness of corporate crime and the widespread knowledge that traditional methods of law enforcment are inadequate against this type of crime, the development of coordinated, multistrategy federal, state, and local responses to corporate crime remains only an ideal and not a reality.

The Prosecutor as Problem Solver

Up to this point, we have tried to describe and explain what local prosecutors currently are thinking and doing about corporate crime. Because there is so little research on local prosecutors and corporate crime, we have concentrated on presenting as much empirical data, both quantitative and qualitative, as possible. Our goal has been to get a clear picture of the attitudes and activities of local prosecutors in regard to corporate crime. In the remaining pages of this book, we turn from examining the contemporary state of affairs to addressing the future.

The prosecutors we interviewed strongly supported the traditional view that their job is to seek criminal convictions and the imposition of appropriate penal sanctions on offenders. Their concern that the guilty be convicted and punished has multiple symbolic and practical justifications. Conviction and punishment function together to make a moral statement about the nature of illegal acts and to vindicate the rule of law; they help satisfy the victims' and the community's need for retribution; and finally, they may deter the convicted offender from committing future crimes as well as other potential offenders contemplating similar crimes (Goldstock 1991, 2).

Yet, while the interviews clearly show that, for most prosecutors, the primary goal is to deter corporate crime by convicting corporate criminals, a broader, more flexible conceptualization of the prosecutor's role in the criminal process also emerged. In this broader view, the reduction of criminal activity is seen as a central function of the prosecutor's role and not as merely a hoped-for by-product of the punishment process. This broader view requires prosecutors to move beyond thinking of themselves as mere presenters of evidence in court and to focus on how best to control criminal activity. It means concentrating on solving problems as opposed to merely enforcing the law (Goldstock 1991). Admittedly, this approach to the corporate crime problem is more the exception than the rule. Nevertheless, we found scattered evidence that such a view may be emerging among local prosecutors.

An example of this approach to corporate crime control, which took place at one of the field sites, involved a well-respected corporation that violated a state law governing the transportation and disposal of toxic materials. The prosecutor had sufficient evidence to pursue a criminal indictment. Yet, after an investigation indicated that this was an isolated incident, he elected not to do so. Instead, he negotiated an agreement with the company in which the corporation paid a substantial civil fine, donated money to a local hazardous waste project, and paid for the entire cost of the investigation. The monies from the civil fine then were used to fund a conference on environmental problems attended by law enforcement and regulatory officials. This case illustrates an innovative use of a prosecutor's office to achieve multiple objectives not all directly related to curbing or punishing the behavior of a particular offender. The prosecutor hoped to achieve both deterrence and educational objectives. Other corporations in the area would learn of and be deterred by the civil fine. Environmental awareness among local officials was fostered by the conference. In effect, ameliorating the problem of corporate environmental violations took precedence over enforcing the law against a particular offender.

This approach, which Goldstock (1991) has labeled "the prosecutor as problem solver," may be especially appropriate for corporate crime. Cases are difficult, time-consuming, and costly to investigate and prosecute successfully. These constraints make it unlikely that prosecutors will be able to raise the certainty of punishment, instrumental for achieving general deterrent effects, by any noticeable amount. By reconceptualizing their approach to the problem of corporate crime, however, prosecutors may be able to affect criminal activity in other ways. For example, one prosecutor we interviewed related how he had given a talk at a meeting of safety engineers. By explaining their legal responsibilities and liabilities, he not only motivated the safety engineers to attend more closely to worker safety but also gave them important information with which to lobby corporate leaders for more resources for worker safety programs.

The potential purposes to which the office of prosecutor can be put are tied to the range of available sanctions. For example, a prosecutor noted that, if corporate probation were available as a sentencing option, it could be used to solve problems or rectify dangerous situations. He used the example of an unsafe nursing home. The home should not be allowed to operate in an unsafe manner, but prosecuting the owners and closing it down would cause a lot of hardship for the patients and their families. If, however, the corporation could be put on probation, it might be possible to arrange supervision so that the patients receive proper care and are not inconvenienced by closure.

We do not recommend that local prosecutors be encouraged to abandon the criminal law as a means of corporate crime control. Criminal conviction and the imposition of penal sanctions are both appropriate and necessary in many instances of corporate wrongdoing. Nevertheless, it should be recognized that perhaps the most important function that criminal penalties can serve in the control of corporate crime is to give local prosecutors leverage to pursue other crime-reducing initiatives with the business community.

Suggestions for Improving Local Responses to Corporate Crime

The prosecutors, investigators, and regulatory officials whom we interviewed at the field study sites had a number of suggestions for improving their ability to handle corporate crimes. Some of their suggestions related specifically to their particular jurisdictions; others were more general and could be usefully applied in many jurisdictions. The suggestions can be divided into two broad categories, according to the level of government or organization at which they can be most feasibly implemented. The first category involves programs and initiatives that would require funding and organization at the national or regional level to be successful. Most likely beyond the capability of any one jurisdiction or even a state to implement in a cost-effective manner, these recommendations could have a national impact on the control of corporate crime. The second set of recommendations can be implemented by individual jurisdictions. In some cases, they are based on practices that seemed to be successful at one or more of the field study sites and that could be used in other jurisdictions. Others are based on ideas that the experienced practitioners we interviewed felt would help improve their efficiency and effectiveness. Taken together, implementation of the national and local recommendations would help to improve the effectiveness of local control of corporate and business-related crime.

National Recommendations

1. *Establish regional laboratories to help local prosecutors investigate and prosecute environmental offenses.* The federal government should investigate the feasibility of setting up regional laboratories to analyze chemical and environmentally related evidence. The laboratories would provide techni-

cal support for local law enforcers by analyzing and identifying chemical samples quickly. State-of-the-art laboratory facilities are too expensive for local jurisdictions, or even the individual states in which they are located, to afford on their own. In addition, the number of times per year that the laboratory may be needed in any given jurisdiction probably would not justify the cost. Regional laboratories that served a multitude of local jurisdictions would make economic sense and would permit local prosecutors to respond to cases that federal agencies may deem as too small or too local in impact to take on. Another advantage of regional laboratories is that they might reduce the number of instances in which cases fall through the cracks because of conflict over goals and procedures among local agencies. They could also provide training for local prosecutors and others in this technically complex area of law enforcement.

These laboratories would provide state-of-the-art and timely testing services for local prosecutors. They would be most useful in cases of illegal disposal or handling of toxic wastes and other potentially harmful chemical materials. Successful investigation and prosecution of these sorts of environmental crimes often depends upon rapid and accurate identification of chemical materials. The expertise to accomplish these tasks often is beyond the capabilities of the traditional crime laboratory facilities available to local prosecutors. Hence, at present prosecutors often must make ad hoc arrangements for testing with other agencies. While these agencies may be willing to do what they can, they ordinarily are not familiar with proper evidence handling procedures, and they have other important work priorities. Evidence may not be handled in a timely and proper manner. Regional laboratories devoted to providing testing services would give prosecutors access to technical expertise in chemical analysis and evidence handling. The public safety implications of rapid testing are obvious.

The laboratories most likely would have to be funded either by the federal government or perhaps by regional combinations of state governments. Although concern over environmental crimes is growing and the threat posed by such offenses is serious, the number of cases likely to occur in any single jurisdiction would not justify the cost of a state-of-the-art facility. Yet, the offenses that do occur need to be handled expeditiously. The questions of whether the laboratories should be funded in part or wholly by user fees and which agencies should have access to services need further investigation and policy analysis. Regional laboratories would reduce unnecessary and expensive duplication of effort among agencies and may help to overcome situations of local interagency rivalries and lack of cooperation.

2. *Establish a national brief bank and information clearinghouse on prosecuting corporate crime.* A brief bank and information clearinghouse would permit local prosecutors to benefit from the collective experience and knowledge of prosecutors nationwide. It is one way in which the experience and wisdom of prosecutors located in larger urban centers can be communicated to their counterparts in smaller jurisdictions. It is well known that corporate offenders often have the financial resources to hire well-financed and well-staffed law firms to defend them against criminal indictments and prosecution. With virtually unlimited financial and legal personnel resources at their disposal, corporate criminals can erect stiff legal obstacles for prosecutors to overcome. While many of the legal challenges raised by corporate defendants can be successfully met, it is expensive and time-consuming to do so. This is especially true for prosecutors who are facing these challenges for the first time. A brief bank would help inexperienced prosecutors respond to these objections. In effect, a brief bank would level the playing field between large corporate law firms and individual local prosecutors. Corporate law firms would have to contend with the collective experience of local prosecutors nationwide instead of just an isolated and overworked assistant district attorney. A brief bank and clearinghouse would be especially useful in helping prosecutors respond to such relatively new areas as environmental and workplace-related crimes.

The clearinghouse could also handle information on alternative sanctions and innovative sentencing. It could acquaint prosecutors nationwide with innovative techniques tried in other jurisdictions.

3. *Establish a program of internships and personnel exchanges between federal and state regulatory agencies and between regulatory agencies and local prosecutors.* The primary benefit of such exchanges is that they would permit agencies to learn of one another's jurisdiction, mandate, standard operating procedures, and problems. With such knowledge, personnel in involved agencies would be in a better position to share information and to recognize when situations should be referred to another agency. While it is well known that such information sharing and case referrals are crucial elements of networking as a crime control strategy, the survey and field study show that there is relatively little cooperation between federal agencies and local prosecutors. A federally sponsored program of interagency internships and exchanges may help increase the level of interaction and

cooperation. The interviews suggested that criminal matters may all too often fall through cracks in the system simply because they are discovered by an agency that has no interest or mandate to pursue them. To the extent that agencies at all levels of government learn about one another, the likelihood increases that potential criminal cases will be referred to an appropriate agency.

Local Recommendations

1. *Recruit prosecutors and investigatory personnel who have an interest in environmental, workplace-safety–related, or other corporate crime prosecutions.* Environmental and workplace-related investigations and prosecutions require special knowledge and expertise. It is easier to develop expertise if one has a personal interest in environmental issues. Yet, in many jurisdictions, assistant district attorneys are recruited with little attention to the types of crimes they may be called on to prosecute. The career path envisioned by new assistants often leads toward the prosecution of serious street crimes. The new assistant assigned to an environmental crime unit may view it as a temporary diversion from his or her real professional goals and not be inclined to develop expertise in the area. As a result, financial and personnel resources may not be used very effectively. By recruiting attorneys with a personal interest in environmental issues, local prosecutors can ensure more effective use of their limited resources.

2. *Create a local area computer network linking agencies, so that investigators can find out quickly if someone in another agency is working a case.* Computers are playing an increasingly important role in law enforcement, and many law enforcement agencies now use computers for record keeping and case management. By accessing computer files, an investigator can quickly learn whether someone else in the agency is working a particular case, thus reducing duplication of effort and facilitating information sharing. However, the full potential of computers to reduce duplication of effort and to increase information sharing among investigators in *different* agencies has not yet been realized. At present, while many agencies have their own computer database of their cases, they have no way of knowing what other agencies are working on. To find out, investigators have to call their counterparts in other agencies. Not surprisingly, such calls often do not get made. Such linkages between agencies in a given area may be particularly important in putting together cases against certain kinds of financial frauds, where victims are spread out and offenders very mobile.

A local area computer network linking agencies would permit investigators in one agency easier access to their counterparts in another agency. Agencies could be linked to a common database of ongoing investigations and cases. The database entries would contain information on the investigator (e.g., name, phone number, and agency) and information on the case (e.g., suspects, modi operandi, and victims). In theory, such a network would permit investigators to learn whether an investigator in another agency in their area was working a case involving particular suspects or a particular modus operandi. In situations where investigators have information on what may be the same case, they could then contact one another directly and coordinate their activities. Such a network would be particularly useful in the largest urban areas, where multiple agencies in different jurisdictions often work in close geographical proximity.

Many technical details would require careful consideration. For example, problems involving access, confidentiality, and hardware compatibility undoubtedly will arise. But these problems are not, in principle, unsolvable. For example, files could be set up so that only the investigator establishing or entering a case in the database could alter information pertaining to it, but other investigators would be able to read the file. Further, all those accessing a file could be required to identify themselves and to have security clearances.

3. *Educate the public as to whom to contact and make it easier for citizens to report corporate crimes.* Effective law enforcement ultimately depends on the support of a concerned citizenry willing to become involved in making the community safer. Public concern over environmental pollution and environmental safety clearly is rising. Local prosecutors and other law enforcement agencies should take advantage of these rising levels of concern by publicizing their activities against corporate environmental crimes. They should make sure that the public knows that environmental crimes are real crimes and educate the public on how to identify and report such crimes.

4. *Increase the number of prosecutors and investigators assigned full time to environmental, workplace-related, and other corporate offenses.* Local prosecutors and law enforcement agencies always have limited resources. During economic downturns, personnel and financial resources often are reduced by state and local governments in response to fiscal emergencies. Nevertheless, it is clear from the interviews that, to be effective against complex corporate environmental and workplace-related crimes, more

prosecutors and investigators need to be assigned full time to such cases. The same is true of regulatory agencies.

5. *Assign investigators to environmental regulatory agencies so that they can cull through cases to identify the ones that should be brought to the attention of prosecutors.* A continuing problem in relationships between local prosecutors and environmental regulatory agencies is that regulatory personnel often are unfamiliar with the types of cases that deserve to be brought to the attention of prosecutors. By assigning investigators trained in criminal environmental investigations to work in regulatory agencies, prosecutors can ensure that prosecutable cases are identified and that agency personnel are sensitized to the prosecutor's priorities. Equally important, establishing a close working relationship between criminal investigators and regulatory officials may spur the use of innovative problem-solving approaches to corporate crime control, thereby reducing overreliance on criminal controls.

6. *Provide more technical training for environmental investigators.* Insofar as possible, investigators assigned to environmental crimes need regular retraining in technical matters. Industrial production and manufacturing techniques continually change, posing new threats to environmental safety. To keep up with these changes, local prosecutors should not overlook the importance of regular training and retraining for their investigators.

Final Thoughts

Criminologists and others have written much about the control of corporate crime and the need to bring corporations within reach of the criminal law (Braithwaite 1982; Geis 1972, 1985; Schlegel 1990; Stone 1975). Yet, except for a handful of case studies, criminologists have largely neglected to study the role of local prosecutors in controlling corporate illegality. This neglect is surprising. In America, criminal justice is predominately a local responsibility, and the local prosecutor is widely recognized as the most powerful person in the local criminal justice system. This is not to deny the importance of federal authorities in the control of corporate crime and the regulation of corporate conduct. Federal prosecutors surely are best suited to respond to the really big cases, such as those that involve major national or multinational corporations or that spread across multiple jurisdictions and harm thousands of victims. But the federal system has its limits. Federal authorities cannot be expected to, and in actual practice do not, respond to the vast majority of smaller-scale corporate crimes. Local prosecutors can and do play a meaningful role in controlling these far more numerous, routine, ordinary offenses.

Whether to regard the current rate of local prosecutions as high or low is, of course, a matter of opinion. We suspect that local prosecutors are conducting more prosecutions of fraud and environmental offenses now than at any time in the past. Further, we suspect that, despite the incredible drain on local resources caused by the war on drugs and the rise in violence among young people, the number of corporate prosecutions will continue to grow. One reason for this is that it is likely that these and other types of white-collar offenses will become more common in the future. The cultural and structural conditions conducive to corporate crime certainly are strongly present in American society. On the one hand, there is the unrelenting pressure of the American dream—that is, our materialistic value system that rewards economic affluence above all else (Messner and Rosenfeld 1994). This value system exerts its criminogenic effects not only on the lower classes but also on the "broad middle of American society" (Weisburd et al. 1991, 184). Small businessowners and those who run the multitudinous small to medium-sized corporations in America are not immune to its effects, and it is from their ranks that the majority of locally handled corporate offenders emerge. Economic motivation for crime is built into American culture.

On the other hand, opportunities for fraud and dishonesty within organizational settings are increasing, giving more people "greater access to the white-collar world of paper fraud" (Weisburd et al. 1991, 183). Small companies represent the fastest growing sector of the American economy. They face an extremely competitive economic environment, where the difference between success and failure often is measured in just a few percentage points of profitability. The auto repair shop owner who makes a few dollars more by billing for repairs that were unnecessary or never made has an advantage over law-abiding competitors. So does the metal-plating plant operator who cuts operating costs by illegally disposing of hazardous waste. As the number of small to medium-sized businesses increases, the number of potential corporate offenders will increase automatically, and in all likelihood, so will the number of offenses. Cultural emphasis on the value of economic affluence combines with the competitive pressures faced by businesses to act, pincer-like, as complementary sources of corporate crime.

Of course, there is no simple one-to-one correspondence between corporate offenses and corporate crime prosecutions on the local level. As we have tried to demonstrate throughout this book, contextual factors influence local reactions to corporate crime. Nevertheless, there are reasons to suspect that an increase in corporate offenses will be met over time with a more or less corresponding increase in local prosecutions. For one thing, the federal government is likely to play a smaller role in corporate crime control in the future than it has in the past. Efforts to balance the federal budget and to downsize the federal workforce inevitably will reduce federal resources available to monitor corporate conduct. In addition, efforts to shift responsibility for programs from the federal government to the states will likely continue. As the federal government scales back, local prosecutors along with other local and state officials will increasingly be called upon to take the initiative against social problems like corporate crime.

The pressure for local officials to keep an eye on corporate misconduct will come from local communities unwilling to put up with either fraud or pollution. While fraud has long been recognized as a straightforward criminal offense, environmental pollution is increasingly being seen in criminal terms. As knowledge of the dangers posed by environmental pollution grows among ordinary citizens, there will be less tolerance for companies that pollute. The evidence clearly indicates that local prosecutors are handling increasing numbers of criminal environmental offenses (Hammett and Epstein 1993a; Rebovich and Nixon 1994). We suspect that this is happening because environmental violations are now being defined in terms of traditional concepts of harm and blameworthiness by both prosecutors and the general public. The social context and legal culture surrounding corporate conduct are changing. In response to this change, local prosecutors will experience increased pressure to prosecute corporate criminals.

Notes

1. Although the connection between economic conditions and perceptions of social problems such as the environment is complex, there is evidence that support for environmental regulation is contingent on economic conditions. Support for stronger governmental regulations tends to decrease during recessions and to increase when the economy is stable or growing (Jones, forthcoming).

2. More recent evidence suggests that this situation may be improving. At least with respect to environmental crimes, more local prosecutors now appear to be involved in formal networks (Rebovich and Nixon 1994).

REFERENCES

Abrams, Norman. 1980. "Assessing the Federal Government's War on White Collar Crime." *Temple Law Review* 53:984–1008.

American Bar Association. 1970. *Standards Relating to the Prosecution Function and the Defense Function*. Chicago: American Bar Association.

Bardach, Eugene, and Robert A. Kagan. 1982. *Going by the Book*. Philadelphia: Temple University Press.

Barnett, Harold. 1981. "Wealth, Crime and Capital Accumulation." In *Crime and Capitalism*, edited by David Greenberg, 182–88. Palo Alto, Calif.: Mayfield.

Becker, Howard S. 1963. *Outsiders: Studies in the Sociology of Deviance*. New York: Free Press.

Benson, Michael L. 1985. "Denying the Guilty Mind: Accounting for Involvement in a White-Collar Crime." *Criminology* 23:583–607.

Benson, Michael L., and Esteban Walker. 1988. "Sentencing the White-Collar Offender." *American Sociological Review* 53:294–302.

Benson, Michael L., William J. Maakestad, Francis T. Cullen, and Gilbert Geis. 1988. "District Attorneys and Corporate Crime: Surveying the Prosecutorial Gatekeepers." *Criminology* 26:505–18.

Bequai, August. 1978. *White-Collar Crime: A 20th-Century Crisis*. Lexington, Mass.: Lexington Books.

Bernstein, Marver H. 1955. *Regulating Business by Independent Commission*. Princeton, N.J.: Princeton University Press.

Bittner, Egon. 1980. *The Functions of the Police in Modern Society*. Cambridge: Oelgeschlager, Gunn, and Hain.

Box, Steven. 1987. *Recession, Crime and Punishment*. Totowa, N.J.: Barnes and Noble.

Box, Steven, and Chris Hale. 1982. "Economic Crises and the Rising Prisoner Population in England and Wales." *Crime and Social Justice* 17:20–35.

Braithwaite, John. 1982. "The Limits of Economism in Controlling Harmful Corporate Conduct." *Law and Society Review* 16:481–504.

———. 1982. "Enforced Self-Regulation: A New Strategy for Corporate Crime Control." *Michigan Law Review* 80:1466–1507.

———. 1985a. *To Punish or Persuade: Enforcement of Coal Mine Safety*. Albany, N.Y.: State University of New York Press.

———. 1985b. "White-Collar Crime." *Annual Review of Sociology* 11:1–25.

———. 1989. *Crime, Shame, and Reintegration*. Cambridge: Cambridge University Press.

Brickey, Kathleen. 1984. *Corporate Criminal Liability*. Wilmette, Ill.: Callaghan & Co.

Brint, Steven. 1984. "'New Class' and Cumulative Trend Explanations of the Liberal Political Attitudes of Professionals." *American Journal of Sociology* 90:30–71.

Brodeur, Paul. 1985. *Outrageous Misconduct.* New York: Pantheon.

Bursik, Robert. 1988. "Social Disorganization and Theories of Crime and Delinquency: Problems and Prospects." *Criminology* 26:519–51.

Cable, Sherry, and Michael Benson. 1993. "Acting Locally: Environmental Injustice and the Emergence of Grassroots Environmental Organizations." *Social Problems* 40:464–77.

Calavita, Kitty, and Henry N. Pontell. 1990. "'Heads I Win, Tails You Lose': Deregulation, Crime, and Crisis in the Savings and Loan Industry." *Crime and Delinquency* 36: 309–41.

Chamlin, Mitchell B. 1992. "Intergroup Threat and Social Control: Welfare Expansion among States during the 1960s and 1970s." In *Social Threat and Social Control,* edited by Allen E. Liska, 151–64. Albany, N.Y.: State University of New York Press.

Clinard, Marshall B. 1946. "Criminological Theories of Violations of Wartime Regulations." *American Sociological Review* 11:258–70.

———. 1983. *Corporate Ethics and Crime.* Beverly Hills: Sage.

Clinard, Marshall B., and Richard Quinney. 1973. *Criminal Behavior Systems: A Typology.* New York: Holt, Rinehart, and Winston.

Clinard, Marshall B., and Peter C. Yeager. 1980. *Corporate Crime.* New York: Free Press.

Coffee, John C. 1981. "'No Soul to Damn, No Body to Kick': An Unscandalized Inquiry into the Problem of Corporate Punishment." *Michigan Law Review* 79:386–459.

Cole, George F. 1970. "The Decision to Prosecute." *Law and Society Review* 4:313–43.

———. 1988. "Prosecution." In *Criminal Justice: Law and Politics,* edited by George F. Cole, 5th ed. 149–59, Pacific Grove, Calif.: Brooks/Cole.

Coleman, James W. 1987. "Toward an Integrated Theory of White-Collar Crime." *American Journal of Sociology* 93:406–39.

———. 1989. *The Criminal Elite: The Sociology of White-Collar Crime.* 2d ed. New York: St. Martin's Press.

———. 1994. *The Criminal Elite: The Sociology of White-Collar Crime.* 3d ed. New York: St. Martin's Press.

Conklin, John E. 1977. *"Illegal but Not Criminal": Business Crime in America.* Englewood Cliffs, N.J.: Prentice-Hall.

Cressey, Donald R. 1953. *Other People's Money.* New York: Free Press.

Cullen, Francis T., and Paula J. Dubeck. 1985. "The Myth of Corporate Immunity to Deterrence: Ideology and the Creation of the Invincible Criminal." *Federal Probation* 49:3–9.

Cullen, Francis T., Bruce Link, and C. Polanzi. 1982. "The Seriousness of Crime Revisited: Have Attitudes towards White-Collar Crime Changed?" *Criminology* 20:83–102

Cullen, Francis T., William J. Maakestad, and Gray Cavendar. 1987. *Corporate Crime under Attack.* Cincinnati, Ohio: Anderson.

Davis, Kenneth C. 1969. *Discretionary Justice: A Preliminary Inquiry.* Baton Rouge, La.: Louisiana State University Press.

Dawson, John M. 1992. *Prosecutors in State Courts, 1990.* Washington, D.C.: Bureau of Justice Statistics.

Dillman, Don A. 1978. *Mail and Telephone Surveys: The Total Design Method.* New York: John Wiley and Sons.

Diver, Colin S. 1979. "The Assessment and Mitigation of Civil Money Penalties in Federal Administrative Agencies." *Columbia Law Review* 79:1435–1502.

————. 1980. "A Theory of Regulatory Enforcement." *Public Policy* 28:257–99.

Dowrie, Mark. 1987. "Pinto Madness." In *Corporate Violence,* edited by Stuart L. Hills, 13–29. Totowa, N.J.: Rowman and Littlefield.

Dunlap, Riley E. 1991. "Trends in Public Opinion toward Environmental Issues: 1965–1990." *Society and Natural Resources* 4:285–312.

Dunlap, Riley E., George H. Gallup Jr., and Alec M. Gallup. 1993. "Of Global Concern: Results of the Health of the Planet Survey." *Environment* 35:7–38.

Eckstein, Otto, Christopher Caton, Roger Brinner, and Peter Duprey. 1984. *The DRI Report on U.S. Manufacturing Industries.* New York: McGraw-Hill.

Edelhertz, Herbert. 1970. *The Nature, Impact and Prosecution of White-Collar Crime.* Washington, D.C.: U.S. Department of Justice.

Edelhertz, Herbert, and Charles H. Rogovin, eds. 1982a. *A National Strategy for Containing White-Collar Crime.* Lexington, Mass.: Lexington Books.

————. 1982b. "Implementing a National Strategy." In *A National Strategy for Containing White-Collar Crime,* edited by Herbert Edelhertz and Charles H. Rogovin, 103–11. Lexington, Mass.: Lexington Books.

————. 1982c. "Symposium Background." In *A National Strategy for Containing White-Collar Crime,* edited by Herbert Edelhertz and Charles Rogovin, 11–18. Lexington, Mass.: Lexington Books.

Epstein, Joel, and Theodore M. Hammett. 1995. *Law Enforcement Response to Environmental Crime.* Washington, D.C.: National Institute of Justice.

Ermann, M. David, and Richard J. Lundman, eds. 1992. *Corporate and Governmental Deviance.* 4th ed. New York: Oxford University Press.

Evans, T. David, Francis T. Cullen, and Paula Dubeck. 1993. "Public Perceptions of Corporate Crime." In *Understanding Corporate Criminality,* edited by Michael B. Blankenship, 85–114. New York: Garland.

Farber, Stephen, and Marc Green. 1988. *Outrageous Conduct: Art, Ego, and the "Twilight Zone" Case.* New York: Morrow.

Feldman, Lenny H., and Richard J. Zeckhauser. 1978. "Some Sober Thoughts on Health Care Regulation." Pp. 103–111 in *Regulating Business: The Search for an Optimum,* edited by Chris Argyris. San Francisco: Institute for Contemporary Studies.

Finn, Peter, and Alan R. Hoffman. 1976. *Exemplary Projects: Prosecution of Economic Crime.* Washington, D.C.: Law Enforcement Assistance Administration.

Fisse, Brent A. 1983. "Reconstructing Corporate Criminal Law: Deterrence, Retribution, Fault and Sanctions." *Southern California Law Review* 56:1141–246.

Frank, James, Francis T. Cullen, Lawrence F. Travis III, and John L. Borntrager. 1989. "Sanctioning Corporate Crime: How Do Business Executives and the Public Compare?" *American Journal of Criminal Justice* 13:139–69.

Frank, Nancy. 1985. *Crimes against Health and Safety.* New York: Harrow and Heston.

Frank, Nancy, and Michael Lombness. 1988. *Controlling Corporate Illegality: The Regulatory Justice System.* Cincinnati: Anderson.

Friedman, Lawrence M. 1975. *The Legal System.* New York: Russell Sage Foundation.

―――. 1985a. *A History of American Law.* 2d ed. New York: Simon and Schuster.

―――. 1985b. *Total Justice.* New York: Russell Sage Foundation.

―――. 1993. *Crime and Punishment in American History.* New York: Basic Books.

Galanter, Mark. 1986. "Adjudication, Litigation, and Related Phenomena." In *Law and the Social Sciences,* edited by Leon Lipson and Stanton Wheeler, 151–257. New York: Russell Sage Foundation.

Galligan, Denis. 1986. *Discretionary Powers: A Legal Study of Official Discretion.* Oxford: Clarendon Press.

Garfinkel, Harold. 1956. "Conditions of Successful Status Degradation Ceremonies." *American Journal of Sociology* 61:420–24.

Geis, Gilbert. 1972. "Criminal Penalties for Corporate Criminals." *Criminal Law Bulletin* 8:372–92.

―――. 1985. "Criminological Perspectives on Corporate Regulation: A Review of Recent Research." In *Corrigible Corporations and Unruly Law,* edited by Brent Fisse and Peter A. French, 63–84. San Antonio, Texas: Trinity University Press.

―――. 1988. "From Deuteronomy to Deniability: A Historical Perlustration on White-Collar Crime." *Justice Quarterly* 5:7–32.

Goldstock, Ronald. 1991. "The Prosecutor as Problem Solver." Occasional paper from the Center for Research in Crime and Justice X. New York: Center for Research in Crime and Justice at New York University School of Law.

Green, Gary S. 1990. *Occupational Crime.* Chicago: Nelson-Hall.

Gross, Edward. 1978. "Organizational Crime: A Theoretical Perspective." In *Studies in Symbolic Interaction,* edited by Norman Denzin, vol. 1, 55–85. Greenwood, Conn.: JAI Press.

Hagan, John. 1977. "Criminal Justice in Rural and Urban Communities: A Study of the Bureaucratization of Justice." *Social Forces* 55:597–612.

―――. 1982. "The Social Organization of White-Collar Sanctions: A Study of Prosecution and Punishment in the Federal Courts." In *White-Collar and Economic Crime,* edited by Peter Wickman and Timothy Dailey, 259–75. Lexington, Mass.: Lexington Books.

Hagan, John, John Hewitt, and Duane Alwin. 1979. "Ceremonial Justice: Crime and Punishment in a Loosely Coupled System." *Social Forces* 58:506–27.

Hagan, John, Ilene Nagel-Bernstein, and Celesta Albonetti. 1980. "The Differential Sentencing of White-Collar Offenders in Ten Federal District Courts." *American Sociological Review* 45:802–20.

Hagan, John, and Alberto Palloni. 1986. "'Club Fed' and the Sentencing of White-Collar Offenders before and after Watergate." *Criminology* 24:603–22.

Hagan, John, and Patricia Parker. 1985. "White-Collar Crime and Punishment: The Class Structure and Legal Sanctioning of Securities Violations." *American Sociological Review* 50:302–16.

Hammett, Theodore M., and Joel Epstein. 1993a. *Local Prosecution of Environmental Crime.* Washington, D.C.: National Institute of Justice.

―――. 1993b. *Prosecuting Environmental Crime: Los Angeles County.* National Institute of Justice, Program Focus. Washington, DC: National Institute of Justice.

Handler, Joel F. 1986. *The Conditions of Discretion: Autonomy, Community, Bureaucracy.* New York: Russell Sage Foundation.

Harding, T. Swann. 1935. *The Popular Practice of Fraud.* New York: Longmans, Green and Co.

Hawkins, Keith. 1984. *Environment and Enforcement.* Oxford: Clarendon Press.

———. 1992. "The Use of Legal Discretion: Perspectives from Law and Social Science." In *The Uses of Discretion,* edited by Keith Hawkins, 11–46. Oxford: Clarendon Press.

Hays, William L., and Robert L. Winkler. 1970. *Statistics: Probability, Inference and Decision.* Vol. 1. New York: Holt, Rinehart and Winston.

Hills, Stuart L., ed. 1987. *Corporate Violence.* Totowa, N.J.: Rowman and Littlefield.

Hirschi, Travis, and Michael R. Gottfredson. 1987. "Causes of White-Collar Crime." *Criminology* 25:949–74.

Hochstedler, Ellen, ed. 1984. *Corporations as Criminals.* Beverly Hills, Calif.: Sage Publications.

Hochstetler, Andrew, and Neal Shover. 1997. "Street Crime, Labor Surplus, and Criminal Punishment, 1980–1990." *Social Problems,* 44:358–68.

Inverarity, James. 1992. "Extralegal Influences on Imprisonment: Explaining the Direct Effects of Socioeconomic Variables." In *Social Threat and Social Control,* edited by Allen E. Liska, 113–28. Albany, N.Y.; State University of New York Press.

Inverarity, James, and D. McCarthy. 1988. "Punishment and Social Structure Revisited: Unemployment and Imprisonment in the United States, 1948–1984. *Sociological Quarterly* 29:263–80.

Isard, Walter. 1960. *Methods of Regional Analysis: An Introduction to Regional Science.* Cambridge, Mass.: MIT Press.

Jackson, Pamela I. 1989. *Minority Group Threat, Crime and Policing.* New York: Praeger.

Jackson, Pamela I., and Leo Carroll. 1981. "Race and the War on Crime: The Socio-Political Determinants of Municipal Expenditures in 90 Non-Southern U.S. Cities." *American Sociological Review* 46:290–305.

Jacobs, Mark D. 1990. *Screwing the System and Making It Work: Juvenile Justice in the No-Fault Society.* Chicago: University of Chicago Press.

Jacoby, Joan E. 1980. *The American Prosecutor.* Lexington, Mass.: Lexington Books.

Jankovic, Irving. 1977. "Labor Market and Imprisonment." *Crime and Social Justice* 8:17–37.

Jones, Robert Emmet. Forthcoming. "Black Concern for the Environment: Myth vs. Reality." *Society and Natural Resources: An International Journal.*

Jones, Robert Emmet, and Riley E. Dunlap. 1992. "The Social Bases of Environmental Concern: Have They Changed over Time?" *Rural Sociology* 57:28–47.

Jowell, Jeffrey. 1986. "Implementation and Enforcement of Law." In *Law and the Social Sciences,* edited by Leon Lipson and Stanton Wheeler, 287–318. New York: Russell Sage Foundation.

Katz, Jack. 1977. "Legality and Equality: Plea Bargaining in the Prosecution of White-Collar Crimes." *Law and Social Review* 13:479–500.

———. 1979. "Concerted Ignorance: The Social Construction of Cover-Up." *Urban Life* 8:295–316.

———. 1980. "The Social Movement against White-Collar Crime." *Criminology Review Yearbook* 2:161–84.

REFERENCES

Kinney, Joseph A., Karen L. Weiss, Kira E. Sufalko, Amy B. Gleason, William J. Maakestad, and Patricia Howe. 1990. *Criminal Job Safety Prosecutions.* Chicago: National Safe Workplace Institute.

Kish, Leslie. 1967. *Survey Sampling.* New York: John Wiley and Sons.

Kramer, Ronald C. 1984. "Corporate Criminality: Development of an Idea." In *Corporations as Criminals,* edited by Ellen Hochstedler, 13–38. Beverly Hills, Calif.: Sage Publications.

Kress, Jack M. 1976. "Progress and Prosecution." *Annals of the American Academy of Political and Social Sciences* 423:99–116.

LaFave, Wayne R. 1965. *Arrest: The Decision to Take a Suspect into Custody.* Boston: Little, Brown.

Lasley, James R. 1988. "Toward a Control Theory of White-Collar Offending." *Journal of Quantitative Criminology* 4:347–62.

Levi, Michael. 1987. *Regulating Fraud.* London: Tavistock.

Lipset, Seymour M., and William Schneider. 1987. *The Confidence Gap: Business, Labor, and Government in the Public Mind.* Rev. ed. Baltimore: Johns Hopkins University Press.

Liska, Allen E. 1992. "Introduction to the Study of Social Control." In *Social Threat and Social Control,* edited by Allen E. Liska, 1–29. Albany, N.Y.: State University of New York Press.

Liska, Allen E., ed. 1992. *Social Threat and Social Control.* Albany, N.Y.: State University of New York Press.

Liska, Allen E., and Mitchell B. Chamlin. 1984. "Social Structure and Crime Control Among Macrosocial Units." *American Journal of Sociology* 90:383–87.

Liska, Allen E., Joseph J. Lawrence, and Michael L. Benson. 1981. "Perspectives on the Legal Order." *American Journal of Sociology* 87:413–26.

Liska, Allen E., and Jiang Yu. 1992. "Specifying and Testing the Threat Hypothesis: Police Use of Deadly Force." In *Social Threat and Social Control,* edited by Allen E. Liska, 53–70. Albany, N.Y.: State University of New York Press.

Lynxwiler, John, Neal Shover, and Donald Clelland. 1984. "Determinants of Sanction Severity in a Regulatory Bureaucracy." In *Corporations as Criminals,* edited by Ellen Hochstedler, 147–65. Beverly Hills, Calif.: Sage.

Maakestad, William J. 1981. "A Historical Survey of Corporate Homicide in the United States: Could It Be Prosecuted in Illinois?" *Illinois Bar Journal* 69:772–79.

———. 1986. "State's Attorneys Stalk Corporate Murderers." *Business and Society Review* 56:21–25.

Maakestad, William J., Michael L. Benson, Francis T. Cullen and Gilbert Geis. 1987. "Prosecuting Corporate Crime in California." Paper presented at Symposium '87: White-Collar and Institutional Crime. Co-sponsored by the California Office of the Attorney General and the University of California, Berkeley. Berkeley, Calif.

Magnuson, Jay, and Gareth Leviton. 1987. "Policy Considerations in Corporate Criminal Prosecutions after *People v. Film Recovery Systems, Inc.*" *Notre Dame Law Review* 62:913–39.

Mann, Kenneth. 1985. *Defending White-Collar Crime: A Portrait of Attorneys at Work.* New Haven, Conn.: Yale University Press.

Mann, Kenneth, Stanton Wheeler, and Austin Sarat. 1980. "Sentencing the White-Collar Offender." *American Criminal Law Review.* 17:479–500.

Mannheim, Hermann. 1965. *Comparative Criminology.* London: Routledge and Kegan Paul.

McAdams, John. 1987. "Testing the Theory of the New Class." *Sociological Quarterly* 28:23–50.

McGarrah, Robert E. 1990. *Manufacturing for the United States.* New York: Quorum Books.

Messner, Steven F., and Richard Rosenfeld. 1994. *Crime and the American Dream.* Belmont, Calif.: Wadsworth.

Moore, Charles A. 1987. "Taming the Giant Corporation: Some Cautionary Remarks on the Deterrability of Corporate Crime." *Crime and Delinquency* 33:379–402.

Myers, Raymond H. 1986. *Classical and Modern Regression with Applications.* Boston: Duxbury.

Myers, Martha, and Suzette Talarico. 1987. *The Social Contexts of Criminal Sentencing.* New York: Springer-Verlag.

Nagel, Ilene H., and John Hagan. 1982. "The Sentencing of White-Collar Criminals in Federal Courts: A Socio-Legal Exploration of Disparity." *Michigan Law Review* 80:1427–65.

National Commission on Law Observance and Enforcement 1931. *Report on Prosecution.* Washington, D.C.: Government Printing Office.

National Product Safety Commission. 1993. *Annual Report.* Washington, D.C.: Government Printing Office.

Newman, Donald J. 1986. *An Introduction to Criminal Justice.* 3d ed. New York: Random House.

Pollack, Harriet, and Alexander B. Smith. 1983. "White-Collar v. Street Crime Sentencing Disparity: How Judges See the Problem." *Judicature* 67:175–82.

Pope, Carl E. 1975. *Sentencing of California Felony Offenders.* National Criminal Justice Information and Statistics Service. Washington, D.C.: Government Printing Office.

President's Commission on Law Enforcement and Administration of Justice. 1967a. *The Challenge of Crime in a Free Society.* Washington, D.C.: Government Printing Office.

———. 1967b. *Task Force Report: The Police.* Washington, D.C.: Government Printing Office.

Rakoff, Jed S. 1985. "The Exercise of Prosecutorial Discretion in Federal Business Fraud Prosecutions." In *Corrigible Corporations and Unruly Law,* edited by Brent Fisse and Peter A. French, 173–86. San Antonio: Trinity University Press.

Rand McNally and Company. 1971. *Rand McNally Cosmopolitan World Atlas.* New York: Rand McNally.

Reasons, Charles, Lee Ross, and C. Patterson. 1981. *Assault on the Worker: Health and Safety in Canada.* Toronto: Butterworth.

Rebovich, Donald J. 1992. *Dangerous Ground: The World of Hazardous Waste Crime.* New Brunswick, N.J.: Transaction Press.

Rebovich, Donald J., and Richard T. Nixon. 1994. *Environmental Crime Prosecution: Results of a National Survey.* Research in Brief. Washington, D.C.: U.S. Department of Justice, National Institute of Justice.

Reiman, Jeffrey H. 1979. *The Rich Get Richer and the Poor Get Prison.* New York: John Wiley and Sons.

Reiman, Jeffrey H. 1995. *The Rich Get Richer and the Poor Get Prison: Ideology, Class, and Criminal Justice.* 4th ed. Boston: Allyn and Bacon.

Reiss, Albert J. 1971. *The Police and the Public.* New Haven: Yale University Press.

Rush, George E. 1986. *Dictionary of Criminal Justice.* 2d ed. Guilford, Conn.: Dushkin.

Sampson, Robert J., and Byron Groves. 1989. "Community Structure and Crime: Testing Social Disorganization Theory." *American Journal of Sociology* 94:774–802.

Schlegel, Kip. 1990. *Just Desserts for Corporate Criminals.* Boston: Northeastern University Press.

Schrager, Laura, and James F. Short. 1980. "How Serious a Crime? Perceptions of Common and Organizational Crimes." In *White-Collar Crime: Theory and Research,* edited by Gil Geis and Ezra Stotland, 14–31. Beverly Hills, Calif.: Sage.

Schudson, Charles B., Ashton P. Onellion, and Ellen Hochstedler. 1984. "Nailing an Omelet to the Wall: Prosecuting Nursing Home Homicide." In *Corporations as Criminals,* edited by Ellen Hochstedler, 131–46. Beverly Hills, Calif.: Sage.

Seidel, John V., Rolf Kjolseth, and Elaine Seymour. 1988. *The Ethnograph,* version 3.0. Littlejohn, Colo.: Qualis Research Associates.

Shapiro, Susan P. 1984. *Wayward Capitalists.* New Haven: Yale University Press.

———. 1990. "Collaring the Crime, Not the Criminal: Reconsidering 'White-Collar Crime.'" *American Sociological Review* 55:346–65.

Shaw, Clifford, and Henry McKay. 1942. *Juvenile Delinquency and Urban Areas.* Chicago: University of Chicago Press.

Shover, Neal, and Kevin M. Bryant. 1993. "Theoretical Explanations of Corporate Crime." In *Understanding Corporate Criminality,* edited by Michael B. Blankenship, 141–76. New York: Garland Publishing, Inc.

Shover, Neal, Donald Clelland, and John Lynxwiler. 1986. *Enforcement or Negotiation: Constructing a Regulatory Bureaucracy.* Albany, N.Y.: State University of New York Press.

Shover, Neal, Greer Fox, and Michael Mills. 1994. "Long-Term Consequences of Victimization by White-Collar Crime." *Justice Quarterly* 11:75–94.

Simcha-Fagan, Ora, and Joseph E. Schwartz. 1986. "Neighborhoods and Delinquency: An Assessment of Contextual Effects." *Criminology* 24:667–704.

Simpson, Sally S. 1986. "The Decomposition of Antitrust: Testing a Multilevel Longitudinal Model of Profit Squeeze." *American Sociological Review* 51:859–75.

———. 1987. "Cycles of Illegality: Antitrust Violations in Corporate America." *Social Forces* 65:943–63.

Skoler, Daniel L. 1977. *Organizing the Non-System.* Lexington, Mass.: Lexington Books.

———. 1982. "White-Collar Crime and the Criminal Justice System: Problems and Challenges." In *A National Strategy for Containing White-Collar Crime,* edited by Herbert Edelhertz and Charles Rogovin, 57–75. Lexington, Mass.: Lexington Books.

Snider, Laureen. 1982. "Traditional and Corporate Theft: A Comparison of Sanctions." In *White-Collar and Economic Crime,* edited by Timothy Wickman and Peter Dailey, 235–58. Lexington, Mass.: Lexington Books.

Sparrow, Malcolm K. 1996. *License to Steal: Why Fraud Plagues America's Health Care System.* Boulder, Colo.: Westview Press.

Stewart, James B. 1987. *The Prosecutors.* New York: Simon and Schuster.

Stinchcombe, Arthur L. 1987. *Constructing Social Theories.* Chicago: University of Chicago Press.

Stone, Christopher D. 1975. *Where the Law Ends: The Social Control of Corporate Behavior.* New York: Harper and Row.

———. 1987. "A Slap on the Wrist for the Kepone Mob." In *Corporate Violence,* edited by Stuart L. Hills, 121–32. Totowa, N.J.: Rowman and Littlefield.

Stotland, Ezra. 1982. "The Role of Law Enforcement in the Fight against White-Collar Crime." In *White-Collar Crime: An Agenda for Research,* edited by Herbert Edelhertz and Thomas D. Overcast, 69–98. Lexington, Mass.: Lexington Books.

Sutherland, Edwin H. 1940. "White-Collar Criminality." *American Sociological Review* 5:1–12.

———. 1949. *White-Collar Crime.* New York: Holt, Rinehart and Winston.

———. 1983. *White-Collar Crime: The Uncut Version.* New Haven: Yale University Press.

Tallmer, Matt. 1987. "Chemical Dumping as a Corporate Way of Life." In *Corporate Violence,* edited by Stuart L. Hills, 111–20. Totowa, N.J.: Rowman and Littlefield.

Tappan, Paul. 1977. "Who is the Criminal?" In *White-Collar Crime: Offenses in Business, Politics, and the Professions–Classic and Contemporary Views,* edited by Gilbert Geis and Robert F. Meier, 272–82. New York: Free Press.

Taylor, Ralph B., and Jeanette Covington. 1988. "Neighborhood Changes in Ecology and Violence." *Criminology* 26:553–89.

Titus, Richard, Fred Heinzelmann, and John M. Boyle. 1995. "Victimization of Persons by Fraud." *Crime and Delinquency* 41:54–72.

Tolnay, Stewart E., and E. M. Beck. 1992. "Toward a Threat Model of Southern Black Lynchings." In *Social Threat and Social Control,* edited by Allen E. Liska, 33–52. Albany, N.Y.: State University of New York Press.

U.S. Bureau of the Census. 1988. *County and City Data Book, 1988, Files on Diskette.* Washington, D.C.: U.S. Bureau of the Census.

———. 1989a. *County Business Patterns, 1987.* Washington, D.C.: U.S. Bureau of the Census.

———. 1989b. *Statistical Abstract of the United States, 109th edition.* Washington, D.C.: Government Printing Office.

U.S. Department of Justice. 1989. *Profile of State and Local Law Enforcement Agencies, 1987.* Washington, D.C.: U.S. Department of Justice.

———. 1990a. *Justice Expenditures and Employment, 1988.* Washington, D.C.: U.S. Department of Justice.

———. 1990b. *Crime in the United States, 1989.* Washington, D.C.: Government Printing Office.

Van Alstyne, W. Scott. 1952. "The District Attorney—A Historical Puzzle." *Wisconsin Law Review* 125–38.

Van Wyk, Judy, and Michael L. Benson. 1997. "Fraud Victimization: Risky Business or Just Bad Luck?" *American Journal of Criminal Justice* 21:163–79.

Vandivier, Kermit. 1992. "Why Should My Conscience Bother Me?" In *Corporate and Governmental Deviance: Problems of Organizational Behavior in Contemporary Society,* edited by M. David Ermann and Richard J. Lundman, 205–26. Oxford: Oxford University Press.

Vaughan, Diane. 1983. *Controlling Unlawful Organizational Behavior.* Chicago: University of Chicago Press.

Weil, Frederick D. 1985. "The Variable Effects of Education on Liberal Attitudes: A Comparative-Historical Analysis of Anti-Semitism Using Public Opinion Survey Data." *American Sociological Review* 50:458–74.

Weisburd, David, Stanton Wheeler, Elin Waring, and Nancy Bode. 1991. *Crimes of the Middle Classes: White-Collar Offenders in the Federal Courts.* New Haven: Yale University Press.

Wheeler, Malcolm E. 1981. "Product Liability: Civil or Criminal—The Pinto Litigation." *The Forum.* 17:250–65.

Wheeler, Stanton, Kenneth Mann, and Austin Sarat. 1988. *Sitting in Judgement: The Sentencing of White-Collar Criminals.* New Haven: Yale University Press.

Wheeler, Stanton, and Mitchell Lewis Rothman. 1982. "The Organization as Weapon in White-Collar Crime." *Michigan Law Review* 80:1403–26.

Wheeler, Stanton, David Weisburd, and Nancy Bode. 1982. "Sentencing the White-Collar Offender: Rhetoric and Reality." *American Sociological Review* 47:641–59.

Whitcomb, Debra, Louis Frisina and Robert L. Spangenberg. 1979. *An Exemplary Project: Connecticut Economic Crime Unit.* Washington, D.C.: National Institute of Law Enforcement and Criminal Justice.

Wilson, James Q. 1968. *Varieties of Police Behavior.* Cambridge: Harvard University Press.

Wright, John P., Francis T. Cullen, and Michael B. Blankenship. 1995. "The Social Construction of Corporate Violence: Media Coverage of the Imperial Food Products Fire." *Crime and Delinquency* 41:20–36.

INDEX